Pocket Rough Guide

PARIS

Written and researched by
RUTH BLACKMORE AND JAMES McCONNACHIE

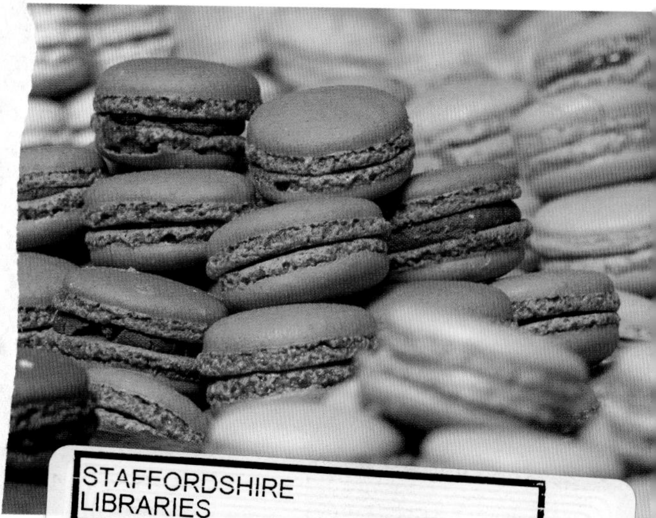

Contents

INTRODUCTION 4

BEST OF PARIS 12

PLACES 32

ACCOMMODATION 168

ESSENTIALS 180

<< PARISIAN *MACARONS*
< NOTRE-DAME IN THE SPRINGTIME

INTRODUCTION TO

PARIS

A trip to Paris, famous as the most romantic of destinations, is one of those lifetime musts. Long the beating heart of European civilization, it remains one of the world's most refined yet passionate cities. The very fabric of the place is exquisite, with its magnificent avenues and atmospheric little backstreets, its grand formal gardens and intimate neighbourhood squares. And for all the famed pride and hauteur of its citizens, the city seems to be opening itself up to visitors more and more, with new schemes to pedestrianize the riverbanks and squares and make more of its splendid monuments accessible.

PLACE ST-MICHEL

JARDIN DU LUXEMBOURG

Best places for a Parisian picnic

Picnicking on the grass is rarely allowed in central Paris – except on the elegant place des Vosges. But public benches make civilized alternatives: try the pedestrian bridge, the Pont des Arts; the lime-tree-shaded square Jean XXIII, behind Notre-Dame; the intimate Jardin du Palais Royal; or the splendid Jardin du Luxembourg. Further out, the parks of Buttes-Chaumont and André-Citroën offer idyllic spots for lounging on the grass.

Paris is a city that has weathered many storms, not least the French Revolution, the student riots of 1968 and most recently the series of devastating terrorist attacks in November 2015, which left 130 people dead and many more wounded. While in the immediate aftermath this inevitably had an impact on visitor numbers, the city is getting back on its feet and the café terraces and restaurants are humming with cosmopolitan chatter.

The city is divided into twenty arrondissements in a spiral, centred on the Louvre. The inner hub comprises arrondissements 1er to 6e, and it's here that most of the major sights and museums are to be found. Through the heart of the city flows the Seine, skirting the pair of islands where Paris was founded. The historic pillars of the city, the church of Notre-Dame and the royal palace of the Louvre, stand on the riverbank, along with one of the world's most distinctive landmarks – the Eiffel Tower. The Louvre has one of the world's truly outstanding museums, while the art collections of the Musée d'Orsay and Pompidou Centre are unrivalled.

Yet there is a host of smaller museums, and alongside the great civic monuments lie distinct *quartiers* that make Paris feel more a collection of sophisticated villages than a modern-day metropolis. Communities still revolve around well-loved cafés and restaurants, and the student, gay and immigrant quarters are, by and large, lively and well-defined. So too are the wealthier districts, with their exclusive boutiques and restaurants. Neighbourhoods such as the elegant Marais, St-Germain and romantic Montmartre are ideal for shopping, sitting in cafés and aimless wandering, while throughout the city you can find peaceful green spaces, ranging from formal gardens and avant-garde municipal parks to ancient cemeteries.

Above all, Paris is a city defined by its food. Few cities can compete with the thousand-and-one cafés, brasseries, *bistrots*, restaurants, bakeries, food shops and markets that line the boulevards and back alleys alike. You'll find anything from ultra-modern fashion temples to traditional mirrored palaces, and from tiny neighbourhood *bistrots* to crowded Vietnamese diners. Parisian nightlife is scarcely less renowned: its theatres and concert halls pull in artists of the highest calibre, while the tiny venues hosting jazz gigs, art events and Parisian *chanson* nights offer a taste of a more local, avant-garde scene. The café-bars and clubs of the Champs-Elysées, northeastern districts and the Left Bank fill with the young and style-conscious from all over.

When to visit

Spring is the classic time to visit Paris; the weather is mild (average daily 6–20°C), and plentiful bright sunny days are balanced by occasional freshening rain showers. Autumn, similarly mild, and winter (1–7°C) can be very rewarding, but on overcast days the city can feel melancholic, and cold winds can really cut down the boulevards; winter sun, however, is the city's most flattering light, and hotels and restaurants are relatively uncrowded in this season. Paris in high summer (15–25°C) is not the best time to go: large numbers of Parisians desert the capital between July 15 and the end of August for the beach or mountains, and many restaurants and shops close down for much of this period.

PARIS PLAGE

PARIS AT A GLANCE

>>EATING

There's a real buzz about the current Paris dining scene, as talented young chefs open up new *bistrots* – the **10e arrondissement and the northeastern districts** are good areas to try. For more traditional French cuisine, you don't have to look far: every *quartier* has its own local *bistrot*, serving staples such as *steak au poivre*. For a really authentic experience, go for a classic brasserie such as *Gallopin* (see p.73) off the **Grands Boulevards**, where you can dine amid splendid original decor. You can almost always eat more cheaply at lunchtime, when most places offer set menus from around €15. Even some of the haute cuisine restaurants become just about affordable at lunch.

>>DRINKING

It's easy to go drinking in Paris: most cafés stay open late and serve alcoholic drinks as well as coffee, and old-fashioned wine bars and English-style "pubs" can be found everywhere. That said, certain areas specialize in late-night drinking. The **Marais** offers trendy but relaxed café-bars; further east, the **Bastille and Oberkampf** areas have lots of youthful venues, many doubling as clubs. On the Left Bank, the **Quartier Latin** has lots of postage-stamp-sized studenty dives, while **St-Germain** is the place for cheery posh partying.

>>SHOPPING

One of the most appealing shopping areas is **St-Germain**, with its wide variety of clothes shops and gourmet food stores. Designer wear and haute couture are concentrated around the Champs-Elysées and on **rue du Faubourg-St-Honoré**, while more alternative fashion boutiques can be found in the Marais, especially around **rue Charlot**, and in Montmartre, in particular on **rue des Martyrs**. If you're short on time, make for one of the department stores, such as Printemps or Galeries Lafayette on the Right Bank, or Bon Marché on the Left Bank. For quirky one-off buys and curios, head for the atmospheric *passages* (nineteenth-century shopping arcades), just off the **Grands Boulevards**.

>>NIGHTLIFE

The best clubs in Paris double up as live venues, but dancefloors rarely warm up before 1am. Good eclectic venues include the boats moored beside the **Bibliothèque Nationale**, and **Oberkampf** classics such as *L'Alimentation Générale* and *Le Nouveau Casino*. Serious clubbers should chase down the latest soirée, though the clubs *Rex*, *Showcase* and *Social Club* are generally good bets. **Rue des Lombards** has some classic venues, notably the jazz club *Le Sunside*.

OUR RECOMMENDATIONS FOR WHERE TO EAT, DRINK AND SHOP ARE LISTED AT THE END OF EACH PLACES CHAPTER

Day One in Paris

1 Ile de la Cité > p.34. Paris was founded on this tiny island, which rises out of the River Seine.

2 Notre-Dame > p.36. The magnificent Gothic cathedral of Notre-Dame is the uplifting, historic heart of the city.

3 Sainte-Chapelle > p.35. This chapel is an exquisite jewel box, walled in medieval stained glass.

4 Pont-Neuf > p.34. The riverbank quays lead west to the Pont-Neuf, the oldest bridge in the city, and beyond to the square du Vert Galant, where you can sit and watch the Seine flow by.

Lunch > p.122. Head away from the tourist bustle, south into St-Germain, for lunch at contemporary *bistrot, L'Epi Dupin.*

5 Jardin du Luxembourg > p.119. These gardens are filled with people playing tennis or chess and couples strolling round the elegant lawns.

6 Pont des Arts > p.114. This handsome pedestrian bridge runs from St-Germain to the Louvre; you can pick up the Batobus beside it and head downriver.

7 Musée d'Orsay > p.115. This grand old railway station houses some of the most beguiling Impressionist works ever painted.

8 Eiffel Tower > p.52. Continue on the Batobus to this world-famous structure, ever more thrilling the closer you get to it.

Dinner > p.132. Head over to Montparnasse for a meal at small but perfect *bistrot, Le Timbre.*

Day Two in Paris

1 Pompidou Centre > p.76. Begin the day with a crash course in modern art – the Musée National d'Art Moderne has an unbeatable collection of Matisses, Picassos, and more.

1

2 Rue Montorgueil > p.79. Stroll down this picturesque market street, where grocers, butchers and fishmongers ply their trade alongside traditional restaurants and trendy cafés.

Lunch > p.72. Stop off at *Bistrot des Victoires*, an old-fashioned *bistrot* serving *confit de canard* and other staples.

3 Galerie Vivienne > p.68. One of a number of nineteenth-century shopping arcades dotted around the area, this is probably the finest, with its lofty glass ceiling, floor mosaics and Grecian motifs.

3

4 Palais Royal > p.67. The handsome arcaded buildings of the Palais Royal enclose peaceful gardens and shelter quirky antique shops selling pipes, Légion d'Honneur medals and lead soldiers.

5 Jardin des Tuileries > p.48. Saunter along the chestnut-tree-lined alleys of the Jardin des Tuileries, admiring the grand vistas, formal flower beds and fountains.

6 Place de la Concorde > p.48. An impressive piece of town planning, with a gold-tipped obelisk at its centre, broad avenues radiating off it, and grand monuments, such as the Arc de Triomphe, in every direction.

6

Dinner > p.50. Eat out on the wonderful terrace or in the classy dining room of the *Mini Palais*.

Art lover's Paris

Paris was long the undisputed international capital of art. The cafés of Montmartre and Montparnasse may now be haunted only by the ghosts of the great Impressionists and Modernists, but in the city's galleries you can come face to face with their living works.

1 Musée d'Art Moderne de la Ville de Paris > p.56. The museum celebrates Paris's Modernists, and has a stunning mural by Matisse and a great view across the Seine.

2 Palais de Tokyo > p.56. The gallery's distressed-chic interior is home to cutting-edge contemporary artists such as Dran.

3 Musée Rodin > p.60. Rodin's stirring sculptures are housed in an elegant mansion, now fully open again after a splendid revamp.

Lunch > p.62. Stop for a hearty lunch at the relaxed *La Fontaine de Mars*.

4 Musée Picasso > p.83. An exceptional collection of works by Picasso set in a beautifully renovated Renaissance mansion.

5 Louvre > p.40. If you're going to tackle the mighty Louvre, take on a less well known wing, such as French sculpture or Objets d'Art.

Dinner > p.81. Wind down with a meal at the excellent *La Régalade Saint Honoré* – be sure to make a reservation, though, as this modern *bistrot* is deservedly popular.

Budget Paris

Despite Paris's reputation as an expensive city, there are many treats to be enjoyed for free, plus plenty of good-value deals to be had at restaurants.

1 Hôtel Bonséjour Montmartre > p.177. Set on a quiet street, this hotel is a steal at €60 for a simple double with sink, or €69 for one with a shower.

2 Buses > p.185. Touring by bus is enjoyable and inexpensive; try the #29 from Gare St-Lazare, which goes past the Opera Garnier, through the Marais, and on to Bastille.

3 Sacré-Coeur > p.138. There's no charge to visit this Parisian landmark, but the real draw is the view from the terrace.

4 Musée Carnavalet > p.86. One of the city's best free museums is the Musée Carnavalet, devoted to the history of Paris.

Lunch > p.92. For a cheap and filling lunch, get a takeaway from *L'As du Fallafel* in the Marais' Jewish Quarter.

5 Place des Vosges > p.87. Lounge on the grass beneath the elegant facades of the place des Vosges, and enjoy the entertainment from buskers playing in the arcades.

6 Maison de Victor Hugo > p.88. It's free to visit the stately place des Vosges mansion that Victor Hugo lived in.

7 Petit Palais > p.46. The Petit Palais hosts free lunchtime classical concerts on Thursdays roughly twice a month, and there's no charge to visit the museum's fine collection of art.

Dinner > p.102. The French cuisine at charming restaurant *L'Encrier* is excellent value, with set menus from €21.

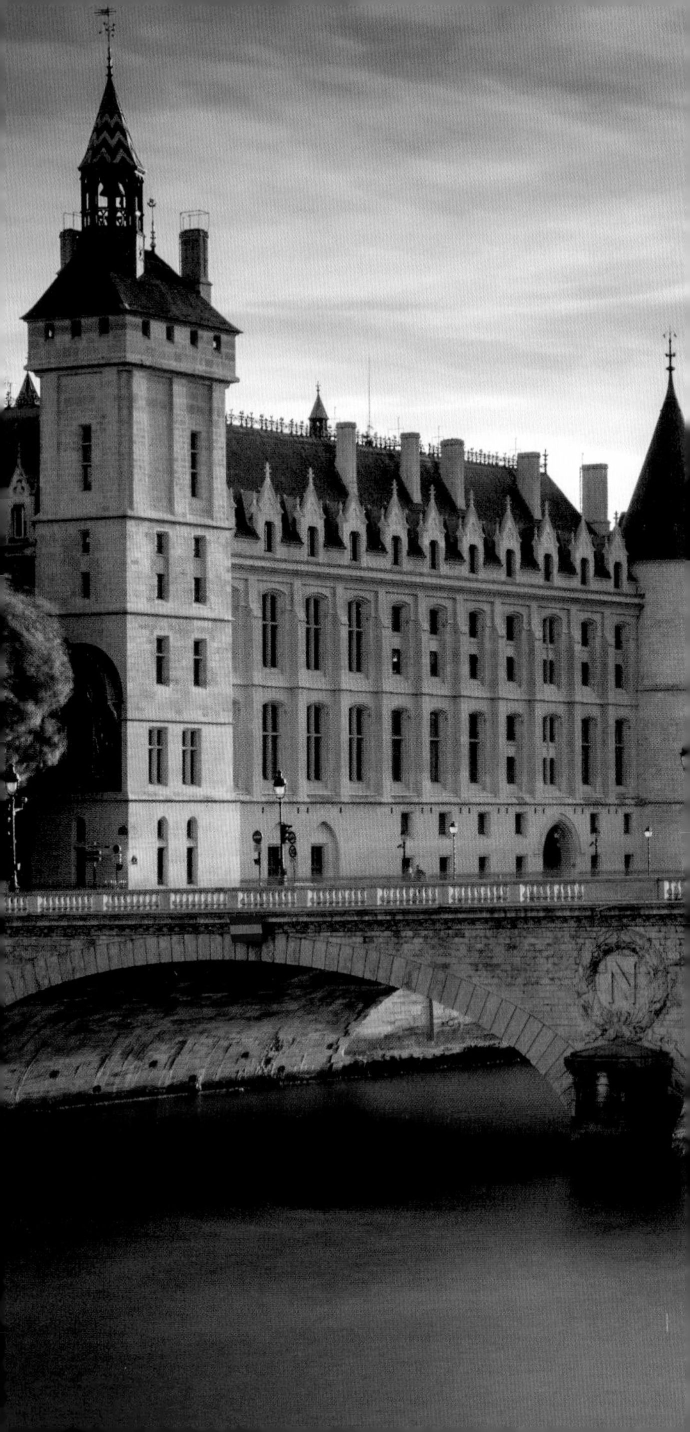

BEST OF PARIS

Big sights

1 Eiffel Tower It may seem familiar from afar, but close up the Eiffel Tower is still an excitingly improbable structure. > **p.52**

2 Pont-Neuf The "new bridge" is actually the oldest in the city, and, with its stone arches, arguably the loveliest. > **p.34**

3 Sacré-Coeur steps From the steps of Sacré-Coeur, atop Montmartre's hill, the silvery roofs of Paris spread to the horizon. > **p.138**

4 Notre-Dame Islanded in the Seine stands one of the world's greatest Gothic cathedrals, Notre-Dame. > **p.36**

5 The Panthéon The domed Panthéon shelters the remains of the French Republic's cultural heroes, from Jean-Jacques Rousseau to Zola. > **p.108**

Cultural Paris

1 Musée Moreau Gustave Moreau's eccentric canvases cover every inch of his studio's walls. > **p.140**

3 Musée Guimet Visiting the Buddhist statues and sculptures at the beautifully designed Musée Guimet is a distinctly spiritual experience. > **p.55**

2 Musée Jacquemart-André The Jacquemart-André couple's sumptuous Second Empire residence displays their choice collection of Italian, Dutch and French masters. > **p.46**

4 Fondation Louis Vuitton Frank Gehry's astonishing "cloud of glass" holds an inspiring collection of modern art. > **p.158**

5 Musée National du Moyen Age Set in a fine Renaissance mansion, Paris's Museum of the Middle Ages houses all manner of exquisite objets d'art. > **p.105**

Dining

1 Le Train Bleu The glamour of the *belle époque* lives on in the Gare de Lyon's restaurant, with its gilt decor and crystal chandeliers. > **p.102**

2 Semilla A refreshingly modern *bistrot* that is deservedly popular for its bold, original and excellent-value cuisine. > **p.123**

2

3 Racines A cosy neighbourhood *bistrot à vins* set in the atmospheric passage des Panoramas, serving simple home-cooked food and natural wines. > **p.73**

3

4 Le Verre Volé This wine-shop-cum-restaurant does perfectly prepared modern and traditional dishes, with a superb wine list. > **p.153**

4

5

5 L'Arpège Alain Passard's unique menu includes exquisitely inventive morsels of unusual vegetables in delicious sauces. > **p.62**

Romantic Paris

1 Lapérouse The private dining rooms at gourmet restaurant *Lapérouse* are full of faded elegance; close the door and summon your waiter with a buzzer.
> **p.123**

2 Lady with the Unicorn Tapestry, Musée du Moyen Age These five medieval tapestries, depicting the senses, comprise perhaps the most sensual work of art ever made. > **p.105**

3 Mixed steam session, Les Bains du Marais At weekends, the fashionable steam rooms of Les Bains du Marais are opened to male–female couples. > **p.87**

4 Time out in the Tuileries Taking time out in one of Paris's elegant gardens can be the most romantic thing of all. > **p.48**

5 Seine-watching Try the Berges de Seine, a lovely spot to sit and watch the river slide by. > **p.118**

Paris shopping

1 Anne Willi Willi designs simple, flattering clothes in luxurious fabrics, as well as cute children's outfits. > **p.100**

2 Galeries Lafayette The queen of Paris's department stores, with floor upon floor of clothes and cosmetics. > **p.70**

2

3

3 Abbesses boutiques Shoppers with a quirky eye should make for the independent designers and boutiques around place des Abbesses. > **p.142**

4 Haut Marais boutiques Currently the city's hottest fashion spot, the Haut Marais is full of stylish independent boutiques. > **p.89**

4

5

5 Isabel Marant Isabel Marant is renowned for her exciting ready-to-wear collections, at prices that won't make your eyes water. > **p.100**

Bars and nightlife

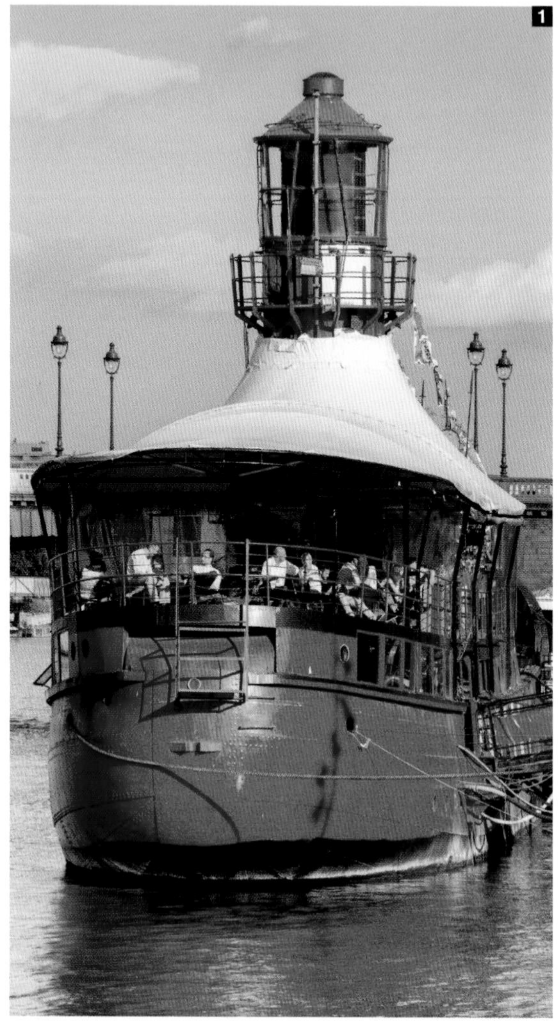

1 Batofar There's not much space for a club on an old lightship, but *Batofar* is a classic, friendly venue. > **p.133**

2 Au Limonaire At this tiny backstreet venue, you can dine while listening to young *chanson* singers, poets and vaudeville acts. > **p.75**

3 Le Comptoir General This is a quirky, exotic place for late-night cocktails, with a cool playlist and occasional live African music. > **p.154**

4 Showcase Set in a former boat hangar, facing onto the river, this club has a fantastic sound system and an up-for-it crowd. > **p.51**

5 Castor Club A fun and relaxed speakeasy-style bar, serving original and inventive cocktails. > **p.123**

Paris for kids

1 Parc Zoologique Paris's recently revamped zoo can't fail to appeal, with its zebras, lions, manatees, giraffes and enormous hothouse. > **p.97**

2 Jardin du Luxembourg boats One of the timeless pleasures of the Luxembourg gardens is hiring a toy boat and sailing it across the circular pond. > **p.119**

3 Parc de la Villette The Géode Omnimax cinema is just one of the many attractions for kids in this futuristic park. > **p.149**

4 Jardin d'Acclimatation No child could fail to be enchanted by this wonderland of mini canal and train rides, adventure parks and farm animals. > **p.157**

5 Jardin des Plantes These delightful gardens have plenty of plants, but also a small zoo and the Grande Galerie de l'Evolution. > **p.109**

Green Paris

1 Jardin des Tuileries The French formal garden par excellence: sweeping vistas, symmetrical flower beds and straight avenues. > **p.48**

2 Jardin du Luxembourg For all its splendid classical design, the Luxembourg is still the most relaxed and friendly of Paris's parks. > **p.119**

3 Jardin du Palais Royal
Enclosed by a collection of arcaded shops, the Jardin du Palais Royal makes a wonderful retreat from the city bustle. > **p.67**

4 Parc des Buttes-Chaumont This enchanting park has a lovely lake, a rocky outcrop topped with a Corinthian temple and plenty of grass which, for once, you can freely wander on. > **p.151**

5 Promenade Plantée This disused railway line, now an elevated walkway, is a great way to see a little-known part of the city. > **p.97**

Parisians' Paris

1 Café de la Mosquée The Paris mosque serves North African snacks and mint tea at its café, and has a hammam (steam bath) next door. > **p.111**

2 Cinema The city's historic cinemas, such as The Rex, are the ideal venues for a French classic. > **p.188**

3 Raspail organic market On Sunday mornings, Paris's fashionable foodies flock to the exquisite Marché Bio, or organic market, which runs down boulevard Raspail. > **p.120**

2

3

4

5

4 Berges de Seine
A pedestrianized stretch of the Seine that's full of activities – climbing wall, table tennis, bikes to rent and board games – or you can simply relax on a sunny terrace over a coffee and enjoy the splendid views. > **p.118**

5 Les Trois Baudets The best place to catch up-and-coming stars of French *chanson* – the classic Parisian singer-songwriter tradition. > **p.145**

PAVILLON RICHELIEU

PLACES

The Islands

There's no better place to start a tour of Paris than its two river islands, Ile de la Cité, the city's ancient core, and charming, village-like Ile St-Louis. The Ile de la Cité is where Paris began. It was settled in around 300 BC by a Celtic tribe, the Parisii, and in 52 BC was overrun by the Romans who built a palace-fortress at the western end of the island. In the tenth century the Frankish kings transformed this fortress into a splendid palace, of which the Sainte-Chapelle and the Conciergerie prison survive today. At the other end of the island they erected the great cathedral of Notre-Dame. The maze of medieval streets that grew up around these monuments was largely erased in the nineteenth century by Baron Haussmann, Napoléon III's Préfet de la Seine (a post equivalent to mayor of Paris), and much of the island is now occupied by imposing Neoclassical edifices, including the Palais de Justice, or law courts.

PONT-NEUF

Ⓜ Pont Neuf. MAP PP.36–37, POCKET MAP C16
Despite its name, the Pont-Neuf is Paris's oldest surviving bridge, built in 1607 by Henri IV, one of the city's first great town planners. A handsome stone construction with twelve arches, the bridge links the western tip of the Ile de la Cité with both banks of the river. It was the first in Paris to be made of stone rather than wood, hence the name. Henri is commemorated with a stately equestrian statue.

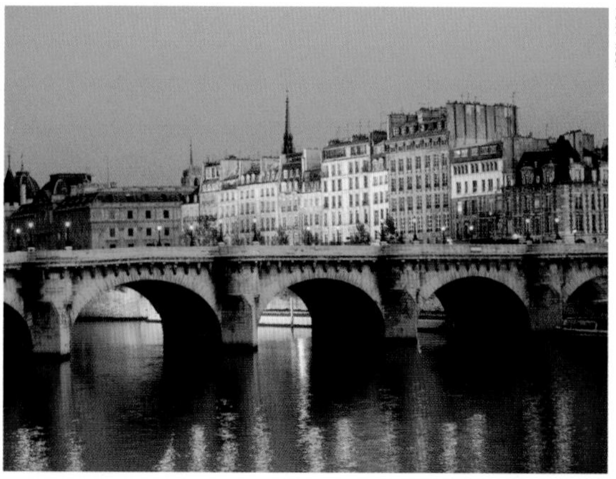

PONT-NEUF

SQUARE DU VERT-GALANT

Ⓜ Pont Neuf. MAP PP.36–37, POCKET MAP C16

Enclosed within the triangular "stern" of the island, the square du Vert-Galant is a tranquil, tree-lined garden and a popular lovers' haunt. The square takes its name (a "Vert-Galant" is a "green" or "lusty" gentleman) from the nickname given to Henri IV, whose amorous exploits were legendary.

PLACE DAUPHINE

Ⓜ Cité. MAP PP.36–37, POCKET MAP C16

Red-brick seventeenth-century houses flank the entrance to place Dauphine, one of the city's most secluded and attractive squares, lined with venerable townhouses. The noise of traffic recedes here, likely to be replaced by nothing more intrusive than the gentle tap of boules being played in the shade of the chestnuts.

INSIDE THE SAINTE-CHAPELLE

THE SAINTE-CHAPELLE

4 bd du Palais Ⓜ Cité. Daily: March–Oct 9.30am–6pm; Nov–Feb 9am–5pm. €10, combined ticket with the Conciergerie €15. MAP PP.36–37, POCKET MAP D16

The slender spire of the Sainte-Chapelle soars high above the Palais de Justice buildings. Though damaged in the Revolution, it was sensitively restored in the mid-nineteenth century and remains one of the finest achievements of French High Gothic, renowned for its exquisite stained-glass windows.

The building was constructed by Louis IX between 1242 and 1248 to house a collection of holy relics, including Christ's crown of thorns and a fragment of the True Cross, bought from the bankrupt empire of Byzantium. First you enter the lower chapel, where servants would have worshipped; very simply decorated, it gives no clue as to the splendour that lies ahead in the upper chapel. Here you're greeted by a truly dazzling sight – a vast, almost uninterrupted expanse of magnificent stained glass, supported by deceptively fragile-looking stone columns. When the sun streams through, the glowing blues and reds of the stained glass dapple the interior and it feels as if you're surrounded by myriad brilliant butterflies. The windows, two-thirds of which are original (the others are from the nineteenth-century restoration), tell virtually the entire story of the Bible, beginning on the north side with Genesis and various other books of the Old Testament, continuing with the Passion of Christ (east end) and ending with the Apocalypse in the rose window.

THE CONCIERGERIE

2 bd du Palais Ⓜ Cité. Daily 9.30am–6pm. €8.50, combined ticket with Sainte-Chapelle €15. MAP PP.36–37, POCKET MAP D16

Located within the Palais de Justice complex, the Conciergerie is Paris's oldest prison, where Marie-Antoinette and, in their turn, the leading figures of the Revolution were incarcerated before execution. It was turned into a prison – and put in the charge of a "concierge", or steward – after Etienne Marcel's uprising in 1358 led Charles V to decamp to the greater security of the Louvre. One of its towers, on the corner of the quai de l'Horloge, bears Paris's first public clock, built in 1370 and now fully restored.

Inside are several splendidly vaulted Gothic halls, among the few surviving vestiges of the original Capetian palace. Elsewhere a number of rooms and prisoners' cells, including Marie-Antoinette's, have been reconstructed to show what they might have been like at the time of the French Revolution.

CATHEDRALE DE NOTRE-DAME

Ⓜ Cité & Ⓜ/RER St-Michel. Ⓦ cathedraledeparis.com. Cathedral daily 8am–6.45pm; free. Towers daily: April–Sept 10am–6.30pm, till 11pm Sat & Sun July & Aug; Oct–March 10am–5.30pm; €10, under-18s and EU residents under 26 free. Guided tours in English Wed & Thurs 2pm, Sat 2.30pm; 1hr–1hr 30min; free; meet at welcome desk. MAP PP.36–37, POCKET MAP E17

One of the masterpieces of the Gothic age, the Cathédrale de Notre-Dame rears up from the Ile de la Cité like a ship moored by huge flying buttresses. It was among the first of the great Gothic cathedrals built in northern France and one of the most ambitious, its nave reaching an unprecedented 33m. It was begun in 1160 and completed around 1345. In the seventeenth and eighteenth centuries it fell into decline, suffering its worst depredations during the Revolution. It was only in the 1820s that the cathedral was at last given a much-needed restoration, a task entrusted to the great

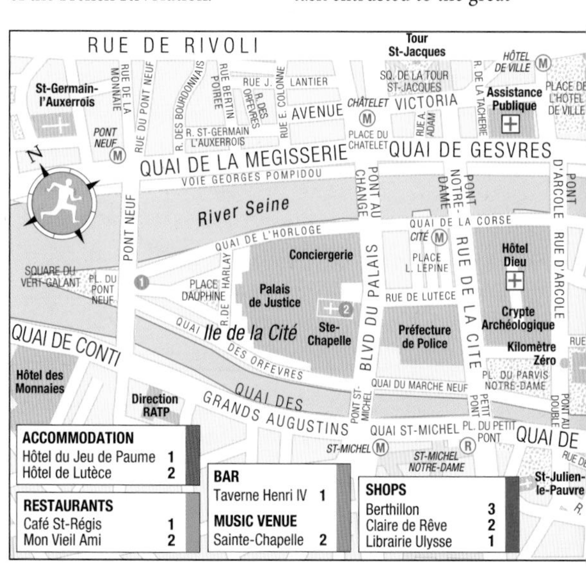

architect-restorer Viollet-le-Duc, who carried out a thorough – some would say too thorough – renovation, remaking much of the statuary on the facade (the originals can be seen in the Musée National du Moyen Age) and adding the steeple and baleful-looking gargoyles, which you can see close up if you climb the towers (entrance outside).

The cathedral's facade is one of its most impressive exterior features; the Romanesque influence is still visible, not least in its solid H-shape, but the overriding impression is one of lightness and grace, created in part by the delicate filigree work of the central rose window and the gallery above.

NOTRE-DAME

Inside, you're struck by the dramatic contrast between the darkness of the nave and the light falling on the first great clustered pillars of the choir. It is the end walls of the transepts which admit all this light, being nearly two-thirds glass, including two magnificent rose windows coloured in imperial purple. These, the vaulting and the soaring shafts reaching to the springs of the vaults, are all definite Gothic elements, while there remains a strong sense of Romanesque in the stout round pillars of the nave and the general sense of four-squareness.

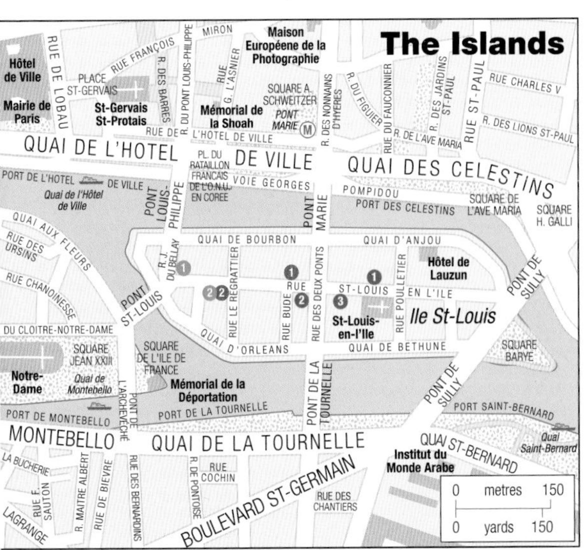

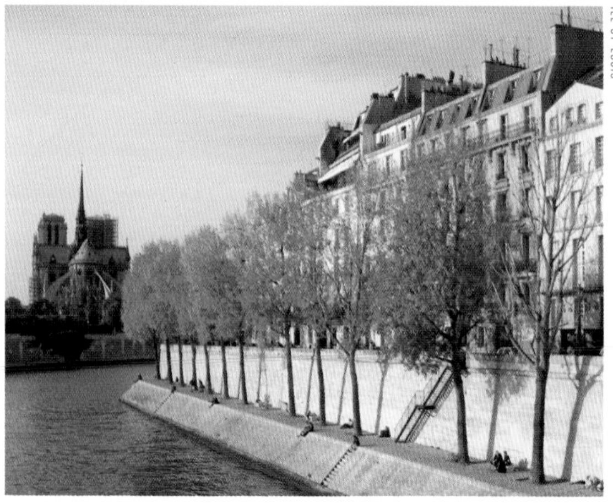
ILE ST-LOUIS

KILOMETRE ZERO

Ⓜ Cité. MAP PP.36–37, POCKET MAP D17

On the pavement by the west door of Notre-Dame is a spot, marked by a bronze star, known as Kilomètre Zéro, from which all main-road distances in France are calculated.

THE CRYPTE ARCHEOLOGIQUE

Parvis-Notre-Dame Ⓜ Cité & Ⓜ/RER St-Michel. Ⓦ crypte.paris.fr. Tues–Sun 10am–6pm. €7. MAP PP.36–37, POCKET MAP D17

The well-presented Crypte Archéologique is a large excavated area under the place du Parvis revealing the remains of the original cathedral, as well as vestiges of the streets and houses that once clustered around Notre-Dame: most are medieval, but some date as far back as Gallo-Roman times.

LE MEMORIAL DE LA DEPORTATION

Ⓜ Cité. Tues–Sun 10am–7pm, closes 5pm Oct–March. Free. MAP PP.36–37, POCKET MAP E17

Scarcely visible above ground, the stark and moving Mémorial de la Déportation is the symbolic tomb of the 200,000 French who died in Nazi concentration camps during World War II – among them Jews, Resistance fighters and forced labourers. Stairs barely shoulder-wide descend into a space like a prison yard and then into a crypt, off which is a long, narrow, stifling corridor, its walls covered in thousands of points of light representing the dead. Above the exit are the words "Pardonne, n'oublie pas" ("Forgive; do not forget").

ILE ST-LOUIS

Ⓜ Pont-Marie. MAP PP.36–37, POCKET MAP E17–F18

The smaller of the two islands, Ile St-Louis, is prime strolling territory. Unlike its larger neighbour, it has no big sights; rather, the island's allure lies in its handsome ensemble of austerely beautiful seventeenth-century houses, tree-lined *quais* and narrow streets, crammed with restaurants, art galleries and gift shops. For centuries the Ile St-Louis was nothing but swampy pastureland, a haunt of lovers, duellists and miscreants on the run, until in the seventeenth century the real-estate developer, Christophe Marie, filled it with elegant mansions.

Shops

BERTHILLON

31 rue St-Louis-en-l'Ile Ⓜ Pont-Marie. Ⓦ berthillon.fr. Wed–Sun 10am–8pm. MAP PP.36–37, POCKET MAP F17

Long queues form for Berthillon's exquisite ice creams that come in unusual flavours such as rhubarb and Earl Grey tea. No credit cards.

CLAIRE DE REVE

35 rue St-Louis-en-l'Ile Ⓜ Pont-Marie. Ⓦ clairedereve.com. Mon–Sat 11am–7pm. MAP PP.36–37, POCKET MAP F17

The shop of your childhood dreams, stuffed with exquisite wind-up toys and handmade puppets on strings, such as The Three Musketeers, Puss in Boots and other fairy-tale characters, many of them one-offs.

LIBRAIRIE ULYSSE

26 rue St-Louis-en-l'Ile Ⓜ Pont-Marie. Tues–Fri 2–8pm. MAP PP.36–37, POCKET MAP F17

A tiny bookshop, piled from floor to ceiling with new and secondhand travel books.

Restaurants

CAFE ST-REGIS

6 rue Jean du Bellay Ⓜ Pont-Marie. Ⓣ 01 46 34 72 34, Ⓦ cafesaintregisparis.com. Daily 7am–2am. MAP PP.36–37, POCKET MAP E17

A buzzy café-restaurant, ideally situated for people-watching. Come for a morning coffee or the good-value happy hour (7–9pm). Tasty French and American snacks and dishes.

MON VIEIL AMI

69 rue St-Louis-en-l'Ile Ⓜ Pont-Marie. Ⓣ 01 40 46 01 35, Ⓦ mon-vieil-ami.com. Wed–Sun noon–2.30pm & 7–11pm; closed 3 weeks in Jan & Aug. MAP PP.36–37, POCKET MAP E17

Overseen by Michelin-starred Alsatian chef Antoine Westermann, this charming *bistrot* offers bold, zesty cuisine made with seasonal ingredients and an emphasis on vegetables; the wine list includes a selection of Alsatian vintages. Mains cost around €24, and there's a €16 *plat du jour* at lunch.

Bar

TAVERNE HENRI IV

13 place du Pont-Neuf Ⓜ Pont-Neuf. Mon–Sat noon–11pm; closed Aug. MAP PP.36–37, POCKET MAP C16

An old-style wine bar, buzziest at lunchtime when lawyers from the Palais de Justice drop in for generous meat and cheese platters (around €15) and toasted sandwiches.

Music venue

SAINTE-CHAPELLE

4 bd du Palais Ⓜ Cité. Ⓣ 01 44 07 12 38; bookings also at any FNAC (see p.81). MAP PP.36–37, POCKET MAP D16

Classical music concerts are held in the splendid surroundings of the chapel more or less daily. Tickets €34–44.

BERTHILLON

The Louvre

The Louvre is one of the world's truly great museums. Opened in 1793, during the Revolution, it soon acquired the largest art collection on earth, thanks to Napoleon's conquests. Today, it houses paintings, sculpture and precious art objects, from Ancient Egyptian jewellery to the beginnings of Impressionism. Separate from the Louvre proper, but within the palace, are three design museums under the aegis of Les Arts Décoratifs, dedicated to fashion and textiles, decorative arts and advertising.

THE PALACE

MAP P.42, POCKET MAP B15-C15

For centuries the site of the French court, the palace was originally little more than a feudal fortress, begun by Philippe-Auguste in 1200. It wasn't until the reign of François I that the foundations of the present-day building were laid, and from then on almost every sovereign added to the Louvre, leaving the palace a surprisingly harmonious building. Even with the addition in 1989 of the initially controversial glass **Pyramide** in the cour Napoléon – an extraordinary leap of imagination conceived by architect I.M. Pei – the overall effect of the Louvre is of a quintessentially French grandeur and symmetry.

THE LOUVRE

PAINTING

The largest of the museum's collections is its paintings. The early **Italians** are perhaps the most interesting, among them Leonardo da Vinci's *Mona Lisa*. If you want to get near her, go during one of the evening openings, or first thing in the day. Other highlights of the Italian collection include two Botticelli frescoes and Fra Angelico's *Coronation of the Virgin*. Fifteenth- to seventeenth-century Italian paintings line the Grande Galerie, including Leonardo's *Virgin and Child with St Anne* and *Virgin of the Rocks*. Epic-scale nineteenth-century French works are displayed in the parallel suite of rooms, among them the *Coronation of Napoleon I*, by David, Ingres' languorous nude, *La Grande Odalisque*, and Géricault's harrowing *Raft of the Medusa*.

A good point to start a circuit of **French paintings** is with the master of French Classicism, Poussin; his profound themes, taken from antiquity, the Bible and mythology, were to influence generations of artists. You'll need a healthy appetite for Classicism in the next suite of rooms, but there are some arresting portraits. When you move into the less severe eighteenth century, the more intimate paintings of Watteau come as a relief, as do Chardin's intense still lifes. In the later part of the collection, the chilly wind of Neoclassicism blows through the paintings of Gros, Gérard, Prud'hon, David and Ingres, contrasting with the more sentimental style that begins with Greuze and continues into the Romanticism of Géricault and Delacroix. The final rooms take in Corot and the Barbizon school, the precursors of Impressionism. The Louvre's collection of French painting stops at 1848, a date picked up by the Musée d'Orsay (see p.123).

Visiting the Louvre

Ⓜ Louvre Rivoli/Palais Royal-Musée du Louvre. Ⓣ 08 92 68 36 22, Ⓦ louvre.fr. Mon, Thurs, Sat & Sun 9am–6pm, Wed & Fri 9am–9.45pm. €15; free to under-26s on Fri after 6pm, and everyone on the first Sunday of each month (Oct–March only). Same-day readmission allowed. You can buy tickets in advance online. The main entrance is via the Pyramide, but you'll find shorter queues at the entrance directly under the Arc du Carrousel (also accessible from 99 rue de Rivoli and from the Palais Royal-Musée du Louvre métro stop). You can join the fast-track queue at the Pyramide if you've pre-booked or have a museum pass (see p.190).

The museum has three cafés: the elegantly modern *Café Richelieu* (first floor, Richelieu) with its wonderful summer-only terrace offering a view of the Pyramide; *Café Mollien* (first floor, Denon), which is the busiest but also has a summer terrace; and the cosy and classy *Café Denon* (lower ground floor, Denon).

The Louvre

ANTIQUITIES

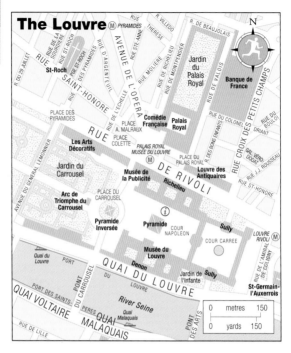

The **Near Eastern Antiquities** category covers the Mesopotamian, Sumerian, Babylonian, Assyrian and Phoenician civilizations, and the art of ancient Persia. One of the collection's most important exhibits is the Code of Hammurabi, a basalt stele from around 1800 BC, covered in Akkadian script setting down King Hammurabi's rules of conduct for his subjects.

The **Egyptian Antiquities** collection starts with the atmospheric crypt of the Sphinx. Everyday life is illustrated through cooking utensils, jewellery, the principles of hieroglyphics, sarcophagi and a host of mummified cats. The collection continues with the development of Egyptian art.

THE GALERIE D'APOLLON

The biggest crowd-pullers after the *Mona Lisa* are found in the **Greek and Roman Antiquities** section: the recently restored *Winged Victory of Samothrace*, and the late second-century-BC *Venus de Milo*, striking a classic model's pose.

OBJETS D'ART

The vast Objets d'Art section presents the finest tapestries, ceramics, jewellery and furniture commissioned by France's wealthiest patrons. It begins with the rather pious Middle Ages section and continues through 81 relentlessly superb rooms to a salon decorated in the style of Louis-Philippe, the last king of France. Walking through the complete chronology gives a powerful sense of the evolution of aesthetic taste at its most refined and opulent. The circuit also passes through the breathtaking apartments of Napoléon III's minister of state.

SCULPTURE

The Sculpture section covers the development of the art in France from the Romanesque to Rodin in the Richelieu wing, and Italian and northern European sculpture in the Denon wing, including Michelangelo's *Slaves*, designed for the tomb of Pope Julius II. The huge glass-covered courtyards of the Richelieu wing – the cour Marly with the Marly Horses, which once graced place de la Concorde, and the cour Puget with Puget's *Milon de Crotone* as the centrepiece – are very impressive.

ISLAMIC ART

The Islamic Art collection was opened in 2012 in the central cour Visconti. The courtyard is covered by an undulating, gold-filigree glass roof – supported by just eight slender columns – that seems to float in mid-air. Suggestive for some of the shimmering wings of an insect, for others a flying carpet or sand dunes, the roof is a fittingly stunning "crown" to the beautiful artworks below. Some 3000 objects are on display, many never before seen by the public, ranging from early Islamic inscriptions to intricate Moorish ivories, and from ninth-century Iraqi moulded glass to exquisite miniature paintings from the courts of Mughal India.

LES ARTS DECORATIFS

107 rue de Rivoli W www.lesartsdecoratifs.fr. Tues–Sun 11am–6pm, Thurs till 9pm (temporary exhibitions only). €11.

Separate from the rest of the Louvre, Les Arts Décoratifs is devoted to design and the applied arts, including fashion, textiles and graphic art. The core of its collection, however, is furnishings, which is arranged chronologically, starting with the medieval and Renaissance rooms, displaying curiously shaped and beautifully carved pieces, religious paintings, tapestries and Venetian glass.

The Art Nouveau and Art Deco rooms include a 1903 bedroom by Hector Guimard – the Art Nouveau designer behind the original Paris métro stations. Individual designers of the 1980s and 90s, such as **Philippe Starck,** are also represented.

The museum also stages regular themed exhibitions, which recently included "Four Centuries of Wallpaper" and "Fashion Unbuttoned", featuring some three thousand buttons by famous designers and artists. Its extensive collection of advertising posters, including Toulouse-Lautrec's posters of Montmartre nightlife, is also the subject of frequent, engaging exhibitions.

The Champs-Elysees and Tuileries

The breathtakingly ambitious Champs-Elysées is part of a grand, nine-kilometre axis, often referred to as the "Voie Triomphale", or Triumphal Way, that extends from the Louvre at the heart of the city to the Défense business district in the west. Combining imperial pomp and supreme elegance, it offers impressive vistas along its entire length and incorporates some of the city's most famous landmarks – the place de la Concorde, Tuileries gardens and the Arc de Triomphe. The whole ensemble is so regular and geometrical it looks as though it might have been laid out by a single town planner rather than successive kings, emperors and presidents, all keen to add their stamp and promote French power and prestige.

THE CHAMPS-ELYSÉES

MAP PP.46–47, POCKET MAP B5–E6

The celebrated avenue des Champs-Elysées, a popular rallying point at times of national crisis and the scene of big military parades on Bastille Day, sweeps down from the Arc de Triomphe towards the place de la Concorde. Its heyday was during the Second Empire when members of the haute bourgeoisie built themselves splendid mansions along its length and fashionable society frequented the avenue's cafés and theatres. Nowadays, this broad, tree-lined avenue is still an impressive sight, especially when viewed from the place de la Concorde, and although fast-food outlets and chain stores tend to predominate, it has been steadily regaining some of its former cachet as a chic address. A number of exclusive designers, such as Louis Vuitton, and major fashion brands including Banana Republic, H&M and Marks & Spencer, have moved in, while remnants of the avenue's glitzy past live on at the *Lido* cabaret, *Fouquet's* café-restaurant, the perfumier Guerlain's shop (occupying an exquisite 1913 building), and the former *Claridges* hotel, now a swanky shopping arcade.

THE ARC DE TRIOMPHE

THE GRAND PALAIS AND THE PONT ALEXANDRE III

THE ARC DE TRIOMPHE

Ⓜ Charles-de-Gaulle. Daily: April–Sept 10am–11pm; Oct–March 10am–10.30pm. €12. MAP PP.46–47, POCKET MAP B5

Crowning the Champs-Elysées, the Arc de Triomphe sits imposingly in the middle of place Charles de Gaulle, also known as l'Etoile ("star") on account of the twelve avenues radiating from it. Modelled on the ancient Roman triumphal arches, this imperial behemoth was built by Napoleon as a homage to the armies of France and is engraved with the names of 660 generals and numerous French battles. The best of the exterior reliefs is François Rude's *Marseillaise*, in which an Amazon-type figure personifying the Revolution charges forward with a sword, her face contorted in a fierce rallying cry. A quiet reminder of the less glorious side of war is the tomb of the unknown soldier placed beneath the arch and marked by an eternal flame that is stoked up every evening by war veterans. The climb up to the top is well worth it for the panoramic views.

THE GRAND PALAIS

Ⓜ Champs-Elysées-Clemenceau. Ⓦ grandpalais.fr. Galeries nationales du Grand Palais: daily except Tues, times vary. €14. MAP PP.46–47, POCKET MAP D6

At the lower end of the Champs-Elysées is the Grand Palais, a grandiose Neoclassical building with a fine glass and ironwork cupola, created for the 1900 Exposition Universelle. The cupola forms the centrepiece of the *nef* (nave), a huge, impressive exhibition space, used for large-scale installations, fashion shows and trade fairs. In the north wing of the building is the Galeries nationales, Paris's prime venue for major art retrospectives.

The Grand Palais' western wing houses the Palais de la Découverte (Ⓦ palais-decouverte.fr; Tues–Sat 9.30am–6pm, Sun 10am–7pm; €9), Paris's original science museum dating from the late 1930s, with interactive exhibits, an excellent planetarium and engaging exhibitions on subjects as diverse as dinosaurs, clay and climate change.

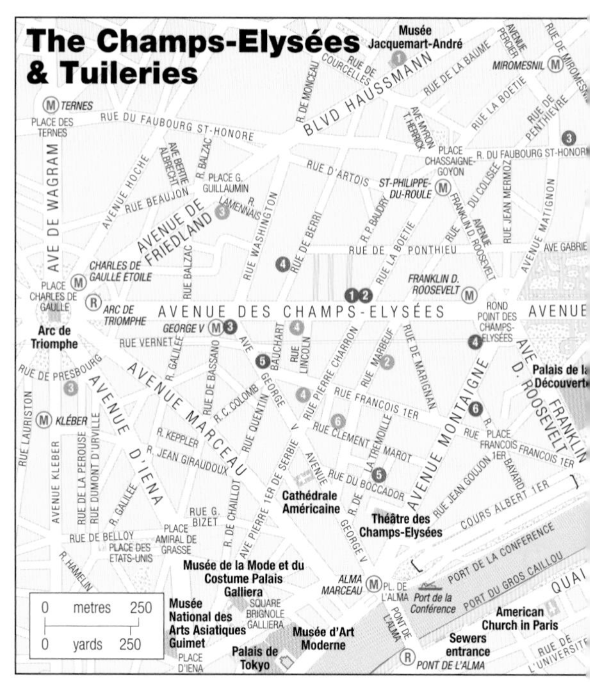

THE PETIT PALAIS

Av Winston Churchill Ⓜ Champs-Elysées-Clemenceau. ⓣ 01 53 43 40 00, Ⓦ petitpalais.paris.fr. Tues–Sun 10am–6pm. Free. MAP PP.46–47, POCKET MAP D6–7

The Petit Palais houses the Musée des Beaux Arts. Built at the same time as its larger neighbour the Grand Palais, the building is hardly "petit" but certainly palatial, with beautiful spiral wrought-iron staircases and a grand gallery on the lines of Versailles' Hall of Mirrors. The museum has an extensive collection of paintings, sculpture and decorative artworks, ranging from the ancient Greek and Roman period up to the early twentieth century. At first sight it looks like it's mopped up the leftovers after the city's other galleries have taken their pick, but there are some real gems here, such as Monet's *Sunset at Lavacourt* and Courbet's provocative *Young Ladies on the Bank of the Seine*. There's also fantasy jewellery of the Art Nouveau period, a fine collection of seventeenth-century Dutch landscape painting, Russian icons and effete eighteenth-century furniture and porcelain. A stylish café overlooks the interior garden, and popular free lunchtime concerts are held every other Thursday at 12.30pm (turn up about an hour in advance to collect a ticket).

MUSEE JACQUEMART-ANDRE

158 bd Haussmann Ⓜ Miromesnil/St-Philippe-du-Roule. ⓣ 01 45 62 11 59, Ⓦ musee-jacquemart-andre.com. Daily 10am–6pm. €12. MAP PP.46–47, POCKET MAP D5

The Musée Jacquemart-André is set in a magnificent nineteenth-century *hôtel particulier* (mansion), hung

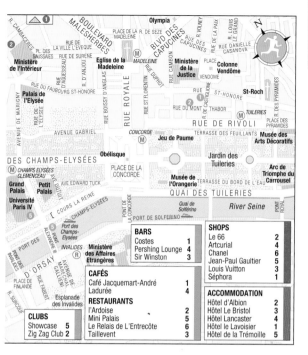

BARS	
Costes	1
Pershing Lounge	4
Sir Winston	3

SHOPS	
Le 66	2
Artcurial	4
Chanel	6
Jean-Paul Gaultier	5
Louis Vuitton	3
Séphora	1

CAFÉS	
Café Jacquemart-André	1
Ladurée	4

RESTAURANTS	
l'Ardoise	2
Mini Palais	5
Le Relais de L'Entrecôte	6
Taillevent	3

ACCOMMODATION	
Hôtel d'Albion	2
Hôtel Le Bristol	3
Hôtel Lancaster	4
Hôtel le Lavoisier	1
Hôtel de la Trémoille	5

CLUBS	
Showcase	5
Zig Zag Club	2

with the superb artworks accumulated on the travels of banker Edouard André and his wife, former society portraitist Nélie Jacquemart. A stunning distillation of fifteenth- and sixteenth-century Italian genius, including works by Tiepolo, Botticelli, Donatello, Mantegna and Uccello, forms the core of the collection. Almost as compelling as the splendid interior and collection of paintings is the insight gleaned into a grand nineteenth-century lifestyle.

THE MUSEE JACQUEMART-ANDRE

PLACE DE LA CONCORDE

Ⓜ Concorde. MAP PP.46–47, POCKET MAP E6–7

The vast place de la Concorde has a much less peaceful history than its name suggests. Between 1793 and 1795, some 1300 people died here beneath the Revolutionary guillotine, Louis XVI, Marie-Antoinette and Robespierre among them. Today, constantly circumnavigated by traffic, the centrepiece of the place is a gold-tipped obelisk from the temple of Ramses at Luxor, offered as a favour-currying gesture by the viceroy of Egypt in 1829.

JARDIN DES TUILERIES

Ⓜ Concorde/Tuileries. Daily: April–June & Sept 7.30am–9pm; July & Aug 7.30am–11.45pm; Oct–March 7.30am–7.30pm. MAP PP.46–47, POCKET MAP E7–F7

The Jardin des Tuileries, the formal French garden par excellence, dates back to the 1570s, when Catherine de Médicis cleared the site of the medieval warren of tile makers (*tuileries*) to make way for a palace and grounds. One hundred years later, Louis XIV commissioned André Le Nôtre to redesign them, and the results are largely what you see today: straight avenues, formal flower beds and splendid vistas. The central alley is lined with clipped chestnuts and manicured lawns, and framed at each end by ornamental pools, surrounded by an impressive gallery of copies of statues by the likes of Rodin.

MUSEE DE L'ORANGERIE

Jardin des Tuileries Ⓜ Concorde. Ⓣ 01 44 77 80 07, Ⓦ musee-orangerie.fr. Daily except Tues 9am–6pm. €9; free for under-26s resident in the EU. MAP PP.46–47, POCKET MAP E7

The Jardin des Tuileries' Orangerie, an elegant Neoclassical-style building designed to protect the garden's orange trees, now houses a private collection of late nineteenth-century art, including eight of Monet's giant water-lily paintings. Highlights from the rest of the collection include sensuous nudes by Renoir and a number of Cézanne still lifes. Book online in advance to avoid long queues.

JEU DE PAUME

Jardin des Tuileries Ⓜ Concorde. Ⓣ 01 47 03 12 50, Ⓦ jeudepaume.org. Tues 11am–9pm, Wed–Sun 11am–7pm. €10. MAP PP.46–47, POCKET MAP E6–7

The Neoclassical Jeu de Paume is a major exhibition space dedicated to photography and video art. It's not as well lit as you might expect from the soaring, light-filled foyer, but it's a top venue for catching major retrospectives of photographers.

JARDIN DES TUILERIES

Shops

LE 66

66 av des Champs-Elysées Ⓜ George V. Mon–Sat 11am–8pm, Sun 1–8pm. MAP PP.46–47, POCKET MAP C6

This stylishly designed glass-walled concept store stocks a great selection of high-end streetwear labels such as Evisu, Raf Simons, American Retro and Acne for both men and women, as well as accessories, international art books and magazines, all in a minimalist space.

ARTCURIAL

61 av Montaigne Ⓜ Franklin-D.-Roosevelt. Ⓦ librairie.artcurial.com. Mon–Fri 9am–7pm, Sat 10.30–7pm; closed two weeks in Aug. MAP PP.46–47, POCKET MAP D6

Arguably the best art bookshop in Paris, set in an elegant townhouse. Sells French and foreign editions, and there's also a gallery, which puts on interesting exhibitions, and a stylish café.

CHANEL

51 av Montaigne Ⓜ Franklin-D.-Roosevelt. Mon–Sat 10am–7pm. MAP PP.46–47, POCKET MAP C6

Born in 1883, Gabrielle "Coco" Chanel engendered a way of life that epitomized elegance, class and refined taste. Her most famous signatures are the legendary No. 5 perfume, the black evening dress and the once-omnipresent tweed suit.

JEAN-PAUL GAULTIER

44 av George V Ⓜ George V. Mon–Sat 10.30am–7pm. MAP PP.46–47, POCKET MAP C6

The primordial young turk of Paris fashion, whose denim collection is within reach of those not being chased by paparazzi.

LOUIS VUITTON SHOP FRONT

LOUIS VUITTON

101 av des Champs-Elysées Ⓜ George V. Mon–Sat 10am–8pm, Sun 11am–7pm. MAP PP.46–47, POCKET MAP C5

You might have to fend off the crowds but the enormous flagship store offers you the best of LV – a "bag bar", jewellery emporium and men's and women's ready-to-wear collections. Don't miss the Espace Culturel exhibition space on the 7th floor – the views over Paris are spectacular.

SEPHORA

70 av des Champs-Elysées Ⓜ Franklin-D.-Roosevelt. Daily 10am–11.30pm. MAP PP.46–47, POCKET MAP C6

A huge perfume and cosmetics emporium, stocking every conceivable brand, including Séphora's own line of fun, girly and reasonably priced cosmetics. There are lots of testers, and you can get free makeovers plus pampering and beauty consultations from the solicitous sales staff. It's also open till midnight, handy if you're out on the town without your lipstick.

THE LADUREE TEA ROOMS

Cafés

CAFE JACQUEMART-ANDRE

158 bd Haussmann Ⓜ Miromesnil/ St-Philippe-du-Roule. Mon–Fri 11.45am–5.30pm, Sat & Sun 11am–5.30pm. MAP PP.46–47, POCKET MAP D5

This, the city's most sumptuously appointed *salon de thé*, is set within the splendid Musée Jacquemart-André. The high ceilings are decorated with detailed frescoes by Tiepolo and the walls hung with antique tapestries. In summer you can sit out on the lovely terrace, set in the mansion's interior courtyard. On the menu are delicious salads and quiches, and the exquisite cakes and pastries are absolutely not to be missed.

LADUREE

75 av des Champs-Elysées Ⓜ George V. Mon–Fri 7.30am–11.30pm, Sat & Sun 8.30am–11.30pm. MAP PP.46–47, POCKET MAP C6

This Champs-Elysées branch of the *Ladurée* tea rooms, with its luxurious gold and green decor, is perfect if you're in need of a shopping break. It's justly famed for its melt-in-the-mouth *macarons* with their gooey fillings (the chocolate and blackcurrant ones are hard to beat), and the light-as-air meringues and millefeuilles are almost as good.

Restaurants

L'ARDOISE

28 rue du Mont Thabor Ⓜ Tuileries. ☎ 01 42 96 28 18, Ⓦ lardoise-paris.com. Mon–Sat noon–2.30pm & 6.30–11pm, Sun 6.30–11pm; closed mid-July to mid-Aug. MAP PP.46–47, POCKET MAP A14

A modern *bistrot* with a friendly atmosphere (the chef frequently pops out of the kitchen to greet diners) and an imaginative take on the classics: think langoustine ravioli, scallops in their shells with herb butter, and banana and caramel crème brûlée. With a three-course set *menu* at €38, this is a good-value, reliable choice.

MINI PALAIS

Av Winston Churchill Ⓜ Champs-Elysées -Clemenceau. ☎ 01 42 56 42 42, Ⓦ minipalais.com. Daily 10am–2am. MAP PP.46–47, POCKET MAP D7

A meal at the Grand Palais' lofty dining room or out on the colonnaded terrace is a real treat. The menu is a sophisticated mix of French classics and more international dishes. You can also come just for a snack, or a drink at the bar. Mains cost €17–39.

LE RELAIS DE L'ENTRECOTE

15 rue Marbeuf Ⓜ Franklin D. Roosevelt. Daily noon–2.30pm & 7–11.30pm; closed Aug. MAP PP.46–47, POCKET MAP C6

Don't worry if a menu isn't forthcoming here – there isn't one. The only dish is *steak frites*, widely considered the best in Paris and served with a delicious sauce, the ingredients of which are a closely kept secret. The set menu of €26.50 includes a salad starter, with desserts around €7 extra. No reservations are taken so you may have to queue, or arrive early.

TAILLEVENT

15 rue Lamennais Ⓜ George V. ⓣ 01 44 95 15 01. Mon–Fri 12.30–2pm & 7.30–10pm; closed Aug. MAP PP.46–47, POCKET MAP C5

The Provençal-influenced cuisine of Alain Solivérés is outstanding, with the emphasis on the classic; dishes include spelt risotto with frogs' legs. The main dining room, with its light-wood panelling and grey-green colour scheme, creates a soothing ambience, and waiters treat you like royalty. There's a set menu for €88 at lunch, otherwise it's around €160–250 a head, excluding wine.

Bars

COSTES

Hôtel Costes, 239 rue St-Honoré Ⓜ Concorde/Tuileries. Mon–Wed & Sun 5pm–2am, Thurs–Sat 7pm–3am. MAP PP.46–47, POCKET MAP A13

A favourite haunt of fashionistas and celebs, this is a glamorous place for an aperitif or late-night drinks amid a decadent nineteenth-century decor of red velvet, swags and columns. Cocktails come in at around €20.

PERSHING LOUNGE

Pershing Hall, 49 rue Pierre Charron Ⓜ George V. Daily 6pm–1am. MAP PP.46–47, POCKET MAP C6

The *Pershing Hall* hotel lounge bar is a delightful retreat from the bustle of the city, with its thirty-metre-high vertical garden. It's a bit of a jetsetters' hangout, with cocktails priced to match.

SIR WINSTON

5 rue du Presbourg Ⓜ Kléber/Charles-de-Gaulle-Etoile. Daily 9am–2am (Thurs–Sat till 4am). MAP PP.46–47, POCKET MAP B5

This British–Indian-themed bar-restaurant boasts a range of comfy leather chesterfields and snug booths that are perfect for lingering over a martini cocktail (€10) or two. Come evening, DJs take to the decks for sets that tend to have a world music slant.

Clubs

SHOWCASE

Below Pont Alexandre III Ⓜ Champs-Elysées-Clemenceau. ⓣ 01 45 61 25 43, Ⓦ showcase.fr. Fri & Sat 11.30pm–dawn. MAP PP.46–47, POCKET MAP D7

This superclub, facing onto the river, has a 1500 capacity, slick decor and a fun crowd. Techno, deep house and drum 'n' bass are the order of the day, with big-name DJs regularly on the decks. Dress up to get in, or sign up online. Entry up to €20.

ZIG ZAG CLUB

32 rue Marbeuf Ⓜ Franklin-D.-Roosevelt. Ⓦ zigzagclub.fr. Fri & Sat 11.30pm–7am. MAP PP.46–47, POCKET MAP C6

This new club has quickly established itself as one of the city's best: it has a huge dancefloor with space for up to 1200 people, a top sound system and an exciting line-up of both established and up-and-coming DJs. Entry €12–27.50.

PERSHING LOUNGE

The Eiffel Tower area

The swathe of the 7e arrondissement from the Eiffel Tower east to St-Germain has little in common with the rest of the Left Bank. Boutique bars and bohemians are few, while mansions and public monuments dominate. Dwarfed by the tower, which casts its timeless spell, the district is also defined by the great military edifices of the Ecole Militaire and Hôtel des Invalides. On a more human scale are the exotic museum of non-Western art, the Musée du Quai Branly, and the intimate Musée Rodin. Across the river, the swish strip of the 16e arrondissement that runs alongside the Seine echoes the staid monumental tone, though a handful of museums – in particular the Site de Création Contemporaine, the Musée Guimet and the Cité de l'Architecture – offer some of the city's most exciting exhibitions.

THE EIFFEL TOWER

RER Champ de Mars–Tour Eiffel. ⓦ toureiffel.paris. Daily: mid-June to Aug 9am–12.45am; Sept to mid-June 9.30am–11.45pm; last entry 45min before closing time. Lift: top level €17; second level €11, or stairs to second level €7; stairs then lift to top level €12 (top level only accessible by lift; access via stairs closes 6pm Sept to mid-June). MAP PP.54–55, POCKET MAP B8

It's hard to believe that the Eiffel Tower, the quintessential symbol both of Paris and the brilliance of industrial engineering, was designed to be a temporary structure for the 1889 Exposition Universelle. When completed, the 300m tower was the tallest building in the world. Outraged critics protested against this "grimy factory chimney", though Eiffel himself thought it was beautiful in its sheer structural efficiency: "To a certain extent," he wrote, "the tower was formed by the wind itself".

THE EIFFEL TOWER AT DUSK

THE PALAIS DE CHAILLOT SEEN FROM THE EIFFEL TOWER

Try and book online well in advance, or turn up before opening time, otherwise you'll face long queues to get in (especially for the lift). It's absolutely worth it, however, not just for the view, but for the exhilaration of being inside the structure, a thrill intensified by the recent renovation of the first level, in which part of the floor has been replaced with glass. The views of the city are usually clearer from the second level, but there's something irresistible about taking the lift all the way up. After dark the tower is lit by a double searchlight, and for the first ten minutes of every hour thousands of effervescent lights fizz about the structure.

PALAIS DE CHAILLOT

Ⓜ Trocadéro. MAP PP.54–55, POCKET MAP A7

From behind its elaborate park and fountains, the sweeping arcs of the Palais de Chaillot seem designed to embrace the view of the Eiffel Tower, which stands on the far side of the river. The totalitarian Modernist-Classical architecture dates the palace to 1937, when it was built as the showpiece of the Exposition Universelle, one of Paris's regular trade and culture jamborees. The central terrace between the palace's two wings provides a perfect platform for photo opportunities, curio-sellers and skateboarders.

CITE DE L'ARCHITECTURE ET DU PATRIMOINE

Palais de Chaillot, 1 place du Trocadéro Ⓜ Trocadéro. ⓣ 01 58 51 52 00, ⓦ www.citechaillot.fr. Mon, Wed & Fri–Sun 11am–7pm, Thurs 11am–9pm; €8.
MAP PP.54–55, POCKET MAP A7–B7

The Cité de l'Architecture et du Patrimoine, in the east wing of the Palais de Chaillot, is a fine museum of architecture. On the loftily vaulted ground floor, the Galerie des Moulages displays giant plaster casts taken from great French buildings at the end of the nineteenth century. You'd never guess these moulds weren't the real thing, and they vividly display the development of national (mainly church) architecture from the Middle Ages to the nineteenth century. The top floor offers a sleek rundown of the modern and contemporary, including a reconstruction of an apartment from Le Corbusier's Cité Radieuse, in Marseille. The Galerie des Peintures Murales, with its radiant, full-scale copies of great French frescoes occupies the top floors.

MUSEE NATIONAL DE LA MARINE

Palais de Chaillot, place du Trocadéro Ⓜ Trocadéro. ⓣ 01 53 65 69 69, Ⓦ musee-marine.fr. Mon & Wed–Sun 11am–6pm. €8.50, €10 including temporary exhibitions. MAP PP.54–55, POCKET MAP A7

While its super-scale models of French ships, ranging from ancient galleys through Napoleon's imperial barges to nuclear submarines, are undeniably impressive, most of the displays in this specialist museum are (ironically) dry as dust – it's best visited if you have a particular interest in one of the lively temporary exhibitions, all on seafaring themes.

CINEAQUA

Jardins du Trocadéro Ⓜ Trocadéro. ⓣ 01 40 69 23 01, Ⓦ cineaqua.com. Daily 10am–7pm. €20.50, children 3–12 €13, children 13–17 €16. MAP PP.54–55, POCKET MAP B7

This high-concept, subterranean aquarium-cum-multimedia complex, consisting of the rather unlikely combination of animation workshops, state-of-the-art tanks, a film museum and classic movie screenings, somehow works and should appeal to any cartoon-loving kid.

MUSEE DE L'HOMME

Palais du Chaillot, place du Trocadéro Ⓜ Trocadéro. ⓣ 01 44 05 72 72, Ⓦ museedelhomme.fr. Mon & Thurs–Sun 10am–6pm, Wed 10am–9pm; €10. MAP PP.54–55, POCKET MAP B7

After six years of closure, the city's anthropological museum reopened in 2015 to much acclaim. The dusty display cabinets have been replaced with a state-of-the-art museum, asking fundamental questions about humankind's origins (and future) through an incredible collection of

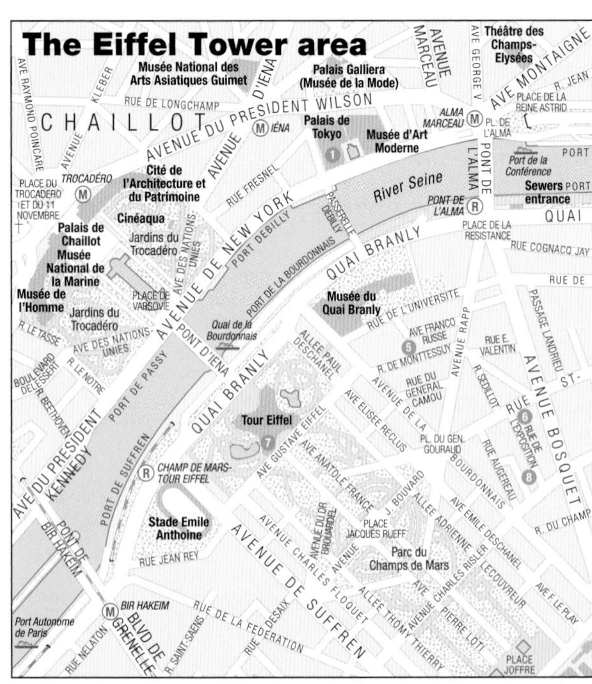

THE MUSEE GUIMET

prehistoric artefacts, including a Cro-Magnon skull and mammoth-tusk sculptures.

MUSEE GUIMET

6 place d'Iéna Ⓜ Iéna. ⓣ 01 56 52 53 00, Ⓦ guimet.fr. Daily except Tues 10am–6pm; €7.50, €9.50 for temporary exhibitions. MAP PP.54–55, POCKET MAP B7

The Musée National des Arts Asiatiques-Guimet boasts a stunning display of Asian, and especially Buddhist, art. Four floors groan under the weight of imaginatively displayed statues of Buddhas and gods, and a roofed-in courtyard provides an airy space in which to show off the museum's world-renowned collection of Khmer sculpture. The Buddhist statues of the Gandhara civilization, on the first floor, betray a fascinating debt to Greek sculpture, while the fierce demons from Nepal, the many-armed gold gods of South India and the pot-bellied Chinese Buddhas are stunningly exotic. One of the most moving exhibits is one of the simplest: a two-thousand-year-old blown-glass fish from Afghanistan.

Founder Emile Guimet's original collection, brought back from Asia in 1876, is exhibited in the temple-like Galeries du Panthéon Bouddhique, at 19 avenue d'Iéna (same hours and ticket as museum).

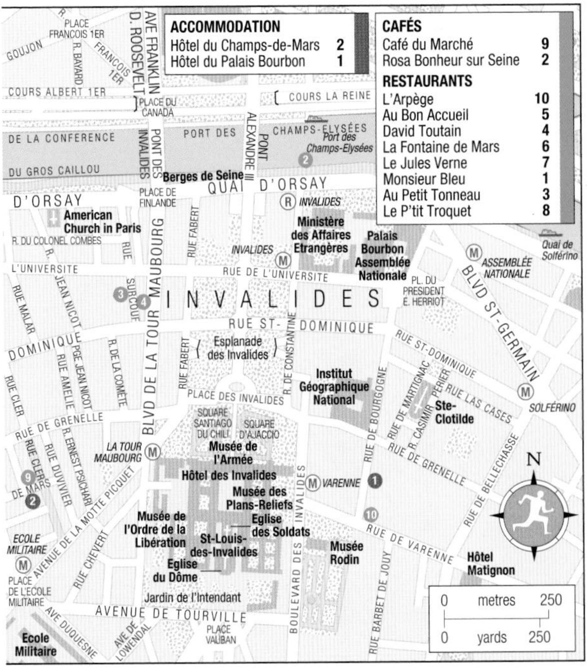

ACCOMMODATION

Hôtel du Champs-de-Mars	2
Hôtel du Palais Bourbon	1

CAFÉS

Café du Marché	9
Rosa Bonheur sur Seine	2

RESTAURANTS

L'Arpège	10
Au Bon Accueil	5
David Toutain	4
La Fontaine de Mars	6
Le Jules Verne	7
Monsieur Bleu	1
Au Petit Tonneau	3
Le P'tit Troquet	8

PALAIS GALLIERA

10 av Pierre 1er de Serbie Ⓜ Iéna/ Alma-Marceau. Ⓣ 01 56 52 86 00, Ⓦ palaisgalliera.paris.fr. Tues, Wed & Fri–Sun 10am–6pm, Thurs 10am–9pm. €8. MAP PP.54–55, POCKET MAP B7

Behind the Palais de Tokyo, the grandiose, recently renovated Palais Galliera – another Neoclassical hulk – is home to the Musée de la Mode, which rotates its magnificent collection of clothes and accessories from the eighteenth century to the present day over the course of a few themed exhibitions a year. During changeovers the museum is closed, so check in advance.

MUSEE D'ART MODERNE DE LA VILLE DE PARIS

11 av du Président Wilson Ⓜ Iéna/ Alma-Marceau. Ⓣ 01 53 67 40 00, Ⓦ mam .paris.fr. Tues–Sun 10am–6pm; during exhibitions also Thurs 10am–10pm. Permanent collection free; temporary shows €5–12. MAP PP.54–55, POCKET MAP B7

While it's no competition for the Pompidou, the cool white Palais de Tokyo is a more contemplative space, offering a fitting Modernist setting for the city's own collection of modern art. Paris-based artists such as Braque, Chagall, Delaunay, Derain, Léger and Picasso are well represented in its strong early twentieth-century collection, and many works have Parisian themes. The enormous centrepieces are two versions of Matisse's *La Danse* and Dufy's giant mural, *La Fée Électricité*, commissioned by the electricity board, which fills an entire curved room with 250 lyrical panels recounting the story of electricity from Aristotle to the 1930s. Temporary exhibitions fill the ground-floor space.

PALAIS DE TOKYO

13 av du Président Wilson Ⓜ Iéna/ Alma-Marceau. Ⓣ 01 47 23 54 01, Ⓦ palaisdetokyo.com. Daily except Tues noon–midnight. €10. MAP PP.54–55, POCKET MAP B7

Spread over four floors, the Palais de Tokyo is one of the largest contemporary art spaces in Europe. Its industrial-looking concrete walls and exposed piping creates a sense of "work in progress", while a changing flow of exhibitions and events – anything from a show by Paris-born Louise Bourgeois to a temporary "occupation" by squatter-artists – keeps the atmosphere lively, with an exciting, countercultural buzz.

PALAIS GALLIERA

PLACE DE L'ALMA

Ⓜ Alma-Marceau. MAP PP.54–55, POCKET MAP C7

From most angles, place de l'Alma looks like just another busy Parisian junction, with cars rattling over the cobbles and a métro entrance on the pavement. Over in one corner, however, stands a replica of the flame from the Statue of Liberty, which was given to France in 1987 as a symbol of Franco-American relations.

This golden torch has been adopted by mourners from all over the world as a memorial to Princess Diana, who was killed in the underpass beneath in 1997.

THE SEWERS

Place de la Résistance, RER Pont de l'Alma/Ⓜ Alma-Marceau. ⓣ 01 53 68 27 81. Sat–Wed: May–Sept 11am–5pm; Oct–April 11am–4pm. €7. MAP PP.54–55, POCKET MAP C7

Opposite the Pont de l'Alma on the northeast side of the busy junction of place de la Résistance, is the entrance to one of Paris's more unusual attractions – a small, visitable section of the sewers, or *les égouts*. Underground, it's dark, damp and noisy from the gushing water; the main exhibition runs along a gantry walk poised above a main sewer. The photographs, lamps, specialized sewermen's tools and other antique flotsam and jetsam render the history of the city's water supply and waste management surprisingly interesting. The air down here is as smelly and unappealing as you might expect, so those of a nervous disposition might want to give it a miss.

RUE CLER AND AROUND

Ⓜ La Tour-Maubourg. MAP PP.54–55, POCKET MAP C8

A little further upstream, the **American Church** on quai

SEWERMEN'S LAMPS ON DISPLAY AT THE SEWERS

d'Orsay, together with the American College nearby at 31 av Bosquet, is a focal point in the well-organized life of Paris's large American community, its notice board usually plastered with job and accommodation offers and requests. Immediately to the south, and in stark contrast to the austerity of much of the rest of the quarter, lies a villagey wedge of early nineteenth-century streets between avenue Bosquet and the Invalides. Chief among them is **rue Cler**, whose food shops act as a kind of permanent market. The cross-streets, rue de Grenelle and rue St-Dominique, are full of neighbourhood shops, posh *bistrots* and little hotels.

PARC DU CHAMPS DE MARS

Ⓜ École Militaire. MAP PP.54–55, POCKET MAP B8–C9

Parading back from the Eiffel Tower are the long, rectangular and tourist-thronged gardens of the **Champs de Mars**, leading to the eighteenth-century **École Militaire**, originally founded in 1751 by Louis XV for the training of aristocratic army officers, and attended by Napoleon, among other fledgling leaders.

MUSEE DU QUAI BRANLY

37 Quai Branly Ⓜ Iéna/RER Pont de l'Alma. Ⓣ 01 56 61 71 72, Ⓦ quaibranly.fr. Tues, Wed & Sun 11am–7pm, Thurs–Sat 11am–9pm. €9, €11 including temporary exhibits. MAP PP.54–55, POCKET MAP B7–8

A short distance upstream of the Eiffel Tower, on quai Branly, stands the intriguing Musée du Quai Branly, designed by the French state's favourite architect, Jean Nouvel. The museum – which gathers together hundreds of thousands of non-European objects bought or purloined by France over the centuries – was the brainchild of President Chirac, whose passion for what he would no doubt call *arts primitifs* helped secure funding. Nouvel's elaborate design, which aims to blur the divide between structure and environment, unfurls in a long glazed curve, pocked with coloured boxes, through the middle of an enormous garden. Inside, areas devoted to Asia, Africa, the Americas and the Pacific ("Oceania") snake through dimly lit rooms lined by curving "mud" walls in brown leather. The 3500 folk artefacts on display at any one time – Hopi kachina dolls, ancient Hawaiian feather helmets – are as fascinating as they are beautiful; the tone of the place, however, is muddled. While the objects are predominantly displayed – and easily experienced – as works of art, there's an uneasy sense that they are being presented above all in terms of their exotic "otherness". This is not helped when the museum loses the courage of its convictions, shifting into outdated anthropological mode, using written (and often poorly translated) panels to give lofty cultural context.

HOTEL DES INVALIDES

Ⓜ Varenne/La Tour-Maubourg. Ⓦ musee-armee.fr. MAP PP.54–55, POCKET MAP D8

There's no missing the overpowering facade of the Hôtel des Invalides, topped by its resplendently gilded dome. Despite its palatial, crushingly grand appearance, it was built as a home for wounded soldiers in the reign of Louis XIV – whose foreign wars gave the building a constant supply of residents, and whose equestrian statue lords it over a massive central arch. It today houses two churches – one for the soldiers, the other intended as a mausoleum for the king but now containing the mortal remains of Napoleon – and the

MUSEE DU QUAI BRANLY

THE DOME OF THE HOTEL DES INVALIDES

Musée de l'Armée, an enormous national war museum. The most interesting sections of the museum are detailed below, but the remainder, dedicated to the history of the French army from Louis XIV up to the 1870s, is really for fanatics only.

MUSEE DE L'ARMEE

Hôtel des Invalides Ⓜ La Tour-Maubourg/Varenne. Ⓣ 01 44 42 38 77, Ⓦ musee-armee.fr. Daily: April–Oct 10am–6pm; Nov–March 10am–5pm; Oct–June closed first Mon of every month. €11 ticket also valid for Napoleon's tomb. MAP PP.54–55, POCKET MAP D8

By far the most affecting galleries of the vast Musée de l'Armée cover the two world wars, beginning with Prussia's annexation of Alsace-Lorraine in 1871 and ending with the defeat of the Third Reich. The battles, the resistance and the slow liberation are documented through imaginatively displayed war memorabilia combined with stirring contemporary newsreels, most of which have an English-language option. The simplest artefacts – a rag doll found on a battlefield, plaster casts of mutilated faces, an overcoat caked in mud from the trenches – tell a stirring human story, while un-narrated footage, from the Somme, Dunkirk and a bomb attack on a small French town, flicker across bare walls in grim silence. The collection of medieval and Renaissance armour in the west wing of the royal courtyard is also worth admiring. Highlights include highly decorative seventeenth-century Italian suits, and two dimly lit chambers of beautifully worked Chinese and Japanese weaponry.

MUSEE DES PLANS-RELIEFS

Same hours and ticket as the Musée de l'Armée. MAP PP.54–55, POCKET MAP D8

Up under the roof of the east wing, the Musée des Plans-Reliefs displays an extraordinary collection of super-scale models of French ports and fortified cities. Essentially giant three-dimensional maps, they were created in the seventeenth and eighteenth centuries to plan defences or plot potential artillery positions. The eerie green glow of their landscapes only just illuminates the long, tunnel-like attic; the effect is rather chilling.

EGLISE DES SOLDATS

Entrance from main courtyard of Les Invalides. Daily 9.30am–5.30pm. Free. MAP PP.54–55, POCKET MAP D8

The lofty "Soldiers' Church" is the spiritual home of the French army, its proud simplicity standing in stark contrast to the elaborate Eglise du Dôme, which lies on the other side of a dividing glass wall – an innovation that allowed worshippers to share the same high altar without the risk of coming into social contact. The walls are hung with almost one hundred enemy standards captured on the battlefield, part of a collection of some three thousand that once adorned Notre-Dame.

NAPOLEON'S TOMB

EGLISE DU DOME

Entrance from south side of Les Invalides. Same hours and ticket as the Musée de l'Armée. MAP PP.54–55, POCKET MAP D8

Some find the lavish Eglise du Dôme, or "royal church", gloriously sumptuous – others find it overbearing. A perfect example of the architectural pomposity of Louis XIV's day, with grandiose frescoes and an abundance of Corinthian columns and pilasters, it is now a monument to Napoleon.

NAPOLEON'S TOMB

Eglise du Dôme. Same hours and ticket as the Musée de l'Armée. MAP PP.54–55, POCKET MAP D8

On December 14, 1840, Napoleon was finally laid to rest in the crypt of the Eglise du Dôme. Brought home from St Helena twenty years after his death, his remains were carried through the streets from the newly completed Arc de Triomphe to the Invalides. As many as half a million people came out to watch the emperor's last journey, and Victor Hugo commented that "It felt as if the whole of Paris had been poured to one side of the city, like liquid in a vase which has been tilted". He now lies in a giant sarcophagus of smooth red porphyry, encircled with Napoleonic quotations of staggering but largely truthful conceit, and overshadowing the nearby tombs of two of his brothers, as well as his son, the King of Rome, whose body was brought here on Hitler's orders in 1940. Another chapel upstairs holds Marshal Foch, the Supreme Commander of Allied forces in World War I.

MUSEE RODIN

79 rue de Varenne Ⓜ Varenne. ☎ 01 44 18 61 10, Ⓦ musee-rodin.fr. Tues & Thurs–Sun 10am–5.45pm, Wed 10am–8.45pm. Museum and garden €10; garden only €4. MAP PP.54–55, POCKET MAP D8

The setting of the recently refurbished Musée Rodin is superbly elegant, a beautiful eighteenth-century mansion which the sculptor leased from the state in return for the gift of all his work upon his death. Bronze versions of major projects like *The Burghers of Calais*, *The Thinker*, *The Gate of Hell* and *Ugolino* are exhibited in the large gardens – the last-named of these works forms the centrepiece of the ornamental pond, and there's also a pleasant outdoor café.

Inside, the passionate intensity of the sculptures contrasts with the graceful wooden panelling and chandeliers. The museum is usually very crowded with visitors eager to see much-loved works like *The Hand of God* and the touchingly erotic *The Kiss*, which was originally designed to portray Paolo and Francesca da Rimini, from Dante's *Divine Comedy*, in the moment before they were discovered and murdered by Francesca's husband. Rodin once self-deprecatingly referred to it as "a large sculpted knick-knack following the usual formula"; art critics today like to think of it as the last masterwork of figurative sculpture before the whole art form was reinvented – largely by Rodin himself. Paris's *Kiss* is one of only four marble versions of the work, but hundreds of smaller bronzes were turned out as money-spinners.

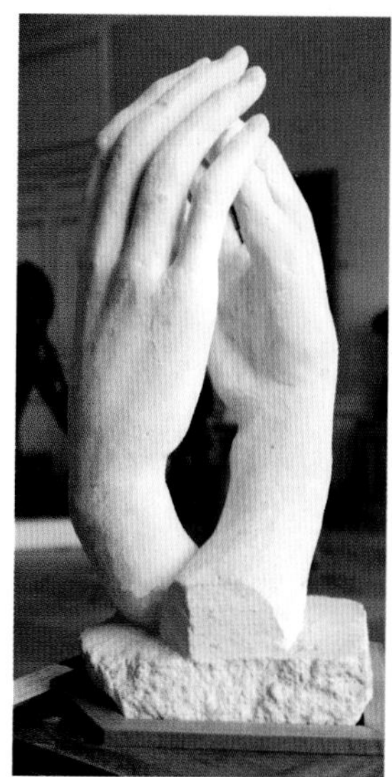
SCULPTURE AT THE MUSEE RODIN

COURTYARD STATUE AT THE MUSEE RODIN

It's well worth lingering over the museum's vibrant, impressionistic clay works, small studies that Rodin took from life. In fact, most of the works here are in clay or plaster, as these are considered to be Rodin's finest achievements – after completing his apprenticeship, he rarely picked up a chisel, in line with the common nineteenth-century practice of delegating the task of working up stone and bronze versions to assistants. Instead, he would return to his plaster casts again and again, modifying and refining them and sometimes deliberately leaving them "unfinished".

Don't miss the room devoted to Camille Claudel, Rodin's pupil, model and lover. Among her works is the painfully allegorical *The Age of Maturity*, symbolizing her ultimate rejection by Rodin, and a bust of the artist himself. Claudel's perception of her teacher was so akin to Rodin's own that he considered it his self-portrait.

Cafés

CAFE DU MARCHE

38 rue Cler Ⓜ La-Tour-Maubourg. Mon–Sat 7am–midnight, Sun 7am–4pm. MAP PP.54–55, POCKET MAP C8

Big, busy café-brasserie in the rue Cler market serving reasonably priced meals, with hearty salads and market-fresh *plats du jour*. Outdoor seating, with a covered terrace in winter.

ROSA BONHEUR SUR SEINE

Near Pont Alexandre III Ⓜ Invalides. Ⓦ rosabonheur.fr. Mon & Tues 5.30pm–2am, Wed–Sun noon–2am. MAP PP.54–55, POCKET MAP D7

On a floating barge moored alongside the Berges de Seine, this café-bar, offshoot of the popular *Rosa Bonheur* in the Parc des Buttes-Chaumont, is the perfect place for a relaxing coffee or cocktail, or a pizza from their riverside food truck.

Restaurants

L'ARPEGE

84 rue de Varenne Ⓜ Varenne. Ⓣ 01 47 05 09 06. Mon–Fri noon–2.30pm & 7.30–10.30pm. MAP PP.54–55, POCKET MAP E8

Elite chef Alain Passard puts the spotlight on vegetables at this Michelin-starred restaurant – grilled turnips with chestnuts, or beetroot baked in salt crust are astonishingly good – but you'll also find plenty of other exhilarating dishes. Lunch *menu* €145, with an incredible *menu dégustation* at €380. Reserve well in advance and dress up.

AU BON ACCUEIL

14 rue de Monttessuy Ⓜ Duroc/Vaneau. Ⓣ 01 47 05 46 11. Mon–Fri noon–2.30pm & 7–10.30pm. MAP PP.54–55, POCKET MAP C8

Practically in the shadow of the Eiffel Tower, this relaxed but upbeat wine-*bistrot* offers fresh, well-considered dishes, such as a salad of prawns and lemon verbena, and veal liver with Jerusalem artichoke purée. There are a few outside tables. Expect to pay around €60 with wine.

DAVID TOUTAIN

29 rue Surcouf Ⓜ Invalides/La Tour Maubourg. Ⓣ 01 45 50 11 10, Ⓦ davidtoutain.com. Mon–Fri noon–2.30pm & 8–10pm; closed two weeks in Aug. MAP PP.54–55, POCKET MAP D7

An intimate, contemporary restaurant, with lots of natural wood and light, serving original, creative cuisine made with seasonal ingredients, especially farm-fresh veg and delicate fish. Typical dishes include beetroot rolls, scallops in Jerusalem artichoke bouillon, and smoked eel with black sesame sauce. No-choice tasting menus at €55 (lunch) and €80/110 (dinner). Booking essential.

LA FONTAINE DE MARS

129 rue Saint-Dominique Ⓜ La Tour-Maubourg. Ⓣ 01 47 05 46 44, Ⓦ fontainedemars.com. Daily noon–2.30pm & 7.30–11pm. MAP PP.54–55, POCKET MAP C8

Pink checked tablecloths, leather banquettes, tiled floor, outside

L'ARPEGE

tables, attentive service: this is quintessential France – the Obama family certainly enjoyed it. The food is meaty, south-western French fare: think snails, *magret de canard* and *boudin* sausages. Starters €9–16, *plat du jour* €22.

LE JULES VERNE

Eiffel Tower Ⓜ Bir-Hakeim. ☎ 01 45 55 61 44, Ⓦ lejulesverne-paris.com. Daily noon–1.30pm & 7–9.30pm. MAP PP.54–55, POCKET MAP B8

It's not only the food, overseen by superchef Alain Ducasse, that's elevated here, but the restaurant too: it's 125m up the Eiffel Tower. Best at dinner (from €190), but the weekday lunch is a more bearable €105. Reserve well in advance and dress smartly.

MONSIEUR BLEU

Palais de Tokyo, 20 Ave de New York Ⓜ Iéna/Alma-Marceau. ☎ 01 47 20 90 47. Daily noon–midnight. MAP PP.54–55, POCKET MAP B7

The more stylish of the two restaurants inside this cutting-edge gallery, *Monsieur Bleu* is an elegant, high-ceilinged Art Deco dining room with an outdoor terrace, perfect in summer for stunning views of the Eiffel Tower. The food – a mix of traditional French and fusion cuisine – is well prepared and tasty, and not too high-priced considering the location (around €55–65 à la carte). The gallery's other restaurant, *Tokyo Eat*, is a more casual, self-consciously hip hangout, serving a fusion of modern Mediterranean and Asian cuisine (mains €18–30).

MONSIEUR BLEU

AU PETIT TONNEAU

20 rue Surcouf Ⓜ Invalides. ☎ 01 47 53 05 59, Ⓦ aupetittonneau.fr. Wed–Sun noon–3pm & 7–11.30pm. Closed Aug. MAP PP.54–55, POCKET MAP D7

Mme Boyer runs this friendly *bistrot*-style restaurant with panache, cooking delicious French cuisine. Wild mushrooms are a speciality, as is the *tarte tatin*. There's a lunch set menu for €24; otherwise count on around €39 for three courses.

LE P'TIT TROQUET

28 rue de l'Exposition Ⓜ Ecole Militaire. ☎ 01 47 05 80 39. Tues–Fri noon–2.30pm & 6.30–10.30pm, Sat 6.30–10.30pm. MAP PP.54–55, POCKET MAP C8

This tiny, discreet family restaurant has a nostalgic feel with its marble tables, tiled floor and ornate zinc bar. Serving refined cuisine to the diplomats of the *quartier*, the well-judged, traditional menu changes seasonally; on a summer *menu du marché* (€35) for example, you might find tabbouleh with herbs, grapefruit and prawns, followed by rabbit with mustard.

The Grands Boulevards and *passages*

Built on the old city ramparts, the Grands Boulevards are the eight broad streets that extend in a long arc from the Eglise de la Madeleine eastwards. In the nineteenth century, the boulevards, with their fashionable cafés, street theatre and puppet shows, were where "Paris vivant" was to be found. A legacy from this heyday, brasseries, cafés, theatres and cinemas (notably the splendid Art Deco cinemas Le Grand Rex and Max Linder Panorama; see p.188) still abound. To the south of the Grands Boulevards lies the city's main commercial and financial district, while just to the north, beyond the glittering Opéra Garnier, are the large department stores Galeries Lafayette and Printemps. Rather more well-heeled shopping is concentrated on the rue St-Honoré in the west and the streets around aristocratic place Vendôme, lined with top couturiers, jewellers and art dealers. Scattered around the whole area are the delightful *passages* – nineteenth-century arcades that hark back to shopping from a different era.

THE OPERA GARNIER

THE CARTIER BOUTIQUE ON PLACE VENDOME

MUSEE GREVIN

10 bd Montmartre Ⓜ Grands-Boulevards. Mon–Fri 10am–6.30pm, Sat & Sun 10am–7pm. €24.50, children €17.50. MAP PP.66–67, POCKET MAP G5

A remnant from the fun-loving times on the Grands Boulevards are the waxworks in the Musée Grévin, comprising mainly French personalities and the usual bunch of Hollywood actors. The best thing about the museum is the original rooms: the magical Palais des Mirages (Hall of Mirrors), built for the Exposition Universelle in 1900; the theatre with its sculptures by Bourdelle; and the 1882 Baroque-style Hall of Columns.

OPERA GARNIER

Ⓜ Opéra. Ⓦ opera-de-paris.fr. Daily 10am–4.30pm. €11; see p.77 for booking information. MAP PP.66–67, POCKET MAP F5

The ornate Opéra Garnier, built by Charles Garnier for Napoléon III, exemplifies the Second Empire in its show of wealth and hint of vulgarity. The theatre's facade is a concoction of white, pink and green marble, colonnades, rearing horses and gleaming gold busts. No less opulent is the interior with its spacious gilded-marble and mirrored lobbies. The auditorium is all red velvet and gold leaf, hung with a six-tonne chandelier; the colourful ceiling was painted by Chagall in 1964 and depicts scenes from well-known operas and ballets jumbled up with Parisian landmarks. You can visit the interior and auditorium outside of rehearsals (your best chance is 1–2pm); entry is on the corner of rues Scribe and Auber.

PLACE VENDOME

Ⓜ Opéra. MAP PP.66–67, POCKET MAP A13

Built by Versailles architect Hardouin-Mansart, place Vendôme is one of the city's most impressive set pieces. It's a pleasingly symmetrical, eight-sided square, enclosed by a harmonious ensemble of elegant mansions, graced with Corinthian pilasters and steeply pitched roofs. Once the grand residences of tax collectors and financiers, they now house such luxury establishments as the *Ritz* hotel, Cartier, Bulgari and other top-flight jewellers, lending the square a decidedly exclusive air. No. 12, now occupied by Chaumet jewellers, is where Chopin died, in 1849.

Somewhat out of proportion with the rest of the square, the centrepiece is a towering triumphal column, surmounted by a statue of Napoleon dressed as Caesar. It was raised in 1806 to celebrate the Battle of Austerlitz and features bronze reliefs of scenes of the battle spiralling their way up.

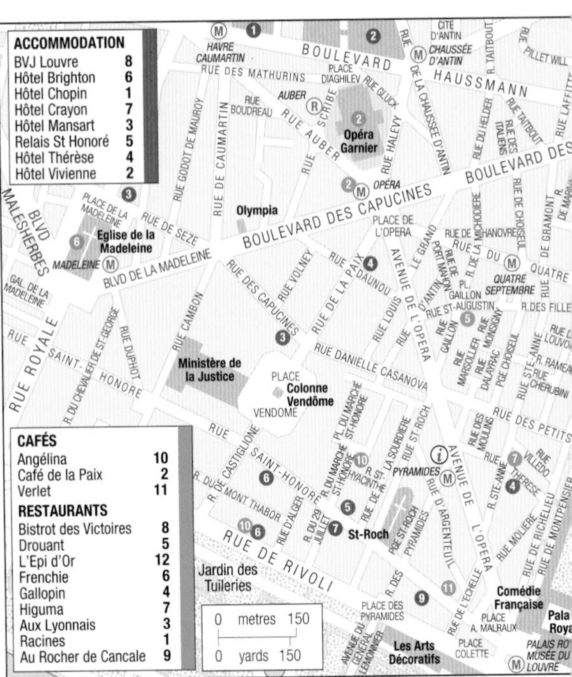

EGLISE DE LA MADELEINE

Ⓜ Madeleine. Ⓦ eglise-lamadeleine.com. Daily 9.30am–7pm. MAP PP.66–67, POCKET MAP E6

Originally intended as a monument to Napoleon's army, the imperious-looking Eglise de la Madeleine is modelled on the Parthenon, surrounded by Corinthian columns and fronted by a huge pediment depicting The Last Judgement. Inside, the wide single nave is decorated with Ionic columns and surmounted by three huge domes – the only source of natural light. A theatrical stone sculpture of the Magdalene being swept up to heaven by two angels draws your eye to the high altar, and above is a half-dome with a fresco commemorating the concordat signed between the Church and Napoleon, healing the rift after the Revolution.

PLACE DE LA MADELEINE

Ⓜ Madeleine. Flower market Tues–Sat 8am–7.30pm. MAP PP.66–67, POCKET MAP E6

Place de la Madeleine is home to some of Paris's top gourmet food stores, one of the best known being Fauchon (see p.70). On the east side is one of the city's oldest flower markets dating to 1832, while nearby, some rather fine Art Nouveau public toilets are worth inspecting.

RUE ST-HONORE

MAP PP.66–67, POCKET MAP A13–D15

Rue St-Honoré – especially its western end and the Faubourg St-Honoré – hosts top fashion designers and art galleries. Admire the beautiful silk scarves at Hermès at no. 24 or join the style-conscious Parisians at the Colette concept store at no. 213 (see p.70).

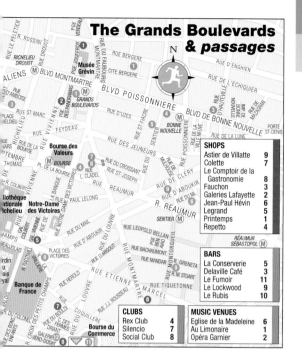

The Grands Boulevards & *passages*

SHOPS
Astier de Villatte 9
Colette 7
Le Comptoir de la Gastronomie 8
Fauchon 3
Galeries Lafayette 2
Jean-Paul Hévin 6
Legrand 5
Printemps 1
Repetto 4

BARS
La Conserverie 5
Delaville Café 3
Le Fumoir 11
Le Lockwood 9
Le Rubis 10

CLUBS
Rex Club 4
Silencio 7
Social Club 8

MUSIC VENUES
Eglise de la Madeleine 6
Au Limonaire 1
Opéra Garnier 2

PALAIS ROYAL

Ⓜ Palais Royal-Musée du Louvre. Gardens daily dawn–dusk. Free. MAP PP.66–67, POCKET MAP B14–C14

The Palais Royal was built for Cardinal Richelieu in 1624, though little now remains of the original palace. The current building, mostly dating from the eighteenth century, houses various governmental bodies and the Comédie Française, long-standing venue for the classics of French theatre. To the rear lie sedate gardens with fountains and avenues of clipped limes, bounded by stately eighteenth-century mansions built over arcades housing quirky antique and designer shops. You'd hardly guess that for a time these peaceful arcades and gardens were a site of gambling dens, brothels and funfair attractions until the prohibition on public gambling in 1838 put an end to the fun. Folly, some might say, has returned – in the form of contemporary artist Daniel Buren's black-and-white-striped pillars. They're rather like sticks of Brighton rock of varying heights, dotted about the main courtyard in front of the palace.

THE PALAIS ROYAL

The *passages*

Conceived by town planners in the early nineteenth century to protect pedestrians from mud and horse-drawn vehicles, the *passages*, elegant glass-roofed shopping arcades, were for decades left to crumble and decay. Many have been renovated and restored to something approaching their former glory, and chic boutiques have moved in alongside the old-fashioned traders and secondhand dealers. Most are closed at night and on Sundays.

GALERIE VERO-DODAT

Between rue Croix-des-Petits-Champs and rue Jean-Jacques Rousseau Ⓜ Palais Royal-Musée du Louvre. MAP PP.66–67, POCKET MAP C14

With its tiled floors, ceiling decorations and mahogany shop fronts divided by faux marble columns, Galerie Véro-Dodat is one of the most attractive and homogeneous *passages*. Fashionable new shops rub shoulders with older businesses, such as R.F. Charle at no. 17, specializing in the repair and sale of vintage stringed instruments.

THE GALERIE VIVIENNE

GALERIE VIVIENNE

Links rue Vivienne with rue des Petits-Champs Ⓜ Bourse. MAP PP.66–67, POCKET MAP C13–14

The flamboyant decor of Grecian and marine motifs in charming Galerie Vivienne establishes the perfect ambience in which to buy Jean-Paul Gaultier gear, or you can browse in the antiquarian bookshop, Librairie Jousseaume, which dates back to the arcade's earliest days.

PASSAGE CHOISEUL

Links rue des Petits Champs and rue St Augustin Ⓜ Pyramides. MAP PP.66–67, POCKET MAP B13

Evocatively described by Louis-Ferdinand Céline in his autobiographical *Death on Credit*, the once dark and dingy passage Choiseul is now flooded with light again after its glass roof was repaired in 2013. It harbours takeaway food stores, discount clothes and shoe shops and art galleries.

PASSAGE DES PANORAMAS

Off rue Vivienne Ⓜ Grands-Boulevards. MAP PP.66–67, POCKET MAP G6

This slightly shabby-looking grid of arcades is known for its stamp dealers and, more recently, a growing number of restaurants. The restaurant at no. 57 is worth a look for its carved wood ornamentation dating from the 1900s, as is *Caffè Stern* at no. 47, which used to house an old print shop and still has its original 1834 decor.

THE PASSAGE DU GRAND-CERF

PASSAGES JOUFFROY AND VERDEAU

Off bd Montmartre Ⓜ Grands-Boulevards. MAP PP.66–67, POCKET MAP G5

Across boulevard Montmartre, passage Jouffroy is full of the kind of stores that make shopping an adventure rather than a chore. M & G Segas sells eccentric walking canes and theatrical antiques opposite a shop stocking every conceivable fitting and furnishing for a doll's house; while near the romantic *Hôtel Chopin* (see p.172), Librairie de Passage displays art books along the passageway, and Ciné-Doc appeals to cinephiles with its collection of old film posters. Crossing rue de la Grange-Batelière, you enter the equally enchanting passage Verdeau, perhaps the lightest of the arcades, with its high glass ceiling sheltering antiquarian books and old prints.

PASSAGE DU GRAND-CERF

Between rue St-Denis and rue Dessoubs Ⓜ Etienne-Marcel. MAP PP.66–67, POCKET MAP D14–E14

The lofty, three-storey passage du Grand-Cerf arcade is stylistically the best of all. The wrought-iron work, glass roof and plain-wood shop fronts have all been cleaned, attracting stylish contemporary design, jewellery and fairtrade boutiques. There's always something quirky and original on display in the window of Le Labo (no. 4), specializing in lamps and other lighting fixtures made from recycled objects, while As'Art, opposite, is a treasure-trove of home furnishings and objects from Africa.

BIBLIOTHEQUE NATIONALE RICHELIEU

58 rue de Richelieu Ⓜ Bourse. Ⓦ bnf.fr. Exhibition times and admission vary. MAP PP.66–67, POCKET MAP C13

The French National Library, a huge, forbidding building that dates to the 1660s, is currently undergoing major renovations, due for completion in 2019. Parts of the library will remain open for exhibitions, but check the website for updates. The Cabinet des Monnaies, Médailles et Antiques, a display of coins and ancient treasures, is currently closed and will be moved to grander rooms as part of the renovations. There's no restriction on entering the library, nor on peering into the atmospheric reading rooms, though many of the books have now been transferred to the new François Mitterrand site in the 13ᵉ (see p.130).

Shops

As well as the shops below, be sure to check out the *passages*, fertile hunting ground for curios and one-off buys.

ASTIER DE VILLATTE

173 rue St-Honoré Ⓜ Palais Royal. Mon–Sat 11am–7.30pm. MAP PP.66–67, POCKET MAP B14

An atmospheric old shop full of oak cabinets displaying stylish ceramic dinnerware. The pieces (starting from around €40) manage to seem elegant and rustic at the same time, with their milky white glaze and slightly unfinished look.

COLETTE

213 rue St-Honoré Ⓜ Tuileries. Ⓦ colette.fr. Mon–Sat 11am–7pm. MAP PP.66–67, POCKET MAP A14

Style-conscious young Parisians peruse the latest Anya Hindmarch handbags and Prada offerings at this cutting-edge concept store, combining high fashion, design and cool gadgetry. Downstairs is the *Water Bar*, with eighty different kinds of bottled H_2O, plus contemporary comfort food.

LE COMPTOIR DE LA GASTRONOMIE

34 rue Montmartre Ⓜ Etienne Marcel. Ⓣ 01 42 33 31 32. Mon–Sat 6am–8pm; restaurant Mon–Sat noon–11pm. MAP PP.66–67, POCKET MAP D14

The walls of this lovely old-fashioned shop are stacked high with foie gras, *saucisses*, hams, terrines, oils and wine. You can also buy takeaway baguettes or dine on delicious cassoulet, onion soup and roast duck in the attached restaurant.

FAUCHON

24–30 place de la Madeleine Ⓜ Madeleine. Ⓦ fauchon.com. Mon–Sat 9am–8pm. MAP PP.66–67, POCKET MAP E6

A cornucopia of extravagant

INSIDE THE GALERIES LAFAYETTE

and beautiful groceries, charcuterie and wines. Just the place for presents of tea, jam, truffles, chocolates, exotic vinegars and mustards.

GALERIES LAFAYETTE

40 bd Haussmann Ⓜ Chaussée d'Antin. Mon–Sat 9.30am–8pm, Thurs until 9pm. MAP PP.66–67, POCKET MAP F5

This venerable department store's forte is high fashion, with two floors given over to the latest creations by leading designers and nearly a whole floor devoted to lingerie. Then there's a host of big names in men's and women's accessories and a huge parfumerie – all under a superb 1900 dome. Just down the road at no. 35 is Lafayette Maison: five floors of quality kitchenware, linen and furniture.

JEAN-PAUL HEVIN

231 rue St-Honoré Ⓜ Tuileries. Mon–Sat 10am–7.30pm; closed 1 week in Aug. MAP PP.66–67, POCKET MAP A14

Jean-Paul Hévin is one of Paris's best chocolatiers. His sleek shop displays an array of elegantly presented tablets of chocolate, bearing little descriptions of their aroma and characteristics as though they were choice wines; try for example the São Tomé, with its "grande intensité aromatique". Upstairs is a cosy *salon de thé*, where you can choose from over thirty cakes and ten different kinds of hot chocolate.

LEGRAND

1 rue de la Banque Ⓜ Bourse. Mon 11am–7pm, Tues–Fri 10am–7.30pm, Sat 10.30am–7.30pm. MAP PP.66–67, POCKET MAP C14

This beautiful old wine shop is the place to stock up on your favourite vintages and discover some little-known ones too. There's also a bar (noon–7pm) for drinks, *saucisson* and pâté.

PRINTEMPS

64 bd Haussmann Ⓜ Havre-Caumartin. Mon–Sat 9.35am–8pm, Thurs until 10pm. MAP PP.66–67, POCKET MAP F5

This venerable old department store stocks a wide range of luxury brands, with three floors devoted to womenswear, plus a whole floor given over to shoes and one to accessories.

REPETTO

The sixth-floor brasserie is right underneath the beautiful Art Nouveau glass dome. Next door is a huge men's store.

REPETTO

22 rue de la Paix Ⓜ Opéra. Mon–Sat 9.30am–7.30pm. MAP PP.66–67, POCKET MAP B13

This long-established supplier of ballet shoes has branched out to produce attractive ballerina pumps in assorted colours, much coveted by the fashion crowd, from €180.

Cafés

ANGELINA

226 rue de Rivoli Ⓜ Tuileries. Mon–Fri 7.30am–7pm, Sat & Sun 8.30am–7.30pm. MAP PP.66–67, POCKET MAP A14

One of the city's best-known *salons de thé*, dating back to 1903 and sporting an ornate decor. The hot chocolate (€8.20) is legendary, and the pastries equally exquisite. It's also good for breakfast or a light lunch.

CAFE DE LA PAIX

Cnr of place de l'Opéra and bd de Capucines Ⓜ Opéra. Daily 9am–12.30am. MAP PP.66–67, POCKET MAP F6

This grand café counts Emile Zola, Tchaikovsky and Oscar Wilde among its illustrious past *habitués*. Sit in the sumptuous interior or watch the world go by from the *terrasse*. Drinks from €8.

VERLET

256 rue St-Honoré Ⓜ Palais Royal-Musée du Louvre. Mon–Sat 9.30am–6.30pm; closed Aug. MAP PP.66–67, POCKET MAP B14

A heady aroma of freshly ground coffee greets you as you enter this old-world coffee merchant and café. Choose from around thirty varieties, such as Mokka Harar d'Ethiopie. There's also a selection of teas and cakes.

AUX LYONNAIS

Restaurants

BISTROT DES VICTOIRES

6 rue de la Vrillère Ⓜ Bourse. ☎ 01 42 61 43 78. Daily 10am–11pm. MAP PP.66–67, POCKET MAP C14

Located just behind the chic place des Victoires, but very reasonably priced for the area, this charming, old-fashioned *bistrot*, with zinc bar, mustard-coloured walls and globe lamps, serves good old standbys such as *confit de canard* and *poulet rôti* for around €11, as well as huge salads and hearty *tartines* – recommended is the *savoyarde* with bacon, potatoes and gruyère. Good-value Sunday brunch, too.

DROUANT

16–18 rue Gaillon Ⓜ Opéra. ☎ 01 42 65 15 16, Ⓦ drouant.com. Daily noon–3pm & 7pm–midnight. MAP PP.66–67, POCKET MAP B13

Legendary restaurant *Drouant*, the setting for the annual Goncourt and Renaudot literary prizes, is run by famed chef Antoine Westermann, who puts a contemporary spin on bourgeois cuisine. The starters and desserts show off the chef's creative flair – you can choose four of each served in small portions, with starters at €28, desserts €18; mains cost €33, and there's a lunchtime *menu* for €45 and a €36 brunch at weekends.

L'EPI D'OR

25 rue Jean-Jacques Rousseau Ⓜ Louvre-Rivoli. ☎ 01 42 36 38 12. Mon–Fri noon–2pm & 8–11pm. MAP PP.66–67, POCKET MAP C14

Christian Louboutin is a fan of this perfect locals' *bistrot* that dishes up comforting, homely standards such as steaks and *tarte tatin*, as well as its signature dish, *agneau à la cuillère* (slow-cooked lamb). Mains from €14.

FRENCHIE

5 rue du Nil Ⓜ Sentier. ☎ 01 40 39 96 19, Ⓦ frenchie-restaurant.com. Mon–Fri 6.30–9.30pm. MAP PP.66–67, POCKET MAP D13

It's famously hard to reserve a table, but definitely worth the effort: *Frenchie*, run by Greg Marchand, is an innovative neo-*bistrot*, reinventing French classics and using only the freshest ingredients. The six-course tasting menu (with countless little extras and *amuse-bouches*) might include dishes such as roast lamb with chickpeas, zaatar and harissa, or beef with ceps and samphire. If you can't get a reservation, try and bag a table (no bookings) at the *Frenchie bar à vins* opposite, where you can sample interesting wines and snack on sharing platters.

GALLOPIN

40 rue Notre-Dame-des-Victoires Ⓜ Bourse. Ⓣ 01 42 36 45 38, Ⓦ gallopin.com. Daily noon–midnight. MAP PP.66–67, POCKET MAP C13

An utterly endearing old brasserie, with all its original brass and mahogany fittings and a beautiful painted glass roof in the back room. The classic French dishes, especially the *foie gras maison*, are well above par; set menus from €22.

HIGUMA

32bis rue Ste Anne Ⓜ Pyramides. Ⓣ 01 47 03 38 59. Daily 11.30am–10pm. MAP PP.66–67, POCKET MAP B14

The pick of the numerous Japanese canteens in this area, *Higuma* serves up cheap, filling staples like pork katsu curry and yaki udon. Sit at the counter and watch the chefs at work, or go for a table in one of the two dining rooms. It's popular and you may have to queue at lunchtime. From €7.50.

DROUANT

AUX LYONNAIS

32 rue St-Marc Ⓜ Bourse/Richelieu-Drouot. Ⓣ 01 42 96 65 04, Ⓦ auxlyonnais.com. Tues–Fri noon–2pm & 7.30–10pm, Sat 7.30–10pm; closed Aug. MAP PP.66–67, POCKET MAP G6

This revamped, attractive old *bistrot*, overseen by top chef Alain Ducasse, sports *belle époque* tiles and mirrored walls, and serves up delicious Lyonnais fare, such as *quenelles* (light, delicate fish dumplings). The lunch set menu costs €34. In the evening count on €70 upwards, including wine.

RACINES

8 passage des Panoramas Ⓜ Grands Boulevards/Bourse. Ⓣ 01 40 13 06 41, Ⓦ racinesparis.com. Mon–Fri noon–2.30pm & 7.30–10.30pm. MAP PP.66–67, POCKET MAP G6

Set in the atmospheric passage des Panoramas, this lovely old, tiled-floored b*istrot à vins* does a short, daily-changing menu of home-cooked food, perhaps scallops or pork with polenta and parmesan, and there's always an excellent cheese platter, which you can pair with one of their natural wines. Be sure to come early or book, as it's very popular.

AU ROCHER DE CANCALE

78 rue Montorgueil Ⓜ Etienne-Marcel. Ⓣ 01 42 21 31 03. Mon–Fri noon–4pm & 7–11.30pm; Sat & Sun food served all day. MAP PP.66–67, POCKET MAP D14

This café-restaurant stands out on the foodie rue Montorgueil owing to the quality and price of its fresh seafood and good wine list. You can also order well-executed burgers and salads and more traditional French food. Desserts are equally good – the Carambar crème brûlée is exceptional. Mains around €16.

THE REX CLUB

Bars

LA CONSERVERIE

37bis rue du Sentier Ⓜ Bonne Nouvelle. Ⓦ laconserveriebar.com. Mon & Tues 7pm–midnight, Wed–Fri 7pm–2am, Sat 8pm–2am. MAP PP.66–67, POCKET MAP H6

This stylishly converted *atelier* mixes some original cocktails such as the Du Maurier, a mix of rum, lemon juice, champagne and raspberries, which comes with rock candy on the side. The food goes beyond the usual charcuterie platters, and you can consume it on low, soft sofas at candlelit tables – appropriately decadent.

DELAVILLE CAFE

34 bd de la Bonne Nouvelle Ⓜ Bonne-Nouvelle. Ⓦ delaville.com. Daily 8.30am–2am. MAP PP.66–67, POCKET MAP H6

This ex-bordello, with grand staircase, gilded mosaics and marble columns, draws crowds of pre-clubbers who sling back a mojito or two before going on to one of the area's nightclubs. DJs reign till the early hours on Thurs, Fri and Sat from 10pm.

LE FUMOIR

6 rue de l'Amiral de Coligny Ⓜ Louvre-Rivoli. Ⓦ lefumoir.com. Daily 11am–2am. MAP PP.66–67, POCKET MAP C15

Animated chatter rises above a mellow jazz soundtrack and the sound of cocktail shakers in this coolly designed and relaxing bar-restaurant, situated just by the Louvre. You can browse the international press and there's also a restaurant and library at the back. Cocktails from €10.

LE LOCKWOOD

73 rue d'Aboukir Ⓜ Grands Boulevards/Sentier. Ⓦ lockwoodparis.com. Mon–Sat 9am–2am. MAP PP.66–67, POCKET MAP D13

A decent coffee shop by day, the *Lockwood* transforms into a bar at night, its candlelit brick-walled cellar filled with a hip crowd sipping creative whisky cocktails and chatting over a soundtrack of rock, soul or blues.

LE RUBIS

10 rue du Marché-St-Honoré Ⓜ Pyramides. Mon–Fri noon–11pm, Sat 9am–3pm; closed mid-Aug. MAP PP.66–67, POCKET MAP B14

This very small and crowded wine bar is one of the oldest in Paris, known for its excellent wines and home-made *rillettes* (a kind of pork pâté). The faded sign and peeling paint just add to the charm.

Clubs

REX CLUB

5 bd Poissonnière Ⓜ Bonne-Nouvelle. Ⓣ 01 42 36 28 83, Ⓦ rexclub.com. Wed–Sat 11.30pm/midnight–7am. Entry up to €20. MAP PP.66–67, POCKET MAP H6

The clubbers' club: serious about its music, which is

strictly electronic, notably techno, played through a top-of-the line sound system. Attracts big-name DJs.

SILENCIO

142 rue Montmartre Ⓜ Bourse. Ⓦ silencio-club .com. Tues–Thurs midnight–4am, Fri & Sat midnight–6am. MAP PP.66–67, POCKET MAP D13

A very cool club, attracting an arty media crowd, hidden away down three flights of stairs underneath the *Social Club*; it's owned by film director David Lynch, who designed the sleek 1950s decor, inspired by the club in *Mulholland Drive*. Up until midnight it's members only; after that doors open to the public, though you still have to look the part to get in.

SOCIAL CLUB

142 rue Montmartre Ⓜ Bourse. Ⓣ 01 43 35 25 48, Ⓦ parissocialclub.com. Thurs–Sat 11pm–6am. Entry price up to €20. MAP PP.66–67, POCKET MAP D13

This unpretentious, grungey club is packed with a mixed clientele, from local students to lounge lizards. Here, it's all about the music, with everything from G-house to trap and hip-hop on the playlist, and regular live bands. Friday is gay night.

Music venues

EGLISE DE LA MADELEINE

Ⓜ Madeleine. Ⓣ 01 42 50 96 18, Ⓦ eglise-lamadeleine.com. MAP PP.66–67, POCKET MAP E6

A grand, regular venue for organ recitals and choral concerts, the church has a long and venerable musical tradition. Gabriel Fauré, who was organist here for a time, wrote his famous Requiem for the church. It also premiered here in 1888. Tickets start at €20.

AU LIMONAIRE

18 Cité Bergère Ⓜ Grands-Boulevards. Ⓣ 01 45 23 33 33, Ⓦ limonaire.free.fr. Tues–Sat. MAP PP.66–67, POCKET MAP H5

This tiny backstreet place is the perfect intimate and informal venue for Parisian *chanson*, often showcasing committed young singers or zany music/poetry/performance acts trying to catch a break. Dinner beforehand (traditional, fairly inexpensive and usually quite good) guarantees a seat for the show at 10pm, otherwise you'll be crammed up against the bar – if you can get in at all.

OPERA GARNIER

Ⓜ Opéra Ⓣ 08 36 69 78 68, Ⓦ operadeparis .fr. MAP PP.66–67, POCKET MAP F5

The Opéra Garnier is generally used for ballets and smaller-scale opera productions than those put on at the Opéra Bastille. For programme and booking details consult their website or phone the box office. Tickets can cost as little as €15 if you don't mind being up in the gods, though most are in the €35–100 range.

OPERA GARNIER

Beaubourg and Les Halles

One of the city's most recognizable and popular landmarks, the Pompidou Centre, or Beaubourg as the building is known locally, draws large numbers of visitors to its excellent modern art museum and high-profile exhibitions. Its groundbreaking architecture provoked a storm of controversy on its opening in 1977, but since then it has won over critics and public alike. By contrast, nearby Les Halles, a huge shopping mall and transport hub built at around the same time as the Pompidou Centre to replace the old food market that once stood there, has struggled to endear itself to the city's inhabitants. However, a recent major revamp, designed to open up the space and make it more appealing, may go some way to rescuing its tarnished image. It's also worth seeking out some of Les Halles' surviving old *bistrots* and food stalls, which preserve traces of the old market atmosphere.

THE POMPIDOU CENTRE

Ⓜ Rambuteau/Hotel-de-Ville.
Ⓣ 01 44 78 12 33, Ⓦ centrepompidou.fr.
MAP P.78, POCKET MAP E15

At the heart of one of Paris's oldest districts stands the resolutely modern Centre Pompidou. Wanting to move away from the traditional idea of galleries as closed treasure-chests and create something more open and accessible, the architects Renzo Piano and Richard Rogers stripped the "skin" off the building and made the "bones" visible. The infrastructure was put on the outside: escalator tubes and utility pipes, brightly colour-coded according to their function, climb around the exterior in a crazy snakes-and-ladders fashion.The centre's main draw is its modern art museum and exhibitions, but there are also cinemas, a performance space and the Galerie de Photographies (free), which organizes exhibitions drawn from the centre's extensive archive of photographs. One of the added treats of the museum is that you get to ascend the transparent escalator on the outside of the building, affording superb views.

THE POMPIDOU CENTRE

MUSEE NATIONAL D'ART MODERNE

MUSEE NATIONAL D'ART MODERNE

Pompidou Centre Ⓜ Rambuteau/Hotel-de-Ville. Daily except Tues 11am–10pm. €14, under-18s & EU residents aged 18–25 free (pick up a pass at the ticket office), free for everyone on first Sun of the month. MAP P.78, POCKET MAP E15

The Musée National d'Art Moderne collection, spread over floors four and five of the Pompidou Centre, is one of the finest of its kind in the world. Only a small fraction of the 100,000-plus works can be displayed at any one time, though with the opening in 2010 of its sister gallery, the Pompidou Metz, and a new "pop-up" gallery in Malaga, Spain, many more can now be enjoyed by the public.

The section covering the years 1905 to 1960, found on floor five, is a near-complete visual essay on the history of modern art: Fauvism, Cubism, Dada, abstract art, Surrealism and Abstract Expressionism are all well represented. There's a particularly rich collection of Matisses, ranging from early Fauvist works to his late masterpieces – a standout is his *Tristesse du Roi*, a moving meditation on old age and memory. Other highlights include a number of Picasso's and Braque's early Cubist paintings and a substantial collection of Kandinskys. A whole room is devoted to the characteristically colourful paintings of Robert and Sonia Delaunay, while the mood darkens in later rooms with unsettling works by Surrealists Magritte, Dalí and Ernst.

The fourth floor is devoted to art from the 1970s to the present day, and undergoes a major rehang every two years. It features installations, photography and video art, as well as displays of architecture and contemporary design. More established artists you might come across include Andy Warhol and Yves Klein, famous for his "body prints", in which the artist turned female models into human paintbrushes, covering them in paint to create his artworks. Other artists regularly featured are Claes Oldenburg, Christian Boltanski, video artist Pierre Huyghe, and Daniel Buren, whose works are easy to spot with their trademark stripes, exactly 8.7cm in width.

ATELIER BRANCUSI

Pompidou Centre Ⓜ Rambuteau/ Hôtel-de-Ville. Daily except Tues 2–6pm. Free. MAP P.78, POCKET MAP E15

The Atelier Brancusi is the reconstructed home and studio of sculptor Constantin Brancusi. He bequeathed the contents of his atelier to the state on condition that the rooms be arranged exactly as he left them, and they provide a fascinating insight into how the artist lived and worked. Studios one and two are crowded with Brancusi's trademark abstract bird and column shapes in highly polished brass and marble, while studios three and four comprise the artist's private quarters.

QUARTIER BEAUBOURG

Ⓜ Rambuteau/Hôtel-de-Ville. MAP P.78, POCKET MAP E15

The lively quartier Beaubourg around the Pompidou Centre also offers much in the way of visual art. The colourful, swirling sculptures and fountains, in the pool in front of the Eglise St-Merri on the south side of the Pompidou Centre, were created by Jean Tinguely and Niki de Saint Phalle. North of the Pompidou Centre, numerous commercial galleries take up the contemporary art theme on rue Quincampoix, a narrow, pedestrianized street lined with fine old houses.

LES HALLES

Ⓜ Les-Halles/RER Châtelet-Les-Halles. Mon–Sat 10am–8pm. MAP P.78, POCKET MAP D15

Described by Zola as "le ventre (stomach) de Paris", Les Halles was Paris's main food market for over eight hundred years until, despite widespread opposition, it was moved out to the suburbs in 1969. It was

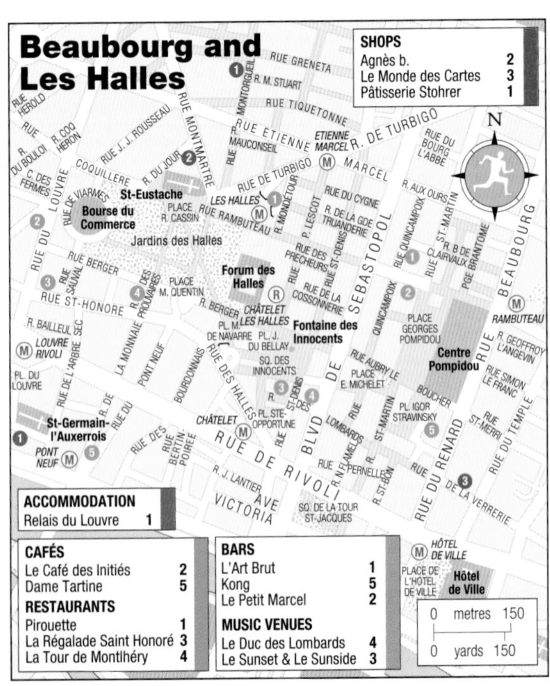

LA CANOPÉE IN THE FORUM DES HALLES

replaced by a large, ugly underground shopping and leisure complex, known as the **Forum des Halles**, as well as a major métro/RER interchange (métro Châtelet-les Halles), the largest in Europe. Widely acknowledged as an architectural disaster, Les Halles has now been rescued by a much-needed, costly facelift, completed in 2016. The most striking feature of the revamp is **La Canopée**, a vast, undulating, metal-and-glass roof, inspired by a rainforest canopy; suspended over the entrance to the complex, it is designed to let light flood into the underground shopping centre. At ground level, the whole area has been made more inviting with re-landscaped gardens, wide promenades, *pétanque* courts and playgrounds.

The Forum des Halles centre stretches underground from the Bourse du Commerce rotunda to rue Pierre-Lescot and is spread over four levels. The shops are mostly devoted to high-street fashion, though there's also a large Fnac bookshop. As part of the revamp, there is also a new library, a music and arts conservatory, and a centre for hip-hop, La Place, the first anywhere of its kind.

Little remains of the old working-class quarter, but you can still catch a flavour of the old market atmosphere in some of the surrounding bars and *bistrots* and on pedestrianized **rue Montorgueil** to the north, where traditional grocers, butchers and fishmongers still ply their trade.

ST-EUSTACHE

Ⓜ Les-Halles/RER Châtelet-Les-Halles.

MAP P.78, POCKET MAP D14

For an antidote to the steel and glass troglodytism of Les Halles, head for the soaring vaults of the beautiful church of St-Eustache. Built between 1532 and 1637, it's Gothic in structure, with lofty naves and graceful flying buttresses, and Renaissance in decoration – all Corinthian columns, pilasters and arcades. Molière was baptized here, and Rameau and Marivaux are buried here.

FONTAINE DES INNOCENTS

Ⓜ Les-Halles/RER Châtelet-Les-Halles.

MAP P.78, POCKET MAP D15

The Fontaine des Innocents, a perfectly proportioned Renaissance fountain, decorated with reliefs of water nymphs, is Paris's oldest surviving fountain, dating from 1549. On warm days shoppers sit around its edge, drawn to the cool of its cascading waters. It is named after the cemetery that used to occupy this site, the Cimetière des Innocents.

Shops

AGNES B.

2–4 & 6 rue du Jour Ⓜ Les-Halles/RER Châtelet-Les-Halles. Mon–Sat 10.30am–7pm. MAP P.78, POCKET MAP D14

Agnès b. pays scant regard to fashion trends, creating chic, timeless, understated clothes for men, women and children. Her best-known staples are the snap cardigan and well-made T-shirts that don't lose their shape.

LE MONDE DES CARTES

50 rue de la Verrerie Ⓜ Hôtel-de-Ville. Mon–Sat 11am–7pm. MAP P.78, POCKET MAP E16

The official (and best) source of maps of France and indeed of the entire world, plus guidebooks, satellite photos, and old and new maps of Paris.

PATISSERIE STOHRER

51 rue Montorgueil Ⓜ Sentier. Daily 7.30am–8.30pm; closed first two weeks of Aug. MAP P.78, POCKET MAP D14

Discover what *pain aux raisins* should really taste like at this wonderful patisserie, in business since 1730 and preserving its lovely old decor.

AGNES B.

Cafés

LE CAFE DES INITIÉS

3 place des Deux-Ecus Ⓜ Châtelet-Les-Halles/Louvre. Mon–Fri 7.30–2am, Sat & Sun 9–2am. MAP P.78, POCKET MAP C14

A smart yet intimate and comfortable café, with dark-red leather banquettes, wooden floor and arty photos on the wall. Locals gather round the zinc bar or tuck into tasty dishes such as grilled king prawns and steak tartare (around €16) and home-made apple crumble. It's also a good spot for an evening drink.

DAME TARTINE

2 rue Brisemiche Ⓜ Rambuteau/Hôtel-de-Ville. Daily noon–11.30pm. MAP P.78, POCKET MAP E15

This classic little café-bar, with its beautiful ceramic-tiled walls decorated with lively market scenes, dates from Les Halles' days as a market. A nice Parisian spot, perfect for a coffee, a glass of wine or a light lunch.

Restaurants

PIROUETTE

5 rue Mondétour ⓂEtienne-Marcel. Ⓣ 01 40 26 47 81, Ⓦ oenolis.com. Mon–Sat 12.30–2.30pm & 7.30–10.30pm MAP P.78, POCKET MAP D14

This sleek restaurant has gained a name for serving beautifully presented, innovative French food in a relaxed, contemporary atmosphere, with fresh, bright flavours, lots of light choices and delicious veggie dishes. There's also a really good wine list, with many wines available by the glass. Mains start at around €22, and set dinner *menus* at €45.

LA REGALADE SAINT HONORE

106 rue St-Honoré Ⓜ Louvre-Rivoli/Les Halles. ⓣ 01 42 21 92 40. Daily noon–2pm & 7.30–11.30pm. MAP P.78, POCKET MAP C15

You'll need to book in advance for a table at this modern *bistrot*, where innovative chef Bruno Doucet's €39 fixed-price, three-course menu offers some of the city's best-value dining. Dishes might include partridge with a celery purée, spinach and sautéed foie gras, followed by pistachio cream pots with raspberry coulis.

LA TOUR DE MONTLHERY (CHEZ DENISE)

5 rue des Prouvaires Ⓜ Louvre-Rivoli/Châtelet. ⓣ 01 42 36 21 82. Mon–Fri noon–3pm & 7.30pm–5am; closed mid-July to mid-Aug. MAP P.78, POCKET MAP D15

An old-style Les Halles *bistrot*, packed with diners at long tables tucking into substantial meaty French dishes, such as *daube* of beef with perfectly cooked chips. Mains around €25.

Bars

L'ART BRUT

78 rue Quincampoix Ⓜ Les Halles/Rambuteau. Daily 4pm–2am. MAP P.78, POCKET MAP E15

A small, friendly bar with a bohemian vibe, partly lent by the changing display of paintings and photos by young artists on the walls. A lively crowd is drawn here in the evenings by its relatively cheap drinks and generous cheese and charcuterie platters.

KONG

5th floor, 1 rue du Pont-Neuf Ⓜ Pont Neuf. ⓣ 01 40 39 09 00, ⓦ kong.fr. Daily 6pm–2am. MAP P.78, POCKET MAP C15

A lift whisks you up to this cool, Philippe Starck-designed bar-restaurant atop the flagship Kenzo building. Happy hour daily 6–8pm. Cocktails from €17. Club nights Fri & Sat.

KONG

LE PETIT MARCEL

63 rue Rambuteau Ⓜ Rambuteau. Daily 8am–midnight. MAP P.78, POCKET MAP E15

A bustling place with tiled floors, a jazz soundtrack and about eight square metres of drinking space. The dining area serves cheap, filling dishes such as sausages with mustard. Mains from €13. No credit cards.

Music venues

LE DUC DES LOMBARDS

42 rue des Lombards Ⓜ Châtelet. ⓣ 01 42 33 22 88, ⓦ ducdeslombards.com. Mon–Sat until 3am. MAP P.78, POCKET MAP D15

Stylish jazz club with nightly performances from 7.30pm of gypsy jazz, blues, ballads and fusion. Most gigs €28–35.

LE SUNSET & LE SUNSIDE

60 rue des Lombards Ⓜ Châtelet. ⓣ 01 40 26 46 20, ⓦ sunset-sunside.com. Daily 6.30pm–2.30am. MAP P.78, POCKET MAP D15

Two clubs in one: *Le Sunside* on the ground floor features mostly traditional jazz; while the downstairs *Sunset* is a venue for electric and fusion jazz. Admission €20–30, with free entry to some jam sessions.

The Marais

Full of splendid old mansions, narrow lanes and buzzing bars and restaurants, the Marais is one of the most seductive areas of central Paris, known for its sophistication and artsy leanings, and for being the neighbourhood of choice for gay Parisians. The quarter boasts a concentration of fascinating museums, including the Carnavalet history museum and the Musée Picasso, as well as some fine commercial art galleries housed in handsome Renaissance buildings.

MUSEE D'ART ET D'HISTOIRE DU JUDAISME

71 rue du Temple Ⓜ Rambuteau. Ⓣ 01 53 01 86 53, Ⓦ mahj.org. Mon–Fri 11am–6pm, Sun 10am–6pm. €8. MAP PP.84–85, POCKET MAP E15–F15

Housed in the attractively restored Hôtel de Saint-Aignan, the Musée d'Art et d'Histoire du Judaïsme traces Jewish culture and history, mainly in France. The result is a comprehensive collection, as educational as it is beautiful.

Highlights include a Gothic-style Hanukkah lamp, one of the very few French-Jewish artefacts to survive from the period before the expulsion of the Jews from France in 1394; an Italian gilded circumcision chair from the seventeenth century; and a completely intact, late nineteenth-century Austrian Sukkah, a temporary dwelling for the celebration of the harvest.

The museum also holds the Dreyfus archives, with one room devoted to the notorious Dreyfus Affair. The wrongful conviction of Captain Alfred Dreyfus caused deep divisions in French society, stoking up anticlerical, socialist sympathies on the one hand and conservative, anti-Semitic feelings on the other.

The last few rooms contain a significant collection of paintings and sculpture by Jewish artists – Marc Chagall, Samuel Hirszenberg, Chaïm Soutine and Jacques Lipchitz – who came to live in Paris at

WEDDING RINGS, MUSEE D'ART ET D'HISTOIRE DU JUDAISME

HOTEL SOUBISE

the beginning of the twentieth century. The Holocaust is only briefly touched on, since it's dealt with in depth by the Mémorial de la Shoah (see p.88).

HOTEL SOUBISE ET HOTEL DE ROHAN

60 rue des Francs-Bourgeois Ⓜ Rambuteau/St-Paul. Ⓦ www.archivesnationales.culture.gouv.fr. Mon & Wed–Fri 10am–12.30pm & 2–5.30pm, Sat & Sun 2–5.30pm. €3–6.
MAP PP.84–85, POCKET MAP F15

The entire block enclosed by rue des Quatre Fils, rue des Archives, rue Vieille-du-Temple and rue des Francs-Bourgeois, was once filled by a magnificent, early eighteenth-century palace complex. Only half remains, but it is utterly splendid, especially the colonnaded courtyard of the Hôtel Soubise, with its Rococo interiors and vestigial fourteenth-century towers on rue des Quatre Fils. The hôtel houses the city archives and mounts changing exhibitions. The adjacent Hôtel de Rohan is also used for exhibitions from the archives, though it is currently closed for a major renovation of its ground floor, which is being restored to its former splendour with wood carvings and decorations salvaged from a demolished mansion in Orléans.

MUSEE PICASSO

5 rue de Thorigny Ⓜ Chemin Vert/St-Paul. Ⓣ 01 85 56 00 36, Ⓦ museepicassoparis.fr. Tues–Fri 11.30am–6pm, Sat & Sun 9.30am–6pm. €12.50, free to under-18s and under-26s resident in the EU; free to everyone first Sun of month. To avoid long queues, reserve tickets online in advance.
MAP PP.84–85, POCKET MAP G15

Behind the elegant classical facade of the seventeenth-century Hôtel Salé lies the Musée Picasso, reopened in 2014 after a major renovation that tripled the display space. The museum is home to the largest collection of Picassos anywhere, representing almost all the major periods of the artist's life from 1905 onwards.

Many of the works were owned by Picasso, and on his death in 1973 were seized by the state in lieu of taxes owed. The result is an unedited body of work, which, although perhaps not among the most recognizable of Picasso's masterpieces, provides an insight into the person behind the myth. Some of the most engaging works on display are his more personal ones, for example the contrasting portraits of his lovers Dora Maar and Marie-Thérèse.

The museum also holds a substantial number of Picasso's ceramics and sculptures, some of which he created from recycled household objects.

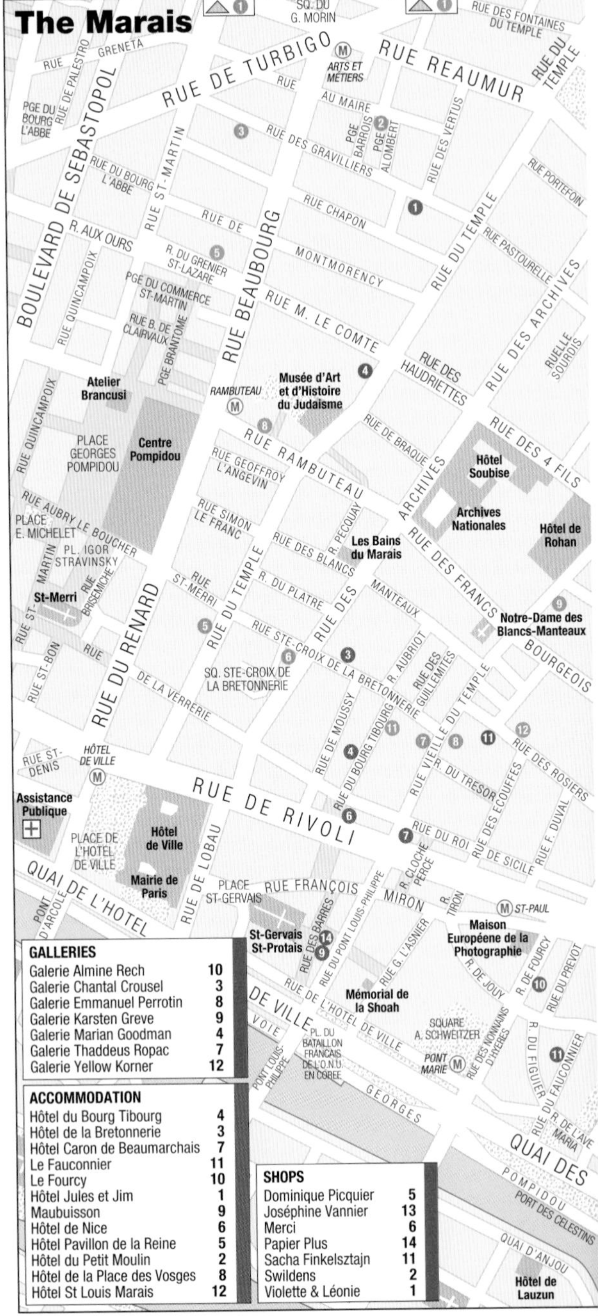
The Marais
RUE DE TURBIGO
RUE REAUMUR
SQ. DU G. MORIN
ARTS ET MÉTIERS
RUE DES FONTAINES DU TEMPLE
RUE DU TEMPLE
RUE GRENETA
RUE DE PALESTRO
PGE DU BOURG L'ABBE
BOULEVARD DE SEBASTOPOL
RUE AU MAIRE
RUE DES GRAVILLIERS
PGE BARROIS
PGE ALOMBERT
RUE DES VERTUS
RUE ST-MARTIN
RUE DU BOURG L'ABBE
RUE CHAPON
RUE PORTEFOIN
R. AUX OURS
RUE DE MONTMORENCY
R. DU GRENIER ST-LAZARE
RUE PASTOURELLE
PGE DU COMMERCE ST-MARTIN
RUE BEAUBOURG
RUE M. LE COMTE
RUE QUINCAMPOIX
RUE B. DE CLAIRVAUX
PGE BRANTOME
RUE DES ARCHIVES
RUELLE SOURDIS
RUE DES HAUDRIETTES
Atelier Brancusi
RAMBUTEAU
Musée d'Art et d'Histoire du Judaïsme
PLACE GEORGES POMPIDOU
Centre Pompidou
RUE RAMBUTEAU
RUE DE BRAQUE
RUE DES 4 FILS
Hôtel Soubise
RUE GEOFFROY L'ANGEVIN
Archives Nationales
Hôtel de Rohan
RUE AUBRY LE BOUCHER
PLACE E. MICHELET
RUE SIMON LE FRANC
R. PECQUAY
Les Bains du Marais
PL. IGOR STRAVINSKY
RUE DES BLANCS MANTEAUX
RUE DES FRANCS BOURGEOIS
St-Merri
RUE BRISEMICHE
RUE ST-MERRI
R. DU PLATRE
Notre-Dame des Blancs-Manteaux
RUE DU RENARD
RUE STE-CROIX DE LA BRETONNERIE
RUE ST-BON
RUE DE LA VERRERIE
SQ. STE-CROIX DE LA BRETONNERIE
R. AUBRIOT
RUE DES GUILLEMITES
RUE VIEILLE DU TEMPLE
RUE DE MOUSSY
RUE DU BOURG TIBOURG
RUE DES ROSIERS
RUE ST-DENIS
HÔTEL DE VILLE
R. DU TRESOR
RUE DES ECOUFFES
RUE DE RIVOLI
Assistance Publique
Hôtel de Ville
PLACE DE L'HOTEL DE VILLE
RUE DE LOBAU
RUE DU ROI DE SICILE
RUE F. DUVAL
R. CLOCHE PERCE
QUAI DE L'HOTEL DE VILLE
Mairie de Paris
PLACE ST-GERVAIS
RUE FRANÇOIS MIRON
R. TIRON
ST-PAUL
PONT D'ARCOLE
St-Gervais St-Protais
RUE DES BARRES
RUE DU PONT LOUIS-PHILIPPE
RUE G. L'ASNIER
Maison Européene de la Photographie
R. DE JOUY
R. DE FOURCY
RUE DU PREVOT
Mémorial de la Shoah
VOIE GEORGES POMPIDOU
PL. DU BATAILLON FRANÇAIS DE L'O.N.U. EN CORÉE
SQUARE A. SCHWEITZER
PONT MARIE
RUE DES NONNAINS D'HYERES
R. DU FIGUIER
RUE DU FAUCONNIER
R. DE L'AVE MARIA
PONT LOUIS-PHILIPPE
QUAI DES CELESTINS
PORT DES CELESTINS
QUAI D'ANJOU
Hôtel de Lauzun
GALLERIES
Galerie Almine Rech 10
Galerie Chantal Crousel 3
Galerie Emmanuel Perrotin 8
Galerie Karsten Greve 9
Galerie Marian Goodman 4
Galerie Thaddeus Ropac 7
Galerie Yellow Korner 12
ACCOMMODATION
Hôtel du Bourg Tibourg 4
Hôtel de la Bretonnerie 3
Hôtel Caron de Beaumarchais 7
Le Fauconnier 11
Le Fourcy 10
Hôtel Jules et Jim 1
Maubuisson 9
Hôtel de Nice 6
Hôtel Pavillon de la Reine 5
Hôtel du Petit Moulin 2
Hôtel de la Place des Vosges 8
Hôtel St Louis Marais 12
SHOPS
Dominique Picquier 5
Joséphine Vannier 13
Merci 6
Papier Plus 14
Sacha Finkelsztajn 11
Swildens 2
Violette & Léonie 1

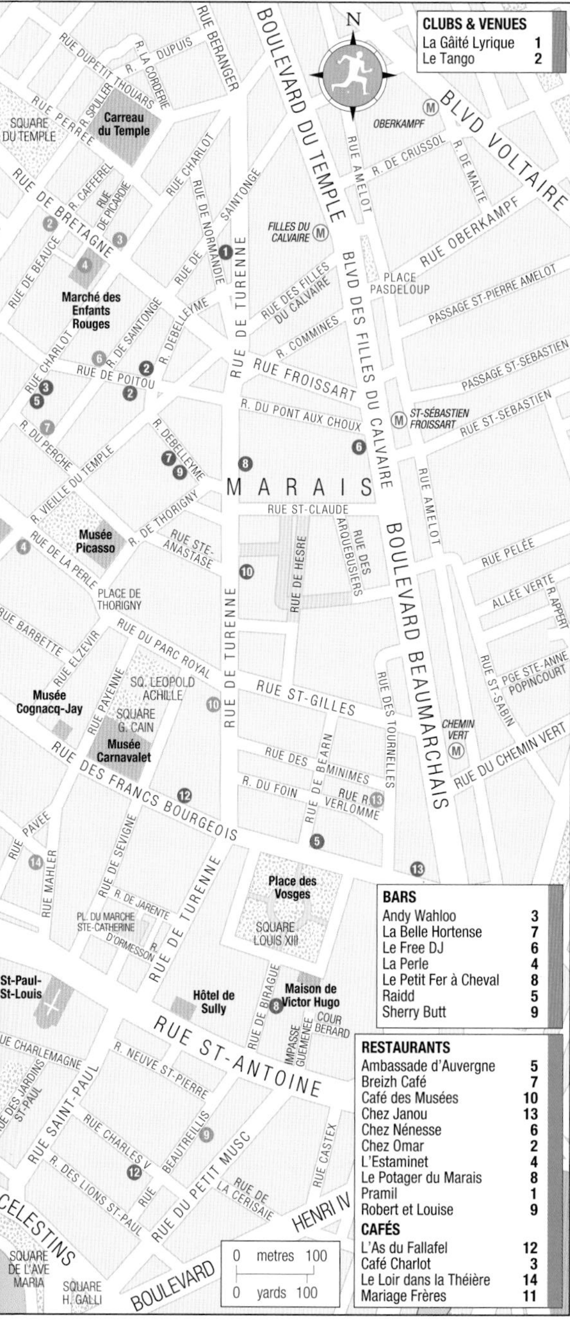
CLUBS & VENUES
La Gâité Lyrique 1
Le Tango 2
BARS
Andy Wahloo 3
La Belle Hortense 7
Le Free DJ 6
La Perle 4
Le Petit Fer à Cheval 8
Raidd 5
Sherry Butt 9
RESTAURANTS
Ambassade d'Auvergne 5
Breizh Café 7
Café des Musées 10
Chez Janou 13
Chez Nénesse 6
Chez Omar 2
L'Estaminet 4
Le Potager du Marais 8
Pramil 1
Robert et Louise 9
CAFÉS
L'As du Fallafel 12
Café Charlot 3
Le Loir dans la Théière 14
Mariage Frères 11
N
MARAIS
BOULEVARD DU TEMPLE
BLVD DES FILLES DU CALVAIRE
BOULEVARD BEAUMARCHAIS
BLVD VOLTAIRE
RUE DE TURENNE
RUE DE BRETAGNE
RUE ST-ANTOINE
RUE DES FRANCS BOURGEOIS
RUE VIEILLE DU TEMPLE
RUE OBERKAMPF
RUE FROISSART
RUE ST-GILLES
RUE DU PARC ROYAL
RUE DE POITOU
RUE CHARLOT
RUE DE SAINTONGE
RUE DE NORMANDIE
RUE BERANGER
RUE AMELOT
RUE DU CHEMIN VERT
RUE PELÉE
RUE ST-CLAUDE
RUE DE THORIGNY
RUE DE LA PERLE
RUE BARBETTE
RUE ELZEVIR
RUE PAYENNE
RUE DE SEVIGNE
RUE PAVEE
RUE MAHLER
RUE DE BIRAGUE
RUE SAINT-PAUL
RUE DU PETIT MUSC
RUE CASTEX
RUE CHARLEMAGNE
RUE BEAUTREILLIS
RUE DES MINIMES
RUE DE BEARN
RUE DE HESRE
RUE DES TOURNELLES
RUE DES ARQUEBUSIERS
RUE DE BEAUCE
RUE PERREE
RUE DUPETIT THOUARS
R. DUPUIS
R. LA CORDERIE
RUE DE PICARDIE
R. CAFFERELLI
R. SPULLER
R. DE CRUSSOL
R. DE MALTE
R. DEBELLEYME
R. DU PERCHE
R. DU PONT AUX CHOUX
R. COMMINES
R. DU FOIN
R. DE JARENTE
R. NEUVE ST-PIERRE
R. DES LIONS ST-PAUL
RUE CHARLES V
RUE DE LA CERISAIE
RUE DES JARDINS ST-PAUL
RUE STE-ANASTASE
RUE DES FILLES DU CALVAIRE
RUE ST-SEBASTIEN
PASSAGE ST-SEBASTIEN
PASSAGE ST-PIERRE AMELOT
ALLÉE VERTE
R. APPERT
RUE ST-SABIN
PGE STE-ANNE POPINCOURT
RUE VERLOMME
PLACE PASDELOUP
PLACE DE THORIGNY
PL. DU MARCHE STE-CATHERINE
R. D'ORMESSON
IMPASSE GUEMENEE
COUR BERARD
HENRI IV
BOULEVARD
CELESTINS
OBERKAMPF
FILLES DU CALVAIRE
ST-SÉBASTIEN FROISSART
CHEMIN VERT
SQUARE DU TEMPLE
Carreau du Temple
Marché des Enfants Rouges
Musée Picasso
Musée Cognacq-Jay
SQ. LEOPOLD ACHILLE
SQUARE G. CAIN
Musée Carnavalet
Place des Vosges
SQUARE LOUIS XIII
Maison de Victor Hugo
Hôtel de Sully
St-Paul-St-Louis
SQUARE DE L'AVE MARIA
SQUARE H. GALLI
0 metres 100
0 yards 100

THE MUSEE COGNACQ-JAY

MUSEE COGNACQ-JAY

8 rue Elzévir Ⓜ St-Paul. Ⓣ 01 40 27 07 21, Ⓦ museecognacqjay.paris.fr. Tues–Sun 10am–6pm. Free. MAP PP.84–85, POCKET MAP G16

The compact Musée Cognacq-Jay occupies the fine Hôtel Donon. The Cognacq-Jay family built up the Samaritaine department store and were noted philanthropists and lovers of European art. Their collection of eighteenth-century pieces on show includes a handful of works by Canaletto, Fragonard, Rubens and Rembrandt, as well as an exquisite still life by Chardin, displayed in beautifully carved wood-panelled rooms filled with Sèvres porcelain and Louis XV furniture.

MUSEE CARNAVALET

16 rue des Francs-Bourgeois Ⓜ St-Paul. Ⓣ 01 44 59 58 58, Ⓦ carnavalet.paris.fr. Tues–Sun 10am–6pm. Free. MAP PP.84–85, POCKET MAP G16

The fascinating Musée Carnavalet charts the history of Paris from its origins up to the *belle époque* through a huge and extraordinary collection of paintings, sculptures, decorative arts and archeological finds, occupying over 140 rooms. The museum's setting in two beautiful Renaissance mansions, Hôtel Carnavalet and Hôtel Le Peletier, surrounded by attractive formal gardens, is worth a visit in itself.

Among the highlights on the ground floor, devoted largely to the early history of Paris, is the orangery, housing a significant collection of Neolithic finds, including a number of wooden pirogues unearthed during the redevelopment of the Bercy riverside area in the 1990s.

On the first floor, decorative arts feature strongly, with numerous re-created salons and boudoirs full of richly sculpted wood panelling and tapestries from the time of Louis XII to Louis XVI. Room 21 is devoted to the famous letter-writer Madame de Sévigné, who lived in the Carnavalet mansion and wrote a series of letters to her daughter, which vividly portray her privileged lifestyle under the reign of Louis XIV. Rooms 128 to 148 are largely devoted to the *belle époque*, evoked through numerous paintings of the period and some wonderful Art Nouveau interiors, among which is the sumptuous peacock-green interior designed by Alphonse Mucha for Fouquet's jewellery shop in the rue Royal. Also well preserved is José-Maria Sert's Art Deco ballroom, with its extravagant gold-leaf decor and grand-scale

Hammams

Hammams, or Turkish baths, are one of the unexpected delights of Paris. Much more luxurious than the standard Swedish sauna, these are places to linger and chat, and you can usually pay extra for a massage and a gommage – a rubdown with a rubber glove – followed by mint tea to recover. One of the most attractive is to be found at **Les Bains du Marais** (31–33 rue des Blancs-Manteaux; Ⓜ Rambuteau/St-Paul; Ⓣ 01 44 61 02 02, Ⓦ lesbainsdumarais.fr), as much a posh health club as a hammam, with a chichi clientele and glorious interior. Sauna and steam room entry costs €35 for two hours; massage/gommage is €35 extra. There are exclusive sessions for women (Tues 10am–11pm, Wed 10am–7pm) and men (Thurs 10am–11pm, Fri 10am–8pm), as well as mixed sessions (Wed 7–11pm, Sat 10am–8pm, Sun 10am–11pm), for which you have to bring a swimsuit.

paintings, including one of the Queen of Sheba with a train of elephants. Nearby is a section on literary life at the beginning of the twentieth century, including a reconstruction of Proust's cork-lined bedroom (room 147). The second floor has rooms full of mementos of the French Revolution.

THE JEWISH QUARTER: RUE DES ROSIERS

Ⓜ St-Paul. MAP PP.84–85, POCKET MAP F16

The narrow, pedestrianized rue des Rosiers has been the city's Jewish quarter ever since the twelfth century. Despite the incursion of trendy boutiques, it just about manages to retain a Jewish flavour, with the odd delicatessen, kosher food shop and Hebrew bookstore, as well as a number of falafel takeaways – testimony to the influence of the North African Sephardim, who, since the end of World War II, have sought refuge here from the uncertainties of life in the former French colonies.

STATUE OF LOUIS XIV AT THE MUSÉE CARNAVALET

PLACE DES VOSGES

Ⓜ St-Paul. MAP PP.84–85, POCKET MAP G16

A grand square of handsome pink brick and stone mansions built over arcades, the place des Vosges is a masterpiece of aristocratic elegance and the first example of planned development in the history of Paris. It was built by Henri IV and inaugurated in 1612 for the wedding of Louis XIII and Anne of Austria; a replica of Louis' statue stands hidden by chestnut trees in the middle of the grass-and-gravel gardens at the square's centre.

Today, well-heeled Parisians pause in the arcades to browse art, antique and clothing shops, and lunch alfresco in the restaurants while buskers play classical music. Unusually for Paris, you're allowed to sprawl on the grass in the garden.

MAISON DE VICTOR HUGO

Place des Vosges Ⓜ St-Paul. Ⓣ 01 42 72 10 16, Ⓦ maisonsvictorhugo.paris.fr. Tues–Sun 10am–6pm, closed hols. Free. MAP PP.84–85, POCKET MAP G17

Among the many celebrities who made their homes in place des Vosges was Victor Hugo; his house, at no. 6, where he wrote much of *Les Misérables*, is now a museum, the Maison de Victor Hugo. Hugo's life is evoked through a sparse collection of memorabilia, portraits and photographs. What the museum conveys, though, is an idea of his prodigious creativity: as well as being a prolific writer, he enjoyed drawing and designed his own furniture. Some of his sketches and Gothic-style furniture are on display, and a Chinese-style dining room that he designed for his house in Guernsey is re-created in its entirety.

HOTEL DE SULLY

62 rue St-Antoine Ⓜ St-Paul. Daily: garden 9am–7pm, bookshop 10am–7pm. MAP PP.84–85, POCKET MAP G17

The exquisite Renaissance Hôtel de Sully (not open to the public) is the headquarters of the Centre des Monuments Nationaux, which looks after more than a hundred national monuments and publishes numerous guides and books, many of which are on sale in the excellent ground-floor bookshop. The mansion's attractive garden is a peaceful place for a rest-stop and a handy shortcut from the place des Vosges to rue St-Antoine.

THE QUARTIER ST-PAUL-ST-GERVAIS

Ⓜ St-Paul. MAP PP.84–85, POCKET MAP E16–F17

The southern section of the Marais, below rues de Rivoli and St-Antoine, is quieter than the northern part and has some picturesque corners. One of these is cobbled rue des Barres, perfumed with the scent of roses from nearby gardens and the occasional waft of incense from the church of St-Gervais-St-Protais, a late Gothic construction that looks somewhat battered on the outside owing to a direct hit from a shell fired from a Big Bertha howitzer in 1918. Its interior contains some lovely stained glass, carved misericords and a seventeenth-century organ – Paris's oldest.

MEMORIAL DE LA SHOAH

17 rue Geoffroy l'Asnier Ⓜ St-Paul/Pont-Marie. Ⓣ 01 42 77 44 72, Ⓦ memorialdelashoah.org. Mon–Fri & Sun 10am–6pm, Thurs until 10pm. Free. MAP PP.84–85, POCKET MAP F17

Since 1956 this has been the

MAISON DE VICTOR HUGO

site of the Mémorial du Martyr Juif Inconnu (Memorial to an Unknown Jewish Martyr), a sombre crypt containing a large black marble Star of David. In 2005 President Chirac opened a new museum here and unveiled a Wall of Names: four giant slabs of marble engraved with the names of the 76,000 Jews sent to death camps from 1942 to 1944.

The excellent museum gives an absorbing account of the history of Jews in France, and especially Paris, during the German occupation. There are last letters from deportees to their families, videotaped testimonies from survivors, numerous ID cards and photos. The museum ends with the Mémorial des Enfants, an overwhelming collection of photos of 2500 French children, each with the dates of their birth and their deportation.

MAISON EUROPEENNE DE LA PHOTOGRAPHIE

5–7 rue de Fourcy Ⓜ St-Paul. Ⓣ 01 44 78 75 00, Ⓦ mep-fr.org. Wed–Sun 11am–8pm. €8. MAP PP.84–85, POCKET MAP F16

A gorgeous Marais mansion, the early eighteenth-century Hôtel Hénault de Cantobre, has been turned into a vast and serene space dedicated to the art of contemporary photography. Temporary shows are combined with a revolving exhibition of the Maison's permanent collection; young photographers and news photographers get a look-in, as well as artists using photography in multimedia creations or installation art.

HOTEL DE VILLE

Ⓜ Rambuteau/Hotel-de-Ville. MAP PP.84–85, POCKET MAP E16

The Hôtel de Ville, the seat of the city's mayor, is a gargantuan mansion in florid neo-Renaissance style, modelled on the

THE HOTEL DE VILLE

previous building which burned down during the Commune in 1871. The huge square in front provides the location for a popular **ice-skating rink** (Dec–Feb Mon–Fri noon–10pm, Sat & Sun 9am–10pm; skate rental €6). The road along the **river** from here to the Port de l'Arsenal is now more pedestrian friendly, with widened pavements and traffic controls; on Sundays cars are banned completely, making it a delightful spot for a stroll.

THE HAUT MARAIS

MAP PP.84–85, POCKET MAP F14/15–G14/15

The northern part of the Marais, the "haut Marais", is currently the favoured strolling ground of bobo (bourgeois-bohemian) Parisians, drawn by the art galleries, design and fashion shops, and the **Carreau du Temple** arts centre (Ⓦ carreaudutemple.eu). The main thoroughfare is rue de Bretagne, with its cafés and traditional shops. The adjacent **Marché des Enfants-Rouges**, one of the smallest and oldest food markets in Paris (Tues–Sat 8.30am–1pm & 4–7.30pm, Sun 8.30am–2pm) makes a good lunchtime stop.

Shops

DOMINIQUE PICQUIER

10 rue Charlot Ⓜ Filles du Calvaire. Ⓦ dominiquepicquier.com. Tues–Fri 11am–7.30pm, Sat 2.30–7.30pm. MAP PP.84–85, POCKET MAP F15

"A tribute from the town to the country" is how this textile designer describes her beautiful hand-printed fabrics of swirling orchids, delicate mimosas and daisies. She also does a stylish range of accessories, such as tote bags, purses and travel bags, starting from around €40.

SWILDENS

JOSEPHINE VANNIER

4 rue du Pas de la Mule Ⓜ Bastille. Ⓦ chocolats-vannier.com. Tues–Sat 11am–1pm & 2–7pm, Sun 2.30–7pm. MAP PP.84–85, POCKET MAP H16

This inventive chocolatier sells chocolate-shaped accordions, violins, books, Eiffel Towers and Arcs de Triomphe – exquisite creations, almost too perfect to eat.

MERCI

111 blvd Beaumarchais Ⓜ St-Sébastien-Froissart. Ⓦ merci-merci.com. Mon–Sat 10am–7pm. MAP PP.84–85, POCKET MAP G15

Set in a huge old wallpaper factory, this hip and original concept store sells an attractive range of women's clothing alongside homeware, jewellery and secondhand books; the clothes are not especially cheap, but all profits go to charity.

PAPIER PLUS

9 rue du Pont-Louis-Philippe Ⓜ Hôtel-de-Ville. Ⓦ papierplus.com. Mon–Sat noon–7pm. MAP PP.84–85, POCKET MAP F16

Fine-quality colourful stationery, including notebooks, photo albums and artists' portfolios, with prices starting around €20.

SACHA FINKELSZTAJN

27 rue des Rosiers Ⓜ Hôtel-de-Ville. Ⓦ laboutiquejaune.fr. Daily except Tues 10am–7pm; closed mid-July to mid-Aug. MAP PP.84–85, POCKET MAP F16

A marvellous Jewish deli for takeaway snacks and goodies: Eastern European breads, apple strudel, *gefilte* fish, aubergine purée, tarama, *blinis* and *borscht*.

SWILDENS

16 rue de Turenne Ⓜ Saint-Paul. Mon–Sat 11am–7.30pm, Sun 2–7pm. MAP PP.84–85, POCKET MAP G15

Womenswear designer Juliette Swildens makes well-cut, affordable clothes, with a hint of rock'n'roll. Typical pieces are off-the-shoulder smocks, slouchy sweatshirts, baggy harem pants and layered knits.

VIOLETTE & LEONIE

114 rue de Turenne Ⓜ St-Sébastien-Froissart/Filles-du-Calvaire. Ⓦ violetteleonie.com. Mon 1–7.30pm, Tues–Sat 11am–7.30pm, Sun 2–7pm. MAP PP.84–85, POCKET MAP G14

This secondhand shop looks so smart, you'd think it was a designer boutique, and its decent range of stock, from high-end labels to H&M and Zara, is in great condition.

Galleries

GALERIE ALMINE RECH

64 rue de Turenne Ⓜ St-Sébastien-Froissart. Ⓣ 01 45 83 71 90, Ⓦ alminerech.com. Tues–Sat 11am–7pm. MAP PP.84–85, POCKET MAP G15

Recently installed in this elegant gallery, Rech represents around fifty artists, including Ugo Rondinone and James Turrell.

GALERIE CHANTAL CROUSEL

10 rue Charlot Ⓜ Filles du Calvaire. Ⓣ 01 42 77 38 87, Ⓦ crousel.com. Tues–Sat 11am–1pm & 2–7pm. MAP PP.84–85, POCKET MAP F15

This gallery, which has been around since 1980, represents mostly foreign and some French artists – such as Gabriel Orozco and Mona Hatoum – who work in a variety of media. It also promotes the work of emerging video artists.

GALERIE EMMANUEL PERROTIN

76 rue de Turenne Ⓜ St-Sébastien-Froissart. Ⓣ 01 42 16 79 79, Ⓦ galerieperrotin.com. Tues–Sat 11am–7pm. MAP PP.84–85, POCKET MAP G15

One of the most influential galleries on the French contemporary art scene, Perrotin has exhibited French artists such as Sophie Calle, as well as international names including the likes of Takashi Murakami and Maurizio Cattelan.

GALERIE KARSTEN GREVE

5 rue Debelleyme Ⓜ St-Sébastien-Froissart Ⓣ 01 42 77 19 37, Ⓦ galerie-karsten-greve.com. Tues–Sat 11am–7pm. MAP PP.84–85, POCKET MAP G15

Paris branch of the German gallery, showing the work of world-renowned artists such as Louise Bourgeois and Willem de Kooning.

GALERIE MARIAN GOODMAN

79 rue du Temple Ⓜ Rambuteau Ⓣ 01 48 04 70 52, Ⓦ www.mariangoodman.com. Tues–Sat 11am–7pm. MAP PP.84–85, POCKET MAP F15

This offshoot of the famed New York gallery has exhibited Jean-Marc Bustamante, Steve McQueen and Rineke Dijkstra, among many other big names.

GALERIE THADDEUS ROPAC

7 rue Debelleyme Ⓜ Filles-du-Calvaire Ⓣ 01 42 72 99 00, Ⓦ ropac.net. Tues–Sat 10am–7pm. MAP PP.84–85, POCKET MAP G15

Recent exhibitions at this well-established gallery include Sturtevant and Robert Longo. Also well worth a visit is Ropac's enormous outpost in Pantin, near La Villette, showing large-scale installations.

GALERIE YELLOW KORNER

8 rue des Francs Bourgeois Ⓜ St-Paul Ⓣ 01 49 96 50 23, Ⓦ yellowkorner.com. Tues–Sun 11am–7pm.30, Mon 1–7.30pm. MAP PP.84–85, POCKET MAP G16

This contemporary photography gallery, which has outposts throughout Europe, showcases both established and up-and-coming talent.

GALERIE KARSTEN GREVE

Cafés

L'AS DU FALLAFEL

34 rue des Rosiers Ⓜ St-Paul. Mon–Thurs & Sun noon–11.30pm, Fri noon–3pm. MAP PP.84–85, POCKET MAP F16

The sign above the doorway of this falafel shop in the Jewish quarter reads "*Toujours imité, jamais égalé*" ("Always copied, but never equalled"), a boast that few would challenge, given the queues. Takeaway falafels cost €6, or pay a bit more and sit in the buzzing little dining room.

CAFE CHARLOT

38 rue de Bretagne Ⓜ Filles du Calvaire. Daily 7am–2am. MAP PP.84–85, POCKET MAP G14

You'll need to fight for a seat on the terrace of this white-tiled retro-chic café, which bursts at the seams on weekends with local hipsters and in-the-know tourists. The food – a mix of French and American standards – is not that special, but it's a great place for a drink and a spot of people-watching.

LE LOIR DANS LA THEIERE

3 rue des Rosiers Ⓜ St-Paul. Ⓦ leloirdanslatheiere.com. Daily 9am–7.30pm. MAP PP.84–85, POCKET MAP F16

A characterful *salon de thé* decorated with antique toys and Alice in Wonderland murals. It's a popular spot for meeting friends and lounging about on comfy sofas, while feasting on delicious home-made cakes and pastries (the lemon meringue pie is to die for) or excellent vegetarian quiches.

MARIAGE FRERES

MARIAGE FRERES

30 rue du Bourg-Tibourg Ⓜ Hôtel-de-Ville. Ⓦ www.mariagefreres.com. Daily noon–7pm. MAP PP.84–85, POCKET MAP F16

A classy, colonial-style *salon de thé* in the *Mariages Frères* tea emporium, with a choice of over five hundred brews.

Restaurants

AMBASSADE D'AUVERGNE

22 rue du Grenier St-Lazare Ⓜ Rambuteau. Ⓣ 01 42 72 31 22, Ⓦ ambassade-auvergne.com. Daily noon–2pm & 7.30–10pm; closed three weeks in Aug. MAP PP.84–85, POCKET MAP E14

Suited, moustachioed waiters serve scrumptious, filling Auvergnat cuisine that would have made Vercingetorix proud. There's a set menu for €33, but you may well be tempted by some of the house specialities such as the roast Marvejols lamb. Among the after-dinner treats are a cheese plate and divine chocolate mousse.

BREIZH CAFE

109 rue Vieille du Temple Ⓜ St-Paul. Ⓣ 01 42 72 13 77, Ⓦ breizhcafe.com. Wed–Sat noon–11pm, Sun noon–10pm; closed three weeks in Aug. MAP PP.84–85, POCKET MAP G15

A Breton café, serving the best crêpes in the Marais (and arguably the city), with traditional fillings like ham and cheese, as well as more exotic options such as smoked herring, which you can wash down with one of around sixty different ciders. Leave room for dessert, as Valrhona chocolate is used in the sweet crêpes. It's very popular, so book ahead.

CAFE DES MUSEES

49 rue de Turenne Ⓜ Chemin Vert. Ⓣ 01 42 72 96 17, Ⓦ lecafedesmusees.fr. Daily noon–3pm & 7–11pm. MAP PP.84–85, POCKET MAP G16

An attractive old *bistrot* (with a less appealing basement room) popular with locals who are drawn here by the reasonably priced and hearty food, such as *steak frites*, terrines and *crème caramel*. There's always a vegetarian dish on the menu, too, usually a vegetable casserole. There's a lunch menu for €17; mains cost around €22.

CHEZ JANOU

2 rue Roger Verlomme Ⓜ Chemin Vert. Ⓣ 01 42 72 28 41, Ⓦ chezjanou.com. Daily noon–3pm & 7pm–midnight. MAP PP.84–85, POCKET MAP G16

A fiercely popular Provençal restaurant serving generous portions of traditional southern food (mains from €17) and over eighty different types of *pastis*, so you can whet your appetite like a true local. Tables are cramped, so unless you can snaffle one on the sunny terrace you'll be elbow to elbow with your neighbours.

CHEZ NENESSE

17 rue Saintonge Ⓜ Filles-du-Calvaire. Ⓣ 01 42 78 46 49. Mon–Fri noon–2.30pm & 8–10.30pm; closed Aug. MAP PP.84–85, POCKET MAP G15

A friendly, family-run restaurant with homely, old-fashioned decor, offering reasonably priced, well-prepared traditional cuisine, such as foie gras, braised veal, *quenelles de brochet* (pike dumplings), and chocolate mousse for dessert. Mains around €20.

CHEZ OMAR

47 rue de Bretagne Ⓜ Temple/ Filles-du-Calvaire. Ⓣ 01 42 72 36 26.

AMBASSADE D'AUVERGNE

Mon–Sat noon–2.30pm & 7–11.30pm, Sun 7–11.30pm; no credit cards. MAP PP.84–85, POCKET MAP G14

No reservations are taken at this popular North African couscous restaurant, but it's no hardship to wait for a table at the bar, taking in the handsome old brasserie decor and spirited atmosphere. Portions are copious and the couscous light and fluffy. The *merguez* (spicy sausage) is good, or go all out for the *royal*, though don't expect to have any room left afterwards for the sticky cakes. Mains around €20.

L'ESTAMINET

Marché des Enfants Rouges Ⓜ Arts-et-Métiers. Ⓣ 01 42 72 28 12, Ⓦ lestaminetdesenfantsrouges.com. Tues–Sat 9am–8pm, Sun 9am–3pm. MAP PP.84–85, POCKET MAP G14

This inexpensive, family-friendly place is set in a buzzing foodie market: sit on the picnic tables outside to soak up the atmosphere and choose from tasty dishes such as moussaka, oysters (in season), soup, charcuterie platters, salads and lots of ice cream. Service is amiable, if a little overwrought. *Formules* from €16. Breakfast served till 11.30am. Free wi-fi.

LE POTAGER DU MARAIS

22 rue Rambuteau Ⓜ Rambuteau. ⓣ 01 42 74 24 66. Wed–Sun noon–3pm & 7–11pm. MAP PP.84–85, POCKET MAP E15

Come early or book in advance for a place at this organic vegetarian restaurant, with only 25 covers at a long communal table. There's plenty for vegans, too. Dishes include goat's cheese with honey and "crusty" quinoa burger. Mains around €17.

PRAMIL

9 rue du Vertbois Ⓜ Temple/Arts-et-Métiers. ⓣ 01 42 72 03 60, ⓦ pramilrestaurant.com. Tues–Sat noon–2.30pm & 7.30–10.30pm, Sun 7.30–10.30pm. MAP PP.84–85, POCKET MAP F13

An elegant restaurant with simple decor, serving a short but appetizing menu of classic French and more unusual dishes, such as cauliflower "cake", squash soup with foie gras ice cream, and raspberry and red pepper tart. The set dinner for €33 (lunch €24) is excellent value.

LE POTAGER DU MARAIS

ROBERT ET LOUISE

64 rue Vieille du Temple Ⓜ Hôtel-de-Ville. ⓣ 01 42 78 55 89, ⓦ robertetlouise.com. Tues & Wed 7–11pm, Thurs–Sun noon–2pm & 7–11pm. MAP PP.84–85, POCKET MAP F15

The welcome at this rustic *bistrot*, with its exposed beams and wooden tables, is as warm and hearty as the meaty dishes on offer. Start with foie gras or a blood sausage, then choose between steak, lamb chops, duck confit or *andouillette* (tripe sausage). Lunch menu for €14, three courses around €30. Booking advisable.

Bars

ANDY WAHLOO

69 rue des Gravilliers Ⓜ Arts-et-Métiers. ⓦ andywahloo-bar.com. Tues–Sat 6pm–2am. MAP PP.84–85, POCKET MAP E14

Great little bar decked out in colourful Arabic Pop Art-inspired decor, and playing a wide range of dance music. Delicious meze are served until midnight, and cocktails (€12–17) include the Wahloo julep (rum, lime, tobacco liqueur and cherries). Thursday to Saturday nights see DJs play a wide range of dance music, including Algerian raï.

LA BELLE HORTENSE

31 rue Vieille du Temple Ⓜ St-Paul. Daily 5pm–2am. MAP PP.84–85, POCKET MAP F16

You can sip a glass of wine while reading or chatting in this friendly little wine/champagne-bar-cum-bookshop with book-lined walls and a zinc bar. There's a snug room with sofas at the back, but you'll be lucky to get a seat there later on.

LE FREE DJ

35 rue Ste-Croix de la Bretonnerie Ⓜ Hôtel-de-Ville. ⓦ freedj.fr. Daily 6pm–4am. MAP PP.84–85, POCKET MAP E16

This stylish gay bar draws the young and très *looké* – beautiful types. It's friendly, though, and features some big sounds (house, disco-funk) in the basement club.

LA PERLE

78 rue Vieille du Temple Ⓜ St-Paul. Mon–Fri 6am–2am, Sat & Sun 8am–2am. MAP PP.84–85, POCKET MAP F15

An Emperor's New Clothes kind of place that maintains a *très cool* reputation. Always packed with an arty indie crowd drinking cheap beer, despite being somewhat scruffy and playing generic dance music.

LE PETIT FER A CHEVAL

30 rue Vieille-du-Temple Ⓜ St-Paul. Daily 9am–2am; food served noon–midnight. MAP PP.84–85, POCKET MAP F16

An attractive, tiny bar with original fin-de-siècle decor, including a marble-topped bar in the shape of a horseshoe (*fer à cheval*). Snack on sandwiches or light meals in the little back room furnished with old wooden métro seats.

RAIDD

23 rue du Temple Ⓜ Hôtel-de-Ville. Daily 5pm–2am. MAP PP.84–85, POCKET MAP E15

A popular gay bar, famous for its sculpted, topless waiters and go-go boys' shower shows. Straights and non-beautiful people need not apply.

SHERRY BUTT

20 rue Beautreillis Ⓜ St-Paul/Bastille. Tues–Sat 6pm–2am, Sun & Mon 8pm–2am. MAP PP.84–85, POCKET MAP G17

This cool, New York-style cocktail bar serves creative drinks such as the popular La Belle en Bulle (pisco, pear syrup, lemon juice and champagne). The leather sofas and low lighting create a laidback, intimate atmosphere.

Clubs and venues

LA GAITE LYRIQUE

3 bis rue Papin Ⓜ Réaumur-Sébastopol/Arts-et-Métiers. Ⓦ gaiete-lyrique.net. Tues–Sat 2–8pm, Sun noon–6pm. MAP PP.84–85, POCKET MAP E13

A centre for digital arts and contemporary music, housed in a venerable theatre. After years of closure, it was given a radical makeover – the architects restored the facade and splendid marble foyer and entrance hall, while opening up the interior to accommodate various performance spaces, including a state-of-the-art concert hall. The busy programme of events includes exhibitions, dance, theatre and art installations.

LE TANGO

13 rue au Maire Ⓜ Arts-et-Métiers. Ⓦ boite-a-frissons.fr. Fri & Sat 10.30pm–5am, Sun 6–11pm. MAP PP.84–85, POCKET MAP F14

Unpretentious gay and lesbian club with a Sunday-afternoon tea dance, with proper slow dances as well as tangos. Friday and Saturday nights start with anything from camp 1980s disco classics to world music, turning into a full-on club around midnight. Entry €6–9.

LE PETIT FER A CHEVAL

Bastille and Bercy

A symbol of revolution since the toppling of the Bastille prison in 1789, the Bastille quarter used to belong in spirit and style to the working-class districts of eastern Paris. After the construction of the opera house in the 1980s, however, it became a magnet for artists, fashion folk and young people, who over the years brought with them stylish shops and an energetic nightlife. However, some of the working-class flavour lingers on in the furniture workshops off rue du Faubourg-St-Antoine, testimony to a long tradition of cabinet making and woodworking in the district. To the south lies Bercy, once the largest wine market in the world, its warehouses now converted into restaurants and shops.

PLACE DE LA BASTILLE

Ⓜ Bastille. MAP P.98, POCKET MAP H17

The huge place de la Bastille is where Parisians congregate to celebrate Bastille Day on July 14, though hardly anything survives of the prison – the few remains have been transferred to square Henri-Galli at the end of boulevard Henri-IV.

COLONNE DE JUILLET, PLACE DE LA BASTILLE

At the centre of the *place* is a column (Colonne de Juillet) surmounted by a gilded Spirit of Liberty, erected to commemorate the July Revolution of 1830 that replaced the autocratic Charles X with the "Citizen King" Louis-Philippe. The square is usually clogged with traffic, though plans are afoot to make it a greener and more pedestrian friendly space.

PLACE D'ALIGRE MARKET

Ⓜ Ledru-Rollin. Tues–Sun 7.30am–1pm. MAP P.98, POCKET MAP L9

The place d'Aligre market, between avenue Daumesnil and rue du Faubourg St-Antoine, is a lively, raucous affair, particularly at weekends. The square itself is given over to clothes and bric-a-brac stalls, selling anything from old gramophone players to odd bits of crockery. It's along the adjoining rue d'Aligre where the market really comes to life though, with the vendors, many of Algerian origin, doing a frenetic trade in fruit and veg.

THE PARC FLORAL, BOIS DE VINCENNES

PROMENADE PLANTEE

Ⓜ Bastille. MAP P.98, POCKET MAP L10

The Promenade Plantée is a stretch of disused railway line, much of it along a viaduct, ingeniously converted into an elevated walkway and planted with trees and flowers. Starting near the beginning of avenue Daumesnil, just south of the Bastille opera house, it is reached via a flight of stone steps – or lifts – with a number of similar access points all the way along. It takes you to the Parc de Reuilly, then descends to ground level and continues nearly as far as the *périphérique*, from where you can follow signs to the Bois de Vincennes. The whole walk is around 4.5km long.

VIADUC DES ARTS

Ⓜ Bastille. MAP P.98, POCKET MAP L9-10

The arches of the Promenade Plantée's viaduct have been converted into attractive spaces for artisans' studios and craft shops, collectively known as the Viaduc des Arts, and include furniture and tapestry restorers, interior designers, cabinet-makers, violin- and flute-makers, embroiderers and fashion and jewellery designers.

PARC FLORAL

Bois de Vincennes Ⓜ Chateau de Vincennes, then bus #112, or a fifteen-minute walk. Daily 9.30am–8pm, winter till dusk. Free except June–Sept Wed, Sat & Sun when entry is €5. POCKET MAP M11

The Parc Floral is one of the city's best gardens. Flowers are always in bloom in the Jardin des Quatre Saisons and there are some enchanting walks amid pines and rhododendrons. Children will enjoy the adventure playground and mini-golf of Parisian monuments, and in spring and summer there are exhibitions and concerts.

PARC ZOOLOGIQUE DE PARIS

Bois de Vincennes Ⓜ Porte Dorée. Ⓦ parczoologiquedeparis.fr. Mid-March to mid-Oct Mon–Fri 10am–6pm, Sat & Sun 9.30am–7.30pm; rest of year daily 10am–5pm. €22, children €14. POCKET MAP M11

Paris's zoo uses fake rocks and boulders to re-create as natural a habitat as possible for the 1000-odd animals, including giraffes, lions and endangered species. Animals are grouped by region, such as Madagascar, Patagonia and Guyana.

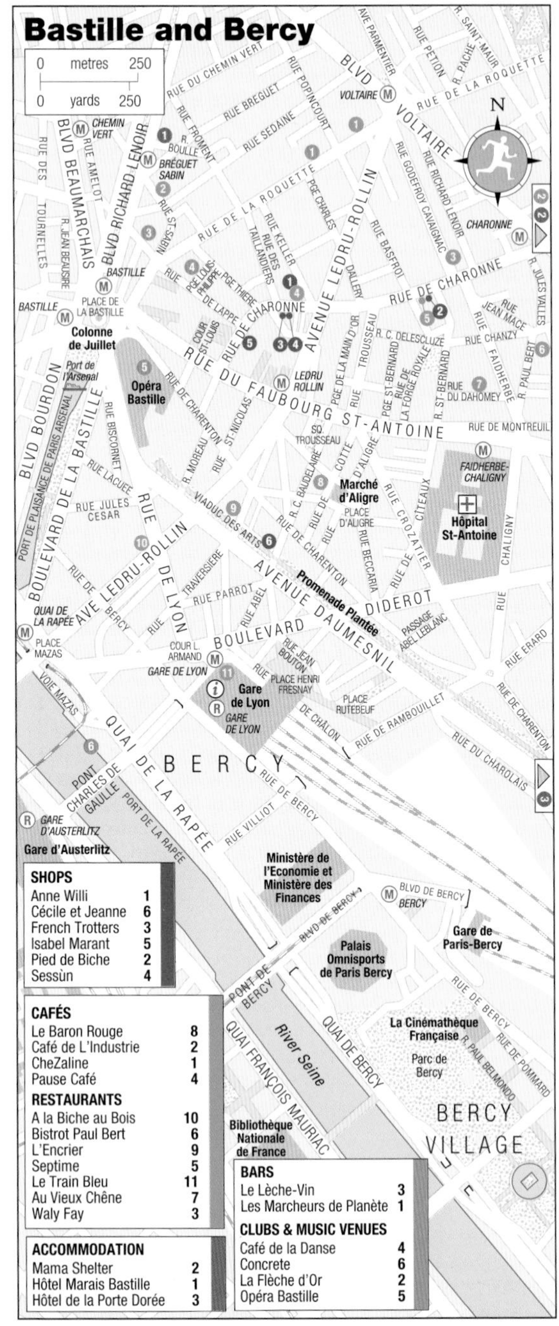
Bastille and Bercy
0 metres 250
0 yards 250
SHOPS
Anne Willi 1
Cécile et Jeanne 6
French Trotters 3
Isabel Marant 5
Pied de Biche 2
Sessùn 4
CAFÉS
Le Baron Rouge 8
Café de L'Industrie 2
CheZaline 1
Pause Café 4
RESTAURANTS
A la Biche au Bois 10
Bistrot Paul Bert 6
L'Encrier 9
Septime 5
Le Train Bleu 11
Au Vieux Chêne 7
Waly Fay 3
ACCOMMODATION
Mama Shelter 2
Hôtel Marais Bastille 1
Hôtel de la Porte Dorée 3
BARS
Le Lèche-Vin 3
Les Marcheurs de Planète 1
CLUBS & MUSIC VENUES
Café de la Danse 4
Concrete 6
La Flèche d'Or 2
Opéra Bastille 5
Colonne de Juillet
Opéra Bastille
Marché d'Aligre
Hôpital St-Antoine
Promenade Plantée
Gare de Lyon
Gare d'Austerlitz
Ministère de l'Economie et Ministère des Finances
Palais Omnisports de Paris Bercy
Gare de Paris-Bercy
La Cinémathèque Française
Parc de Bercy
Bibliothèque Nationale de France
River Seine
BERCY
BERCY VILLAGE
PLACE DE LA BASTILLE
RUE DU FAUBOURG ST-ANTOINE
AVENUE LEDRU-ROLLIN
RUE DE CHARONNE
RUE DE LA ROQUETTE
BLVD VOLTAIRE
BLVD BEAUMARCHAIS
BLVD RICHARD LENOIR
BOULEVARD DE LA BASTILLE
BLVD BOURDON
RUE DE LYON
AVENUE DAUMESNIL
BOULEVARD DIDEROT
QUAI DE LA RAPÉE
QUAI DE BERCY
QUAI FRANÇOIS MAURIAC
PONT CHARLES DE GAULLE
PONT DE BERCY
RUE DE BERCY
BLVD DE BERCY
RUE DE CHARENTON
VIADUC DES ARTS
RUE DE MONTREUIL

CHATEAU DE VINCENNES

Château-de-Vincennes. 01 48 08 31 20, chateau-de-vincennes.fr. Daily: May–Aug 10am–6pm; Sept–April 10am–5pm. €8.50. POCKET MAP M10

On the northern edge of the *bois* is the Château de Vincennes – erstwhile royal medieval residence, then state prison, porcelain factory, weapons dump and military training school. It presents a rather austere aspect on first sight, but is worth visiting for its beautiful Flamboyant-Gothic **Chapelle Royale**, completed in the mid-sixteenth century and decorated with superb Renaissance stained-glass windows. Nearby, in the renovated fourteenth-century *donjon* (keep), you can see some fine vaulted ceilings and Charles V's bedchamber, as well as graffiti left by prisoners.

BERCY VILLAGE

Cour St-Emilion. MAP P.98, POCKET MAP M12

Bercy village is a complex of rather handsome old wine warehouses stylishly converted into shops, restaurants and wine bars – popular spots before or after a film at the giant Bercy multiplex cinema at the eastern end of Cour Saint Emilion.

PARC DE BERCY

Bercy/Cour St-Emilion. MAP P.98, POCKET MAP M12

The contemporary-style Parc de Bercy incorporates elements of the old warehouse site, such as disused railway tracks and cobbled lanes. The western section of the park is a fairly unexciting expanse of grass, but the area to the east has arbours, rose gardens, lily ponds and an orangerie.

LA CINEMATHEQUE FRANCAISE

51 rue de Bercy Bercy. 01 71 19 33 33, cinematheque.fr. MAP P.98, POCKET MAP M11-12

The Cinémathèque, a striking glass, zinc and stone building designed by Guggenheim architect Frank Gehry and resembling a falling pack of cards, houses a huge archive of films dating back to the earliest days of cinema. Regular retrospectives of French and foreign films are screened in its four cinemas and it also has an engaging **museum** (Mon and Wed–Sun noon–7pm; €5), with early cinematic equipment, silent film clips and costumes such as the dress worn by Vivienne Leigh in *Gone With The Wind*.

LA CINEMATHEQUE FRANCAISE

ANNE WILLI

Shops

ANNE WILLI

13 rue Keller Ⓜ Ledru-Rollin/Voltaire. Mon 2–6pm, Tues–Sat 11am–7pm. MAP P.98, POCKET MAP L9

Completely original pieces of clothing in gorgeous, luxurious fabrics, from layered, casual-chic sets to one-piece geometric studies of the body. Prices from €120 upwards. There are also cute clothes for kids.

CECILE ET JEANNE

49 av Daumesnil Ⓜ Gare-de-Lyon. Mon–Sat 11am–7pm. MAP P.98, POCKET MAP L10

Reasonably priced and innovative jewellery from local artisans in one of the Viaduc des Arts showrooms. Many pieces under €100.

FRENCH TROTTERS

430 rue de Charonne Ⓜ Ledru-Rollin. Ⓦ frenchtrotters.fr. Mon 1.30–7.30pm, Tues–Sat 11.30am–7.30pm. MAP P.98, POCKET MAP L9

Trendy concept store, stocking homeware, bath products and above all men's and women's clothing, including covetable own-brand Breton shirts, as well as unusual international and French labels, such as Commune de Paris and Filippa K.

ISABEL MARANT

16 rue de Charonne Ⓜ Ledru-Rollin. Mon–Sat 10.30am–7.30pm. MAP P.98, POCKET MAP L9

Marant has established an international reputation for her feminine and flattering clothes in quality fabrics such as silk and cashmere. Prices are above average, but not exorbitant.

PIED DE BICHE

86 rue de Charonne Ⓜ Charonne. Ⓦ lepieddebiche.com. Tues–Fri 11.30am–8pm, Sat 11am–8pm. MAP P.98, POCKET MAP M9

An inviting little indie store, with a lovingly curated cache of underground, cult and international books and graphic novels, plus regular in-store events and exhibitions.

SESSUN

34 rue de Charonne Ⓜ Ledru-Rollin. Ⓦ sessun.com. Mon–Sat 11am–7pm. MAP P.98, POCKET MAP L9

This bright and spacious boutique on the trendy rue de Charonne sells all the womenswear you could want, from pretty prints and basic Ts to elegant winter coats and cosy knits. Prices start at around €100 – good value given the quality.

Cafés

LE BARON ROUGE

1 rue Théophile-Roussel Ⓜ Ledru-Rollin. Mon 5–10pm, Tues–Fri 10am–2pm & 5–10pm, Sat 10am–10pm, Sun 10.30am–3.30pm. MAP P.98, POCKET MAP L9

This *bar à vins* is as close as you'll get to the spit-on-the-floor, saloon stereotype of the old movies. Stallholders and shoppers from the place d'Aligre market gather for a light lunch or an *apéritif* during the day, especially on Sundays, with a younger crowd appearing later on. Join the locals on the pavement lunching on *saucisson*, mussels or Cap Ferrat oysters washed down with a glass of Muscadet.

CAFE DE L'INDUSTRIE

16 rue St-Sabin Ⓜ Bastille. Daily 10am–2am; closed 3 weeks in Aug. MAP P.98, POCKET MAP H16

One of the best Bastille cafés (actually two cafés, across the road from each other), packed out every evening. Rugs on the floor around solid old wooden tables, mounted rhinoceros heads, old black-and-white photos on the walls and an unpretentious crowd.

CHEZALINE

85 rue de la Roquette Ⓜ Voltaire. Mon–Fri 11am–7pm. MAP P.98, POCKET MAP L8

This great-value gourmet deli puts a creative spin on picnic food – eat in if you're lucky to bag one of the few tables, or take out baguettes (ham, artichoke and pesto; roasted cod with tapenade), deli salads and daily changing specials.

PAUSE CAFE

41 rue de Charonne, cnr rue Keller Ⓜ Ledru-Rollin. Tues–Sat 8am–2am, Sun 9am–8pm. MAP P.98, POCKET MAP L9

Or maybe "Pose Café" – given its popularity with the *quartier*'s young and fashionable (sunglasses are worn at all times) who bag the pavement tables at lunch and *apéritif* time. Service is predictably insouciant. *Plats du jour* around €14.

LE BARON ROUGE

Restaurants

A LA BICHE AU BOIS

45 av Ledru-Rollin Ⓜ Gare de Lyon. Ⓣ 01 43 43 34 38. Mon 7–11pm, Tues–Fri noon–2pm & 7–10.30pm; closed four weeks July–Aug. MAP P.98, POCKET MAP H18

The queues leading out through the conservatory at the front are a strong indicator of the popularity of this restaurant, which mixes charming service with keenly priced, well-produced food. The house speciality is a rich *coq au vin*, and you can start off with a pâté or terrine. Four-course lunch and dinner *menu* (with magnificent cheese platter included) €31.

BISTROT PAUL BERT

18 rue Paul Bert Ⓜ Faidherbe-Chaligny. Ⓣ 01 43 72 24 01. Tues–Sat noon–2pm & 7.30–11pm; closed Aug. MAP P.98, POCKET MAP M9

A quintessential Parisian *bistrot*, with little wooden tables and white tablecloths, tobacco-stained ceiling and old posters. A mix of locals and visitors flock here for the cosy ambience and high-quality simple fare, such as *poulet rôti*, as well as more sophisticated dishes such as guinea fowl with morel mushrooms. Save room for the perfectly cooked Grand Marnier soufflé. Dinner set menu is €39.

L'ENCRIER

55 rue Traversière Ⓜ Ledru-Rollin. Ⓣ 01 44 68 08 16. Mon–Fri noon–2.15pm & 7.30–11pm, Sat 7.30–11pm; usually closed Aug. MAP P.98, POCKET MAP L10

The interior of exposed brick walls and wood beams complements the good-value, homely fare served up by pleasant staff in this cooperative-run restaurant near the Viaduc des Arts. The food has a southwestern influence and might include goose breast in honey or pear with roquefort. Lunch *menu* from €15, evening *menus* from €21.

SEPTIME

80 rue de Charonne Ⓜ Charonne. Ⓣ 01 43 67 38 29, Ⓦ septime-charonne.fr. Mon 7.30–10pm, Tues–Fri 12.15–2pm & 7.30–10pm. MAP P.98, POCKET MAP M9

This highly acclaimed neo-*bistrot* turns out inventive, delicate food matched with a fine list of natural wines. Dishes might include asparagus with oranges and ricotta or steamed cod with pickled turnips and yuzu sauce. The three-course €32 lunch menu is particularly good value; dinner is a five-course tasting menu for €55. Book three weeks in advance. If you can't get a table, you could try its affiliated seafood tapas bar, *Clamato*, two doors up, which takes walk-ins only (Wed–Fri 7–11pm, Sat & Sun noon–11pm; turn up early).

LE TRAIN BLEU

LE TRAIN BLEU

Gare de Lyon Ⓜ Gare de Lyon. Ⓣ 01 43 43 09 06, Ⓦ le-train-bleu.com. Daily 11.30am–3pm & 7–10pm. MAP P.98, POCKET MAP L10

Le Train Bleu's decor is straight out of a bygone era – everything drips with gilt, and chandeliers hang from frescoed ceilings. The French cuisine is good, if a tad overpriced. Set menus from €49; mains around €40.

AU VIEUX CHENE

7 rue du Dahomey Ⓜ Faidherbe-Chaligny. Ⓣ 01 43 71 67 69. Mon–Fri noon–2pm & 8–10.30pm; closed one week in July and two in Aug. MAP P.98, POCKET MAP M9

A relaxed, traditional neighbourhood restaurant with attentive service and attractive decor. Try smoked haddock on a bed of carrots, followed by a perfect *tarte tatin*. Mains €22–27.

WALY FAY

6 rue Godefroy-Cavaignac Ⓜ Charonne/Faidherbe-Chaligny. Ⓣ 01 40 24 17 79, Ⓦ walyfay.com. Mon–Fri noon–3pm & 7pm–12.30am, Sat & Sun 7pm–12.30am. MAP P.98, POCKET MAP M8

West African restaurant with a cosy, stylish atmosphere. Smart young Parisians come here to dine on richly spiced stews and other West African delicacies at a moderate cost (mains €13–19).

Bars

LE LECHE-VIN

13 rue Daval Ⓜ Bastille. Daily 6pm–2am. MAP P.98, POCKET MAP H16

Appealing, rough-around-the edges little bar, dotted with kitsch religious decor. The statue of Mary in the window sets the tongue-in-cheek tone; the pictures in the toilet, on the other hand, are far from pious. It gets packed very quickly at night with a young, cosmopolitan crowd.

LES MARCHEURS DE PLANETE

73 rue de la Roquette Ⓜ Voltaire. Ⓦ lesmarcheursdeplanete.com. Tues–Sat 5.30pm–2am, Sun 11am–11pm. MAP P.98, POCKET MAP L8

Good old-fashioned Parisian atmosphere, with an effortlessly cool, vaguely retro vibe, with chess tables, posters and a wild-haired owner. More than 150 wines are on offer, plus excellent cheeses and charcuterie dishes, as well as traditional French dishes such as *pot au feu* and steak. Live music Thurs at 10pm.

CAFE DE LA DANSE

Clubs and music venues

CAFE DE LA DANSE

5 passage Louis-Philippe Ⓜ Bastille. Ⓣ 01 47 00 57 59, Ⓦ cafedeladanse.com. Open nights of concerts only. MAP P.98, POCKET MAP H17

Rock, pop, world and folk music played in an intimate and attractive space.

CONCRETE

Port de la Rapée Ⓜ Gare de Lyon. Ⓦ concreteparis.fr. Fri–Sun hours vary. MAP P.98, POCKET MAP K10

On a boat moored on the Seine, this is one of the hottest spots on the clubbing scene, putting on all-night and all-day techno parties, and featuring big-name DJs.

LA FLECHE D'OR

102bis rue de Bagnolet Ⓜ Porte-de-Bagnolet/Alexandre-Dumas (15min walk from both). Ⓣ 01 44 64 01 02, Ⓦ flechedor.fr. Opening times and admission vary. MAP P.98, POCKET MAP C21

Housed in the old Bagnolet station on the defunct *petite ceinture* railway, this much-loved bar and live music venue is one of the hottest tickets in town, programming indie-pop, ska, rock, *chanson* and punk.

OPERA BASTILLE

120 rue de Lyon Ⓜ Bastille. Ⓣ 08 36 69 78 68, Ⓦ opera-de-paris.fr. MAP P.98, POCKET MAP H17

Opened in 1989 to a rather mixed reception, the amorphous glass-and-steel opera house building still inspires a fair amount of controversy, but its performances are nearly always a sell-out. Tickets start from €15, but most are in the €35–100 range.

The Quartier Latin

The Quartier Latin has been associated with students ever since the Sorbonne was established in the thirteenth century. The name derives from the Latin spoken at the medieval university, which perched on the slopes of the Montagne Ste-Geneviève. Many colleges remain in the area to this day, along with some fascinating vestiges of the medieval city, such as the Gothic church of St-Séverin and the Renaissance Hôtel de Cluny, site of the national museum of the Middle Ages. Some of the quarter's student chic may have worn thin in recent years – notably around the now-too-famous place St-Michel – and high rents have pushed scholars and artists out of their garrets; but the cafés, restaurants and arty cinemas are still packed with students, making this one of the most relaxed areas of Paris for going out.

THE RIVERBANK

Ⓜ St-Michel. MAP PP.106–107, POCKET MAP D17–E18

The riverbank *quais* east of place St-Michel are ideal for wandering and enjoying a good browse among the old books, postcards and prints sold from the **bouquinistes**, whose green kiosks line the parapets. There are wonderful views across the river to Notre-Dame from square Viviani, a welcome patch of grass around the corner from the celebrated English-language bookshop **Shakespeare and Company** (see p.110). The mutilated church behind the square is **St-Julien-le-Pauvre** (daily 9.30am–1pm and 3–6.30pm; Ⓜ St-Michel/Maubert-Mutualité). The same age as Notre-Dame, it used to be the venue for university assemblies until rumbustious students tore it apart in 1524. For the most dramatic view of Notre-Dame, walk along the riverbank as far as the tip of the Ile St-Louis and the Pont de Sully.

A CAFE TERRACE IN THE QUARTIER LATIN

THE HUCHETTE QUARTER

Ⓜ St-Michel. MAP PP.106–107, POCKET MAP D17

The touristy bustle is at its worst around **rue de la Huchette**, just east of the place St-Michel, but look beyond the cheap bars and overpriced Greek kebab-and-disco tavernas and you'll find some evocative

INSIDE THE MUSEE NATIONAL DU MOYEN AGE

remnants of medieval Paris. Connecting rue de la Huchette to the riverside is the narrow rue du Chat-qui-Pêche, a tiny slice of how Paris looked before Baron Haussmann flattened the old alleys to make room for his wide boulevards. One block south of rue de la Huchette, just west of rue St-Jacques, is the mainly fifteenth-century church of **St-Séverin**, whose entrance is on rue des Prêtres St-Séverin (Mon–Sat 11am–7.30pm, Sun 9am–8.30pm; Ⓜ St-Michel/Cluny-La Sorbonne). It's one of the city's more intense churches, its windows filled with edgy stained glass by the modern French painter Jean Bazaine.

MUSEE NATIONAL DU MOYEN AGE

6 place Paul-Painlevé Ⓜ Cluny-La Sorbonne. Ⓣ 01 53 73 78 16, Ⓦ musee-moyenage.fr. Daily except Tues 9.15am–5.45pm. €8.50. Medieval music concerts throughout the week; see website for details; €8. MAP PP.106–107, POCKET MAP C18–D18

The walls of the third-century **Roman baths** are visible in the garden of the **Hôtel de Cluny**, a sixteenth-century mansion built by the abbots of the Cluny monastery as their Paris pied-à-terre. It now houses the rewarding Musée National du Moyen Age, a treasure-trove of medieval art. There's a feast of medieval sculpture throughout, along with wonderful stained glass, books and curious objets d'art, but the real beauties are the **tapestries** that hang in most rooms, including vivid depictions of a grape harvest, a lover making advances and a woman in a bath that overflows into a duck pond. The greatest of all is the stunning **La Dame à la Licorne** ("The Lady with the Unicorn") series, displayed in its own chapel-like chamber. Made in the late fifteenth century, the set depicts the five senses – along with an ambiguous image that may represent the virtue in controlling them – in six luxuriantly detailed allegoric scenes, each featuring a richly dressed woman flanked by a lion and a unicorn. On the ground floor, the vaults of the Roman baths are preserved intact.

The museum also has a busy progamme of medieval music **concerts**; look out for the regular "heure musicale".

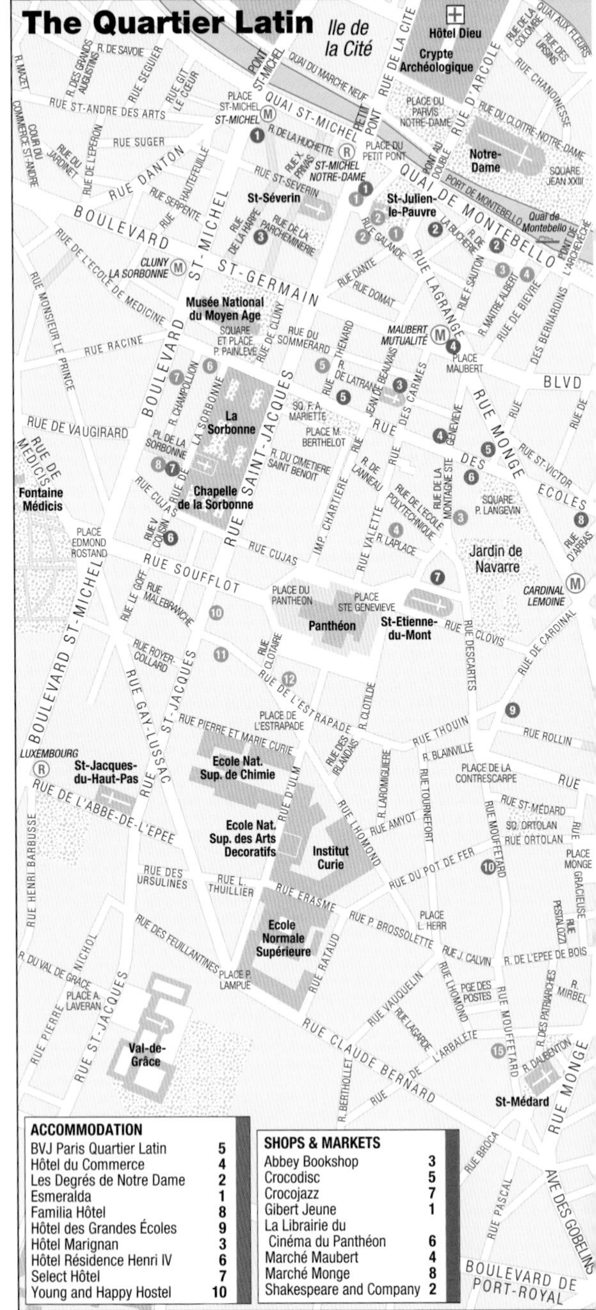
The Quartier Latin
Ile de la Cité
Hôtel Dieu
Crypte Archéologique
Notre-Dame
Square Jean XXIII
Place du Parvis Notre-Dame
Place St-Michel
St-Michel
St-Michel Notre-Dame
Quai St-Michel
Quai du Marché Neuf
Quai de Montebello
Quai de Montebello
Quai aux Fleurs
Petit Pont
Place du Petit Pont
Pont au Double
Pont de Montebello
Pont de l'Archevêché
Pont St-Michel
Rue de la Cité
Rue d'Arcole
Rue du Cloître-Notre-Dame
Rue Chanoinesse
Rue de la Colombe
Rue des Ursins
R. de Savoie
R. des Grands Augustins
Rue Séguier
Rue Gît le Coeur
Rue St-André des Arts
Rue Suger
Rue Danton
Rue de l'Eperon
Rue du Jardinet
Cour du Commerce St-André
R. Mazet
Rue Hautefeuille
Rue Serpente
R. de la Huchette
Rue St-Séverin
St-Séverin
Rue de la Harpe
Rue de la Parcheminerie
St-Julien-le-Pauvre
Rue Galande
Rue Lagrange
La Bûcherie
Rue F. Sauton
R. Maître Albert
Rue de Bièvre
Rue des Bernardins
Boulevard St-Michel
Boulevard St-Germain
Cluny La Sorbonne
Rue de l'Ecole de Médecine
Rue Monsieur le Prince
Rue Racine
Musée National du Moyen Age
Square et Place P. Painlevé
Rue de Cluny
Rue du Sommerard
Rue Dante
Rue Domat
Maubert Mutualité
Place Maubert
Rue Thénard
R. de Latran
Rue Jean de Beauvais
Rue des Carmes
Rue de Vaugirard
Rue de Médicis
Fontaine Médicis
R. Champollion
Rue de la Sorbonne
La Sorbonne
Pl. de la Sorbonne
Chapelle de la Sorbonne
Rue Saint-Jacques
Sq. F.A. Mariette
Place M. Berthelot
R. du Cimetière Saint Benoît
Imp. Chartière
R. de Lanneau
Rue Valette
R. Laplace
Rue de l'Ecole Polytechnique
Rue de la Montagne Ste Geneviève
Rue des Ecoles
Rue Monge
Rue St-Victor
Square P. Langevin
Jardin de Navarre
Rue d'Arras
Cardinal Lemoine
Rue Cujas
Rue V. Cousin
Place Edmond Rostand
Rue Soufflot
Rue Le Goff
Rue Malebranche
Place du Panthéon
Place Ste Geneviève
Panthéon
St-Etienne-du-Mont
Rue Clovis
Rue Descartes
Rue du Cardinal
Rue Royer-Collard
Rue Clotaire
Rue de l'Estrapade
Place de l'Estrapade
R. Clotilde
Rue Thouin
R. Blainville
Rue Rollin
Rue Gay-Lussac
Rue Pierre et Marie Curie
Rue des Irlandais
Place de la Contrescarpe
Luxembourg
St-Jacques-du-Haut-Pas
Ecole Nat. Sup. de Chimie
Rue d'Ulm
R. Laromiguière
Rue Tournefort
Rue Mouffetard
Rue St-Médard
Sq. Ortolan
Rue Ortolan
Rue de l'Abbé-de-l'Epée
Ecole Nat. Sup. des Arts Decoratifs
Institut Curie
Rue Lhomond
Rue Amyot
Rue du Pot de Fer
Place Monge
Rue Gracieuse
Rue Henri Barbusse
Rue des Ursulines
Rue L. Thuillier
Rue Erasme
Rue P. Brossolette
Place L. Herr
Rue Pestalozzi
Rue des Feuillantines
Ecole Normale Supérieure
Rue Rataud
Rue J. Calvin
R. de l'Epée de Bois
R. du Val de Grâce
Rue Nicole
Place A. Laveran
Place P. Lampué
Rue Vauquelin
Rue Lagarde
Pge des Postes
R. des Patriarches
R. Mirbel
Rue Pierre
Rue St-Jacques
Val-de-Grâce
Rue Claude Bernard
Rue de l'Arbalète
R. Daubenton
St-Médard
R. Berthollet
Rue Broca
Rue Pascal
Ave des Gobelins
Boulevard de Port-Royal
ACCOMMODATION
BVJ Paris Quartier Latin 5
Hôtel du Commerce 4
Les Degrés de Notre Dame 2
Esmeralda 1
Familia Hôtel 8
Hôtel des Grandes Écoles 9
Hôtel Marignan 3
Hôtel Résidence Henri IV 6
Select Hôtel 7
Young and Happy Hostel 10
SHOPS & MARKETS
Abbey Bookshop 3
Crocodisc 5
Crocojazz 7
Gibert Jeune 1
La Librairie du Cinéma du Panthéon 6
Marché Maubert 4
Marché Monge 8
Shakespeare and Company 2

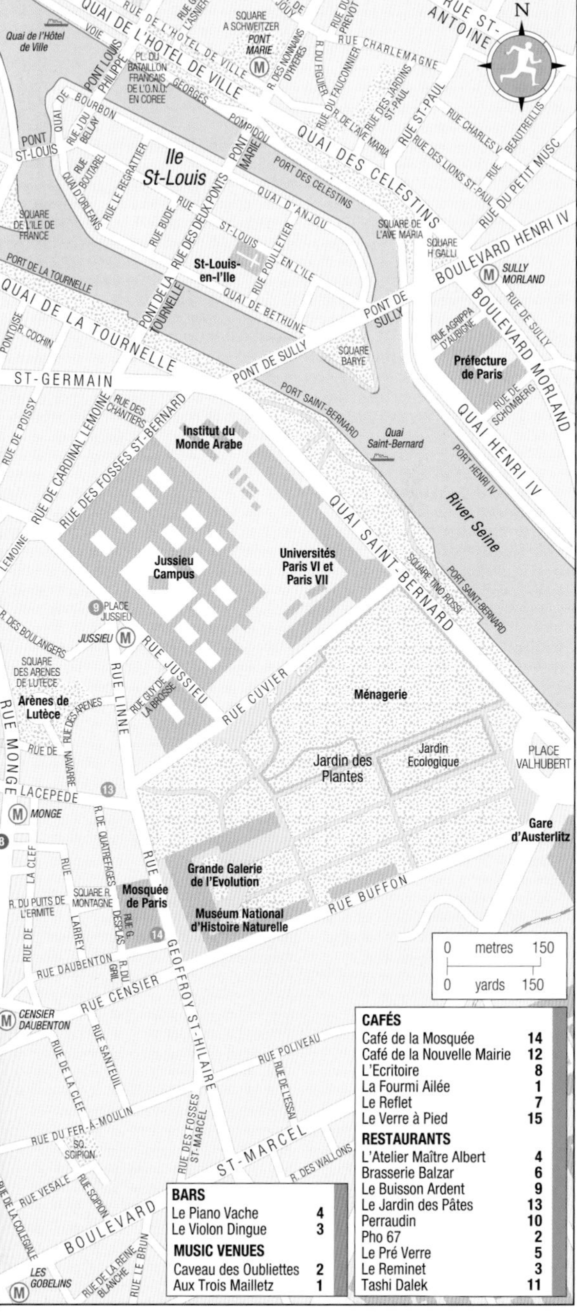
Quai de l'Hôtel de Ville
Ile St-Louis
St-Louis-en-l'Ile
Quai de l'Hotel de Ville
Quai des Celestins
Quai d'Anjou
Quai de Bethune
Quai de la Tournelle
Pont de Sully
Pont Marie
Pont Louis Philippe
Pont St-Louis
Pont de la Tournelle
Square Barye
Boulevard Henri IV
Sully Morland
Boulevard Morland
Préfecture de Paris
Quai Henri IV
Port Henri IV
River Seine
Quai Saint-Bernard
Port Saint-Bernard
Square Tino Rossi
Institut du Monde Arabe
Jussieu Campus
Universités Paris VI et Paris VII
Place Jussieu
Jussieu
Rue Jussieu
Rue Cuvier
Rue Linne
Ménagerie
Jardin des Plantes
Jardin Ecologique
Place Valhubert
Gare d'Austerlitz
Arènes de Lutèce
Square des Arenes de Lutece
Rue Monge
Monge
Rue Lacepede
Grande Galerie de l'Evolution
Muséum National d'Histoire Naturelle
Mosquée de Paris
Rue Buffon
Rue Geoffroy St-Hilaire
Rue Censier
Censier Daubenton
Rue Daubenton
Rue Poliveau
St-Marcel
Boulevard
Les Gobelins
Rue St-Antoine
St-Germain
Rue des Fosses St-Bernard
Rue de Cardinal Lemoine
Rue de Poissy
N
0 metres 150
0 yards 150
CAFÉS
Café de la Mosquée 14
Café de la Nouvelle Mairie 12
L'Ecritoire 8
La Fourmi Ailée 1
Le Reflet 7
Le Verre à Pied 15
RESTAURANTS
L'Atelier Maître Albert 4
Brasserie Balzar 6
Le Buisson Ardent 9
Le Jardin des Pâtes 13
Perraudin 10
Pho 67 2
Le Pré Verre 5
Le Reminet 3
Tashi Dalek 11
BARS
Le Piano Vache 4
Le Violon Dingue 3
MUSIC VENUES
Caveau des Oubliettes 2
Aux Trois Mailletz 1

THE SORBONNE

Ⓜ Cluny-La Sorbonne/RER Luxembourg. MAP PP.106–107, POCKET MAP C18–D18

The traffic-free place de la Sorbonne is a great place to sit back and enjoy the Quartier Latin atmosphere. Frowning over it are the high walls of the Sorbonne, which was once the most important of the medieval colleges huddled atop the Montagne Ste-Geneviève. More recently it was a flashpoint in the student riots of 1968 – and again in the spring of 2006. The frontage is dominated by the Chapelle Ste-Ursule, built in the 1640s by the great Cardinal Richelieu, whose tomb it contains.

THE CAFE AT THE PARIS MOSQUE

THE PANTHEON

Ⓜ Cardinal-Lemoine/RER Luxembourg. Ⓣ 01 44 32 18 00, Ⓦ paris-pantheon.fr. Daily: April–Sept 10am–6.30pm; Oct–March 10am–6pm. €8.50, €10.50 including ascent of dome. MAP PP.106–107, POCKET MAP D19

Crowning the Montagne Ste-Geneviève, the largest and most visible of Paris's domes graces the bulky Panthéon, Louis XV's thank-you to Ste-Geneviève, patron saint of Paris, for curing him of illness. Completed only in 1789, after the Revolution it was transformed into a mausoleum, emblazoned with the words "Aux grands hommes la patrie reconnaissante" ("The nation honours its great men") beneath the pediment of the giant portico. The remains of giants of French culture, including Voltaire, Rousseau, Hugo and Zola, are entombed in the vast, barrel-vaulted crypt, along with Marie Curie, and Alexandre Dumas, who was "panthéonized" in 2002. The Classical nave displays a working model of **Foucault's Pendulum** swinging from the dome. French physicist Léon Foucault devised the experiment, conducted here in 1851, to demonstrate that while the pendulum appeared to rotate over a 24-hour period, it was in fact the Earth beneath it turning. The dome was recently restored and is once again open to the public, though currently only from April to October; numbers are limited to fifty at a time.

ST-ETIENNE-DU-MONT

Ⓜ Cardinal Lemoine. MAP PP.106–107, POCKET MAP D19

The remains of Pascal and Racine, two seventeenth-century literary giants who didn't make it into the Panthéon, and a few relics of Ste-Geneviève, lie in the church of St-Etienne-du-Mont. The main attraction, however, is the fabulously airy interior, formed of a Flamboyant Gothic choir joined to a Renaissance nave, the two parts linked by a sinuous catwalk that runs around the interior, arching across the nave in the form of a carved rood screen – an extremely rare survival, as most French screens fell victim to Protestant iconoclasts, reformers or revolutionaries.

INSTITUT DU MONDE ARABE

1 rue des Fossés St-Bernard Ⓜ Jussieu/Cardinal-Lemoine. ☎ 01 40 51 38 38, Ⓦ www.imarabe.org. Museum Tues–Fri 10am–6pm, Sat & Sun 10am–7pm. Museum €8. MAP PP.106–107, POCKET MAP F18

A bold slice of glass and steel, the stunning exterior of the Institut du Monde Arabe betrays architect Jean Nouvel's obsession with light – its broad southern facade, which mimics a *moucharabiyah*, or traditional Arab latticework, is made up of thousands of tiny metallic shutters. Originally designed to be light-sensitive, they now open and close just once an hour, and the exhibition spaces are consequently quite gloomy. Inside, a thoughtful **museum** explores five themes – Arabs, the sacred, cities, beauty and daily life – through a collection of exquisite ceramics, metalwork and textiles.

THE PARIS MOSQUE AND HAMMAM

Entrance on rue Daubenton Ⓜ Jussieu. ☎ 01 45 35 97 33, Ⓦ mosqueedeparis.net. Daily except Fri & Muslim hols 9am–noon & 2–6pm. €3. MAP PP.106–107, POCKET MAP J11

Even in this quiet area, the Paris mosque, built by Moroccan craftsmen in the early 1920s, feels like an oasis of serenity behind its crenellated walls. You can walk in the sunken garden and patios with their polychrome tiles and carved ceilings, and relax at the laidback café (see p.111), but non-Muslims are asked not to enter the prayer room. The **hammam** (women Mon, Wed, Thurs and Sat 10am–9pm, Fri 2–9pm; men Tues 2–9pm, Sun 10am–9pm. €18; towels extra) is one of the most atmospheric in the city, with its vaulted cooling-off room and marble-lined steam chamber.

JARDIN DES PLANTES

Entrances at the corners of the park and opposite rue Jussieu Ⓜ Jussieu/Censier Daubenton. Ⓦ jardindesplantes.net. Daily: April–Aug 7.30am–7.45pm; Sept–March 8am–5.30pm. Free. MAP PP.106–107, POCKET MAP F19–G19

Behind the mosque, the Jardin des Plantes, a medicinal herb garden from 1626, now hosts Paris's botanical gardens, with avenues of trees, lawns, hothouses, museums and an old-fashioned **menagerie**, also France's oldest zoo.

GRANDE GALERIE DE L'EVOLUTION

Jardin des Plantes; entrance off rue Buffon Ⓜ Censier-Daubenton/Gare d'Austerlitz. Daily except Tues 10am–6pm. €9. MAP PP.106–107, POCKET MAP J11

Magnificent floral beds make a fine approach to the collection of buildings that forms the **Muséum National d'Histoire Naturelle** (Ⓦ mnhn.fr). Skip the musty displays of paleontology, anatomy, mineralogy and paleobotany in favour of the Grande Galerie de l'Evolution, housed in a restored nineteenth-century glass-domed building. It doesn't actually tell the story of evolution, but it does feature a huge cast of life-sized animals, some of them striding dramatically across the space.

STROLLING IN THE JARDIN DES PLANTES

Shops and markets

ABBEY BOOKSHOP

29 rue de la Parcheminerie Ⓜ St-Michel. Mon–Sat 10am–7pm. MAP PP.106–107, POCKET MAP D17

An overstuffed warren with lots of used British and North American fiction and travel guides, plus knowledgeable, helpful staff – and free coffee.

CROCODISC

40–42 rue des Ecoles Ⓜ Maubert-Mutualité. Ⓦ crocodisc.com. Tues–Sat 11am–7pm. Closed first two weeks of Aug. MAP PP.106–107, POCKET MAP D18

Everything from folk and Afro-Antillais to salsa and movie soundtracks, new and used, at good prices.

CROCOJAZZ

64 rue de la Montagne-Ste-Geneviève Ⓜ Maubert-Mutualité. Tues–Sat 11am–1pm & 2–7pm. MAP PP.106–107, POCKET MAP D19

Mainly new jazz and blues imports, with some inexpensive used titles.

GIBERT JEUNE

5 place St-Michel and around Ⓜ St-Michel. Ⓦ gibertjeune.fr. Mon–Sat 9.30am–7.30pm; closed first two weeks of Aug. MAP PP.106–107, POCKET MAP D17

A Latin Quarter institution for student/academic books, with nine stores on and around place St-Michel. There's a secondhand selection at no. 2 and foreign-language titles at no. 10.

LA LIBRAIRIE DU CINEMA DU PANTHEON

15 rue Victor Cousin Ⓜ Cluny-La Sorbonne. Ⓦ cinelitterature.fr. Mon–Fri 1–8pm, Sat 11am–8pm. MAP PP.106–107, POCKET MAP C18

Superb store devoted to cinema, with books, not all in French, plus magazines and posters.

SHAKESPEARE AND COMPANY

MARCHE MAUBERT

Place Maubert Ⓜ Maubert-Mutualité. Tues & Thurs 7am–2.30pm, Sat 7am–3pm. MAP PP.106–107, POCKET MAP D18.

One of the city's classic food markets, with a wonderful array of cheese, *saucisson* and fresh fruit and veg.

MARCHE MONGE

Place Monge Ⓜ Monge. Wed & Fri 7am–2.30pm, Sun 7am–3pm. MAP PP.106–107, POCKET MAP H11.

Just off "La Mouff" (the city's famed rue Mouffetard market, now mostly given over to classy food shops), this authentic market is set around the pretty Monge fountain and sells fabulous, pricey produce. Organic stalls on Sundays.

SHAKESPEARE AND COMPANY

37 rue de la Bûcherie Ⓜ Maubert-Mutualité. Ⓦ shakespeareandcompany.com. Mon–Fri 10am–11pm, Sat & Sun 11am–11pm. MAP PP.106–107, POCKET MAP D17

A Latin Quarter institution, this cosy, crowded literary haunt, run by Americans and staffed by earnest young Hemingway wannabes, sells Paris's best selection of English-language books. There are readings in the week; and check out the new café next door.

Cafés

CAFE DE LA MOSQUEE

39 rue Geoffroy-St-Hilaire Ⓜ Monge. Daily 9am–11pm. MAP PP.106–107, POCKET MAP J11

Drink mint tea and eat sweet cakes beside the courtyard fountain and fig trees of the Paris mosque – a haven of calm (except on weekend lunchtimes when it's a popular spot for festive families). The indoor salon has a beautiful Arabic interior, where tasty tagines and couscous are served for €16 and up.

CAFE DE LA NOUVELLE MAIRIE

19 rue des Fossés-St-Jacques Ⓜ Cluny-La Sorbonne/RER Luxembourg. Mon–Fri 8am–midnight. MAP PP.106–107, POCKET MAP D19

Sleek café/wine bar with some pavement seating and a relaxed feel generated by its older, university clientele. Serves good, modern food and plates of cheese or charcuterie (all around €10). No credit cards.

LUNCH AT THE CAFE DE LA NOUVELLE MAIRIE

L'ECRITOIRE

3 place de la Sorbonne Ⓜ Cluny-La Sorbonne/RER Luxembourg. Daily 7am–midnight. MAP PP.106–107, POCKET MAP C18

This classic university café is right beside the Sorbonne, and has outside tables by the fountain.

LA FOURMI AILEE

8 rue du Fouarre Ⓜ Maubert-Mutualité. Ⓦ la-fourmi-ailee.zenchef.com. Daily noon–11pm; food served noon–3pm & 7–10pm. MAP PP.106–107, POCKET MAP D17

Simple, classically French food and speciality teas are served in this former feminist bookshop, now a relaxed *salon de thé* with a pretty, tiled exterior. The high, cloud-painted ceiling, book-lined walls and background jazz add to the atmosphere. Around €10 for a quiche, €7 for home-made cake.

LE REFLET

6 rue Champollion Ⓜ Cluny-La Sorbonne. Daily 11am–2am. MAP PP.106–107, POCKET MAP C18

This artsy cinema café has a strong flavour of the *nouvelle vague*, with its scruffy black paint scheme, lights rigged up on a gantry and rickety tables packed with film-goers and chess players. Perfect for a drink either side of a film at one of the art cinemas on rue Champollion, perhaps accompanied by a steak, quiche or salad from the short list of blackboard specials.

LE VERRE A PIED

118bis rue Mouffetard Ⓜ Monge. Ⓦ leverreapied.fr. Tues–Sat 9am–9pm, Sun 9am–4pm. MAP PP.106–107, POCKET MAP H11

Wonderfully old-fashioned little market bar where traders take their morning glass of wine at the bar, or sit down to eat a delicious *plat du jour* for €12 and engage in lively conversation. Simple *menus* €15.

Restaurants

L'ATELIER MAITRE ALBERT

1 rue Maître Albert Ⓜ Maubert-Mutualité. Ⓣ 01 56 81 30 01, Ⓦ ateliermaitrealbert.com. Mon–Wed noon–2.30pm & 6.30–11pm, Thurs & Fri noon–2.30pm & 6.30pm–1am, Sat 6.30pm–1am, Sun 6.30–11pm. MAP PP.106–107, POCKET MAP E18

One of chef-entrepreneur Guy Savoy's ventures, this contemporary rôtisserie specializes in top-notch spit-roast meats, though you can also find lighter dishes like cod casseroled with seasonal veg or a delicious starter of prawns stuffed with citrus butter. Set menus €28–70.

BRASSERIE BALZAR

49 rue des Ecoles Ⓜ Maubert-Mutualité. Ⓣ 01 43 54 13 67, Ⓦ brasseriebalzar.com. Daily 8.30am–11pm. MAP PP.106–107, POCKET MAP D18

Classic, high-ceilinged brasserie, long frequented by the literary intelligentsia of the Latin Quarter – along with hordes of delighted tourists. Steak tartare, roast chicken or sauerkraut with sausage cost around €35, but there are *menus* from €27–41.50.

LE BUISSON ARDENT

25 rue Jussieu Ⓜ Jussieu. Ⓣ 01 43 54 93 02, Ⓦ lebuissonardent.fr. Mon–Fri noon–2pm & 7.30–10pm, Sat 7.30–10pm, Sun noon–3pm. Closed two weeks in Aug. MAP PP.106–107, POCKET MAP E19

Generous helpings of first-class cooking with vivacious touches: *velouté* of watermelon followed by lamb noisettes with a fennel and blue cheese fondant, for instance. The panelled dining room is grand, but the atmosphere is never less than convivial – and there's a cosy back room. Lunch *menu* €28, dinner €39.

BRASSERIE BALZAR

LE JARDIN DES PATES

4 rue Lacépède Ⓜ Jussieu. Ⓣ 01 43 31 50 71, Ⓦ restaurant-lejardindespates.fr. Daily noon–2.30pm & 7–11pm. MAP PP.106–107, POCKET MAP E19

Delicious home-made pasta that uses all manner of freshly ground, organic grains and is served with wonderful flourishes and garnishes. The room is stylish, fresh-feeling and airy – almost like a conservatory – and you'll pay no more than €15 for a plate of pasta.

PERRAUDIN

157 rue St-Jacques. RER Luxembourg. Ⓣ 01 46 33 15 75, Ⓦ restaurant-perraudin.com. Daily noon–2.30pm & 7.30–10.30pm. MAP PP.106–107, POCKET MAP D19

Quintessential Left Bank *bistrot* featuring solid cooking and an atmosphere thick with Parisian chatter floating above packed tables. *Menus* €19.50 (lunch) and €34.50 (dinner).

PHO 67

59 rue Galande Ⓜ Maubert-Mutualité. Ⓣ 01 43 25 56 69. Daily except Mon lunchtime 11.30am–3pm & 6.30–11pm. MAP PP.106–107, POCKET MAP D17

The Vietnamese proprietors work in an open kitchen, preparing a range of inexpensive dishes, including sour pig ears; the less adventurous should go for the delicious *pho* soup (€14), or one of the four good-value *menus*. No credit cards.

LE PRE VERRE

8 rue Thénard Ⓜ Maubert-Mutualité. Ⓣ 01 43 54 59 47. Tues–Sat noon–2pm & 7.30–10.30pm. MAP PP.106–107, POCKET MAP D18

Unusually relaxed, contemporary *bistrot à vins*, with a great wine menu and adventurous food such as swordfish on a bed of quinoa. Stunning-value *menus*: evening €32, lunchtime two-courser €14.50.

LE REMINET

3 rue des Grands-Degrés Ⓜ Maubert-Mutualité. Ⓣ 01 44 07 04 24. Daily noon–2.30pm & 7–10.30pm. MAP PP.106–107, POCKET MAP E17

This tiny *bistrot* is effortlessly stylish, with gilded mirrors and brass candlesticks at every table, and French windows opening out onto a leafy square. The classy food incorporates quality French ingredients and imaginative sauces. The weekday-only €18 lunch *menu* is a bargain. Pricier in the evenings when the crowds arrive.

TASHI DALEK

4 rue des Fossés-St-Jacques. RER Luxembourg. Ⓣ 01 43 26 55 55. Mon–Sat noon–2.30pm & 7–11pm; closed two weeks in Aug. MAP PP.106–107, POCKET MAP D19

Sober-looking but cheery Tibetan restaurant serving tasty dishes from robust, warming noodle soups to the addictive, ravioli-like beef *momok* and a salty, soupy yak-butter tea. It's good value, with evening *menus* at €17 and €22.

Bars

LE PIANO VACHE

8 rue Laplace Ⓜ Cardinal-Lemoine. Ⓦ lepianovache.fr. Mon–Fri noon–2am, Sat 6pm–2am. MAP PP.106–107, POCKET MAP D18

Left Bank favourite crammed with students, with cool music and a laidback atmosphere.

LE PIANO VACHE

LE VIOLON DINGUE

46 rue de la Montagne-Ste-Geneviève Ⓜ Maubert-Mutualité. Tues–Sat from 7pm (from 10pm in Aug), happy hour 7–10pm. MAP PP.106–107, POCKET MAP D18

A long, dark student pub that's noisy and popular with young travellers. English-speaking bar staff and cheap drinks. The cellar bar stays open until 4.30am on busy nights.

Music venues

CAVEAU DES OUBLIETTES

52 rue Galande Ⓜ St-Michel. Ⓣ 01 46 34 23 09, Ⓦ caveau-des-oubliettes.com. Tues & Sun 5pm–2am, Wed–Sat 5pm–4am; music from 10pm. Free. MAP PP.106–107, POCKET MAP D17

Lively jazz jams – blues, Latin, African – in a gloomy, smoky dungeon setting, once a medieval prison.

AUX TROIS MAILLETZ

56 rue Galande Ⓜ St-Michel. Ⓣ 01 43 25 96 86, Ⓦ lestroismailletz.fr. Daily 6pm–5am. MAP PP.106–107, POCKET MAP D17

This corner café-resto transforms into a convivial piano bar (after 6pm); later (after 8.30pm), a good jazz/cabaret bar sets up in the basement, often featuring fabulous world music artists.

St-Germain

St-Germain, the westernmost section of Paris's Left Bank, has long been famous as the haunt of bohemians and intellectuals. A few famous cafés preserve a strong flavour of the old times, but the dominant spirit these days is elegant, relaxed and seriously upmarket. At opposite ends of the quarter are two of the city's busiest and best-loved sights: to the east, bordering the Quartier Latin, spreads the huge green space of the Jardin du Luxembourg, while to the west stands the jaw-dropping Musée d'Orsay, a converted railway station with a world-beating collection of Impressionist paintings. Between the two, you can visit the churches of St-Sulpice and St-Germain-des-Prés, or intriguing museums dedicated to the artists Delacroix and Maillol, but really, shopping is king. The streets around place St-Sulpice swarm with international fashion brands, while on the north side of boulevard St-Germain, antique shops and art dealers dominate.

PONT DES ARTS

Ⓜ Pont Neuf. MAP PP.116–117, POCKET MAP C16
The much-loved Pont des Arts offers a classic upstream view of the Ile de la Cité, and provides a grand entrance to St-Germain under the watchful eye of the Institut de France, an august academic institution. It had become dangerously weighed down with thousands of "love locks" left by couples wanting to leave a symbol of their undying love, but these have now been removed and replaced with plates of glass.

MUSEE D'ORSAY

MUSEE D'ORSAY

1 rue de la Légion d'Honneur Ⓜ Solférino/RER Musée-d'Orsay. ⓣ 01 40 49 48 14, Ⓦ musee-orsay.fr. Tues–Sun 9.30am–6pm, Thurs till 9.45pm. €12, free on first Sun of the month & to under-18s. MAP PP.116-117, POCKET MAP A15

Along the riverfront, on the western edge of St-Germain, the Musée d'Orsay dramatically fills a vast former railway station with paintings and sculptures dating between 1848 and 1914, including an unparalleled Impressionist and Post-Impressionist collection.

The museum's **ground floor**, spread out under a giant glass arch, is devoted to pre-1870 work, contrasting Ingres, Delacroix and other serious-minded painters and sculptors acceptable to the mid-nineteenth-century salons, with the relatively unusual works of Puvis de Chavannes, Gustave Moreau and the younger Degas. The influential Barbizon school and the Realists are also showcased, with works by Daumier, Corot and Millet preparing the ground for the early controversies of Monet's violently light-filled *Femmes au Jardin* (1867) and Manet's provocative *Olympia* (1863), which heralded the arrival of Impressionism. It's on **level five**, given a major revamp recently, replacing cramped attic rooms with large, open spaces, that Impressionism proper is displayed. Hung against warmly lit, charcoal-grey walls, the vibrant colours and vigorous brushstrokes of even the almost-too-familiar Monets and Renoirs strike you afresh and seem almost to jump off the walls. The first painting to greet you, magnificent in its isolation, is Manet's scandalous *Déjeuner sur l'Herbe*, the work held to have announced the arrival of **Impressionism**. Thereafter follows masterpiece after masterpiece: Degas' *Dans un café (L'Absinthe)*, Renoir's *Bal du Moulin de la Galette*, Cézanne's *Joueurs de Cartes* and Monet's *Femme à l'Ombrelle* and *Coquelicots* ("Poppies"). You'll also find Degas' ballet dancer sculptures and small-scale landscapes, and outdoor scenes by Renoir, Sisley, Pissarro and Monet that owed much of their brilliance to the novel practice of setting up easels in the open. Berthe Morisot, the first woman to join the early Impressionists, is represented by her famous *Le Berceau*, among others.

VAN GOGH SELF-PORTRAIT AT THE MUSEE D'ORSAY

On the **middle level** you'll find the various offspring of Impressionism. In works such as **Van Gogh**'s *La Nuit Etoilée*, with its fervid colours and disturbing rhythms, and **Gauguin**'s Tahitian paintings, there's an edgier, modern feel. More decorative effects are attempted by Pointillists such as Seurat and Signac. On the **sculpture terraces**, Rodin's works are far and away the stand-outs. Try to find time, too, for the last few rooms, as well as levels two, three and four of the restructured Pavillon Amont, which contain superb Art Nouveau furniture and objets d'art.

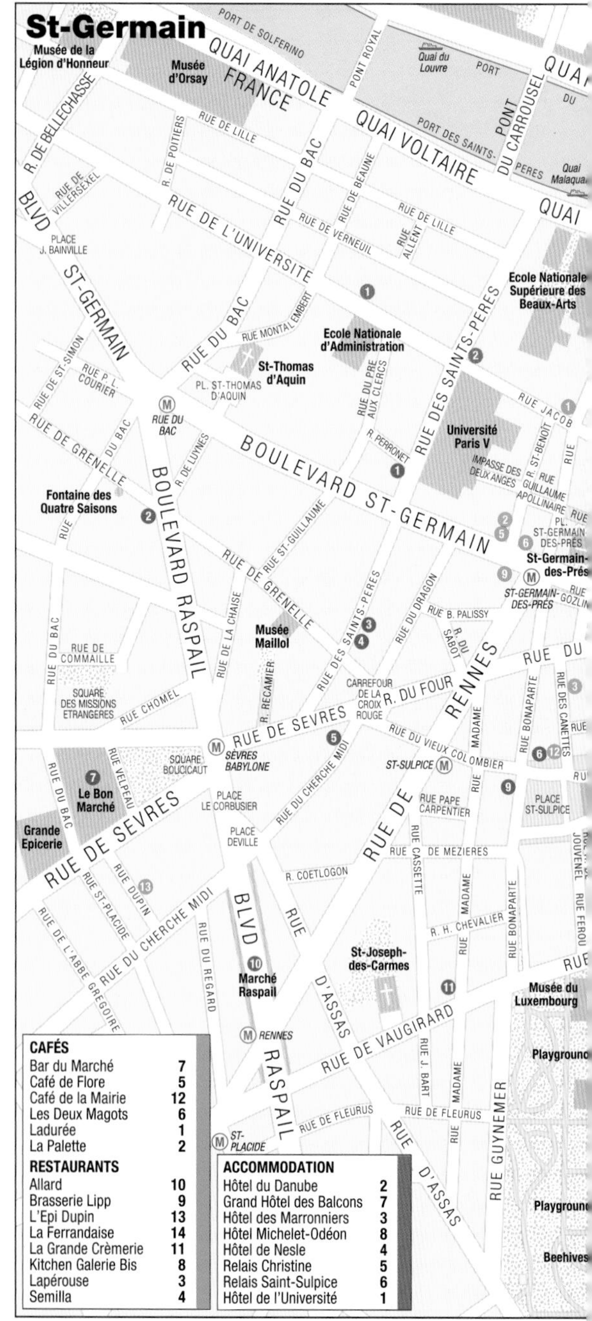
St-Germain
Musée de la Légion d'Honneur
Musée d'Orsay
PORT DE SOLFERINO
QUAI ANATOLE FRANCE
PONT ROYAL
Quai du Louvre
PORT
QUAI
DU
PONT DU CARROUSEL
PORT DES SAINTS-PERES
QUAI VOLTAIRE
Quai Malaquai
QUAI
R. DE BELLECHASSE
R. DE POITIERS
RUE DE LILLE
RUE DU BAC
RUE DE BEAUNE
RUE DE VILLERSEXEL
RUE DE L'UNIVERSITE
RUE DE VERNEUIL
RUE DE LILLE
RUE ALLENT
BLVD ST-GERMAIN
PLACE J. BAINVILLE
Ecole Nationale Supérieure des Beaux-Arts
RUE MONTALEMBERT
Ecole Nationale d'Administration
RUE DES SAINTS-PERES
RUE DU BAC
St-Thomas d'Aquin
PL. ST-THOMAS D'AQUIN
RUE DU PRE AUX CLERCS
RUE DE ST-SIMON
RUE P. L. COURIER
RUE DU BAC
RUE JACOB
Université Paris V
R. PERRONET
RUE DE GRENELLE
R. DE LUYNES
BOULEVARD ST-GERMAIN
IMPASSE DES DEUX ANGES
R. ST-BENOIT
RUE GUILLAUME APOLLINAIRE
RUE
Fontaine des Quatre Saisons
BOULEVARD RASPAIL
PL. ST-GERMAIN DES-PRÉS
St-Germain-des-Prés
RUE ST-GUILLAUME
RUE DE GRENELLE
RUE DES SAINTS-PERES
RUE DU DRAGON
ST-GERMAIN-DES-PRÉS
RUE GOZLIN
RUE B. PALISSY
R. DU SABOT
RUE DU BAC
RUE DE COMMAILLE
RUE DE LA CHAISE
Musée Maillol
RUE DE RENNES
RUE DU
SQUARE DES MISSIONS ETRANGERES
RUE CHOMEL
R. RECAMIER
CARREFOUR DE LA CROIX ROUGE
R. DU FOUR
RUE BONAPARTE
RUE DES CANETTES
RUE DE SEVRES
SÈVRES BABYLONE
RUE DU CHERCHE MIDI
RUE DU VIEUX COLOMBIER
ST-SULPICE
RUE MADAME
RUE VELPEAU
SQUARE BOUCICAUT
Le Bon Marché
RUE DU BAC
PLACE LE CORBUSIER
RUE PAPE CARPENTIER
PLACE ST-SULPICE
Grande Epicerie
RUE DE SEVRES
PLACE DEVILLE
RUE CASSETTE
RUE DE MEZIERES
RUE FEROU
R. COETLOGON
RUE ST-PLACIDE
RUE DUPIN
RUE MADAME
RUE DU CHERCHE MIDI
BLVD RASPAIL
RUE D'ASSAS
R. H. CHEVALIER
RUE BONAPARTE
RUE DE L'ABBE GREGOIRE
RUE DU REGARD
St-Joseph-des-Carmes
Marché Raspail
Musée du Luxembourg
RENNES
RUE DE VAUGIRARD
RUE J. BART
Playground
RUE GUYNEMER
RUE DE FLEURUS
RUE DE FLEURUS
ST-PLACIDE
Playground
Beehives
CAFÉS
Bar du Marché 7
Café de Flore 5
Café de la Mairie 12
Les Deux Magots 6
Ladurée 1
La Palette 2
RESTAURANTS
Allard 10
Brasserie Lipp 9
L'Epi Dupin 13
La Ferrandaise 14
La Grande Crèmerie 11
Kitchen Galerie Bis 8
Lapérouse 3
Semilla 4
ACCOMMODATION
Hôtel du Danube 2
Grand Hôtel des Balcons 7
Hôtel des Marronniers 3
Hôtel Michelet-Odéon 8
Hôtel de Nesle 4
Relais Christine 5
Relais Saint-Sulpice 6
Hôtel de l'Université 1

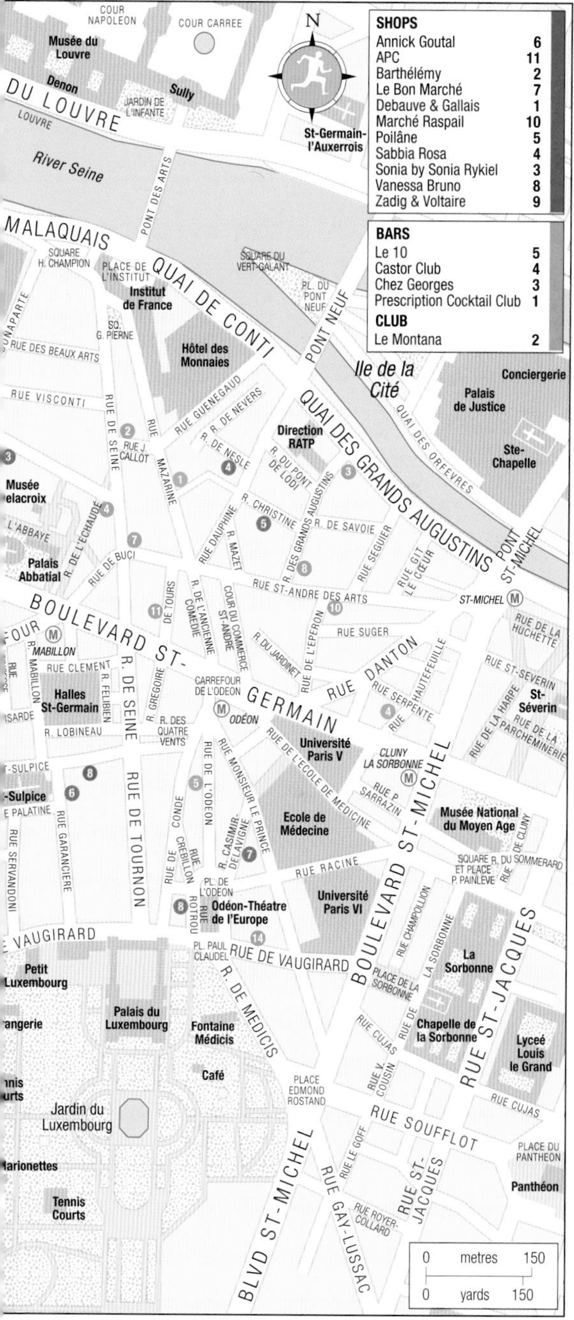
SHOPS
Annick Goutal 6
APC 11
Barthélémy 2
Le Bon Marché 7
Debauve & Gallais 1
Marché Raspail 10
Poilâne 5
Sabbia Rosa 4
Sonia by Sonia Rykiel 3
Vanessa Bruno 8
Zadig & Voltaire 9
BARS
Le 10 5
Castor Club 4
Chez Georges 3
Prescription Cocktail Club 1
CLUB
Le Montana 2
Musée du Louvre
Cour Napoleon
Cour Carree
Denon
Sully
Jardin de l'Infante
St-Germain-l'Auxerrois
River Seine
Quai de Conti
Quai des Grands Augustins
Quai des Orfevres
Pont Neuf
Pont des Arts
Pont St-Michel
Ile de la Cité
Institut de France
Hôtel des Monnaies
Conciergerie
Palais de Justice
Ste-Chapelle
Direction RATP
Musée Delacroix
Palais Abbatial
Boulevard St-Germain
Halles St-Germain
Carrefour de l'Odeon
Odéon
Université Paris V
Cluny La Sorbonne
St-Michel
St-Séverin
Ecole de Médecine
Musée National du Moyen Age
Université Paris VI
Odéon-Théatre de l'Europe
Rue de Vaugirard
Boulevard St-Michel
La Sorbonne
Chapelle de la Sorbonne
Lycée Louis le Grand
Rue St-Jacques
Petit Luxembourg
Palais du Luxembourg
Fontaine Médicis
Café
Jardin du Luxembourg
Tennis Courts
Place Edmond Rostand
Rue Soufflot
Place du Pantheon
Panthéon
Blvd St-Michel
Rue Gay-Lussac
0 metres 150
0 yards 150

INSIDE ST-SULPICE

BERGES DE SEINE

Ⓜ Assemblée Nationale Ⓦ lesberges.paris.fr. MAP PP.116–117, POCKET MAP C7, D7 & E7

The stretch of river between the Musée du Quai Branly and Musée d'Orsay has been turned into a pedestrianized promenade, where you can listen to occasional concerts, play a game of chess over a cup of coffee, or simply relax in a deckchair and enjoy some of the finest views in the city.

MUSEE DELACROIX

6 rue de Furstenberg Ⓜ Mabillon/St-Germain-des-Prés. ⓣ 01 44 41 86 50, Ⓦ musee-delacroix.fr. Daily except Tues 9.30am–5pm. €7. MAP PP.116–117, POCKET MAP B17

The Musée Delacroix is tucked away halfway down rue de Furstenberg, opposite a tiny square and backing onto a secret garden. Although the artist's major work is exhibited permanently at the Louvre (see p.40) and the Musée d'Orsay (see p.115), this museum, housed in the studio where the artist lived and worked from 1857 until his death in 1863, displays a refreshingly intimate collection, including a scattering of personal belongings and minor exhibitions of his work.

PLACE ST-GERMAIN-DES-PRÉS

Ⓜ St-Germain-des-Prés. MAP PP.116–117, POCKET MAP B17

Place St-Germain-des-Prés is the hub of the *quartier*, with the *Deux Magots* café (see p.121) on the corner of the square, *Flore* (see p.121) adjacent and *Lipp* (see p.122) across the boulevard St-Germain. All are renowned for the number of philosophico-politico-literary backsides that have shone – and continue to shine – their seats, along with plenty of celebrity-hunters. Picasso's bust of a woman, dedicated to the poet Apollinaire, recalls the district's creative heyday.

ST-GERMAIN-DES-PRÉS

Place St-Germain-des-Prés Ⓜ St-Germain-des-Prés. Daily 7.30am–7.30pm. MAP PP.116–117, POCKET MAP B17

The ancient tower overlooking place St-Germain-des-Prés belongs to the church of St-Germain, all that remains of an enormous Benedictine monastery. Inside, the transformation from Romanesque to early Gothic is just about visible under the heavy green and gold nineteenth-century paintwork. The last chapel on the south side contains the tomb of the philosopher René Descartes.

ST-SULPICE

Place St-Sulpice Ⓜ St-Sulpice. Daily 7am–7.30pm. MAP PP.116–117, POCKET MAP B18

The enormous, early eighteenth-century church of St-Sulpice is an austerely Classical building with Doric and Ionic colonnades and Corinthian pilasters in the towers. There are three Delacroix murals in the first chapel on the right, but most visitors come to see the gnomon, a kind of solar clock whose origins and purpose were so compellingly garbled in *The Da Vinci Code*.

JARDIN DU LUXEMBOURG

Ⓜ Odéon/RER Luxembourg. Daily dawn to dusk. MAP PP.116–117, POCKET MAP B18/19–C18/19

Fronting onto rue de Vaugirard, the Jardin du Luxembourg is the chief green space of the Left Bank, its atmosphere a beguiling mixture of the formal and the relaxed. At the centre, the round pond and immaculate floral parterres are overlooked by the haughty Palais du Luxembourg, seat of the French Senate. Students sprawl on the garden's famous metal chairs, children sail toy yachts, watch the puppets at the *guignol*, or run about in the playgrounds, and old men play boules or chess. The southwest corner is dotted with the works of famous sculptors.

MUSEE DU LUXEMBOURG

19 rue de Vaugirard Ⓜ Odéon/RER Luxembourg. Ⓣ 01 42 34 25 95, Ⓦ museeduluxembourg.fr. Hours and prices vary. MAP PP.116–117, POCKET MAP B18

The Musée du Luxembourg, at the top end of rue de Vaugirard, hosts temporary art exhibitions that rank among the most ambitious in Paris – recent shows have included Henri Fantin-Latour and masterpieces from Budapest.

MUSEE MAILLOL

61 rue de Grenelle Ⓜ Rue du Bac. Ⓣ 01 42 22 59 58, Ⓦ museemaillol.com. Check online for opening times and admission. MAP PP.116–117, POCKET MAP A17

Temporarily closed, but due to reopen towards the end of 2016, the Musée Maillol is stuffed with Aristide Maillol's sculpted female nudes, of which the curvaceous *Mediterranean* is his most famous. Other rooms house work by Matisse, Bonnard, Camille Bombois, and the odd minor work by Picasso, Degas, Cézanne, Gauguin and Suzanne Valadon.

OUTDOOR GAMES IN THE JARDIN DU LUXEMBOURG

Shops

ANNICK GOUTAL

12 place St-Sulpice Ⓜ St-Sulpice. Ⓦ annickgoutal.com. Mon–Sat 10am–7pm. MAP PP.116–117, POCKET MAP B17

This family-run business, started by Goutal in the 1980s, is still going strong, producing exquisite perfumes, all made from natural essences and presented in old-fashioned ribbed-glass bottles.

APC

38 rue Madame Ⓜ St-Sulpice. Ⓦ apc.fr. Mon–Sat 11am–7.30pm. MAP PP.116–117, POCKET MAP B18

This chain is perfect for young, urban basics. Simple cuts and fabrics create a minimal, Parisian look. Prices start at under €100.

BARTHELEMY

51 rue de Grenelle Ⓜ Rue du Bac. Tues–Fri 8.30am–1pm & 4–7.15pm, Sat 8.30am–1.30pm & 3–7pm; closed Aug. MAP PP.116–117, POCKET MAP E8

This aromatic nook sells carefully ripened seasonal cheeses to the rich and powerful, with attendants on hand to offer expert advice.

SONIA BY SONIA RYKIEL

LE BON MARCHE

38 rue de Sèvres Ⓜ Sèvres-Babylone. Mon–Wed & Sat 10am–8pm, Thurs & Fri 10am–9pm. MAP PP.116–117, POCKET MAP E9

The world's oldest department store, founded in 1852, is a beautiful building and a classy place to shop – despite its name, this is a luxury emporium – with a legendary food hall.

DEBAUVE & GALLAIS

30 rue des Saints-Pères Ⓜ St-Germain-des-Prés/Sèvres-Babylone. Ⓦ debauve-et-gallais.fr. Mon–Sat 9am–7pm. MAP PP.116–117, POCKET MAP A16

A beautiful, ancient shop specializing in expensive, ambrosial chocolates.

MARCHE RASPAIL

Bd Raspail, between rue du Cherche-Midi & rue de Rennes Ⓜ Rennes. Tues, Fri & Sun 7am–2.30pm. MAP PP.116–117, POCKET MAP A18

The Sunday organic market which takes over the broad central reservation of the boulevard is one of the classic experiences of bourgeois Paris. Come to people-watch as well as to browse, taste and shop.

POILANE

8 rue du Cherche-Midi Ⓜ Sèvres-Babylone. Ⓦ poilane.com. Mon–Sat 7.15am–8.15pm. MAP PP.116–117, POCKET MAP A17

This delicious-smelling bakery is the ultimate source of traditional sourdough *pain Poilâne*, and great for other baked treats.

SABBIA ROSA

71–73 rue des Saints-Pères Ⓜ St-Germain-des-Prés. Mon–Sat 10am–7pm. MAP PP.116–117, POCKET MAP A17

Supermodels' knickers – they all shop here – at supermodel prices in this famed store. Exquisite lingerie in buttery silk and Calais lace.

SONIA BY SONIA RYKIEL

6 rue de Grenelle Ⓜ St-Sulpice. Mon–Sat 10.30am–7pm. MAP PP.116–117, POCKET MAP A17

Sonia Rykiel has been an area institution since opening a store on bd St-Germain in 1968; this is a younger, less expensive offshoot.

VANESSA BRUNO

25 rue St-Sulpice Ⓜ Odéon. Mon–Sat 10.30am–7.30pm. MAP PP.116–117, POCKET MAP B17

Prices start in the hundreds for these effortlessly beautiful women's fashions with a hint of hippy chic.

ZADIG & VOLTAIRE

1 & 3 rue du Vieux Colombier Ⓜ St-Sulpice. Mon–Sat 10.30am–7.30pm. MAP PP.116–117, POCKET MAP B18

The clothes at this pricey Parisian chain have a wayward flair. There are two shops next door to each other selling clothes for women, men and children, the other only womenswear.

Cafés

BAR DU MARCHE

75 rue de Seine Ⓜ Mabillon. Daily 8am–1.45am. MAP PP.116–117, POCKET MAP B17

Buzzing café in the heart of the Buci market bustle, with *serveurs* kitted out in flat caps and market-trader dungarees.

CAFE DE FLORE

172 bd St-Germain Ⓜ St-Germain-des-Prés. Ⓦ cafedeflore.fr. Daily 7.30am–1.30am. MAP PP.116–117, POCKET MAP B17

The rival and neighbour of *Les Deux Magots*, with a trendier and more local clientele. Sartre, De Beauvoir, Camus et al used to hang out here – and there's still the odd reading or debate. Come for the famous morning hot chocolate. Prices are high.

CAFE DE FLORE

CAFE DE LA MAIRIE

8 place St-Sulpice Ⓜ St-Sulpice. Mon–Sat 7am–2am, Sun 9am–9pm. MAP PP.116–117, POCKET MAP B17

A pleasant, ever-popular café on the sunny north side of the square, opposite the church.

LES DEUX MAGOTS

170 bd St-Germain Ⓜ St-Germain-des-Prés. Ⓦ lesdeuxmagots.fr. Daily 7.30am–1am. MAP PP.116–117, POCKET MAP B17

This historic Left Bank intellectual hangout has fallen victim to its own fame. Prices are ridiculous, but it's irresistible for people-watching. Come for breakfast (around €25).

LADUREE

21 rue Bonaparte Ⓜ St-Germain-des-Prés. Ⓦ laduree.com. Mon–Fri 8.30am–7.30pm, Sat 8.30am–8.30pm, Sun 10am–7.30pm. MAP PP.116–117, POCKET MAP B16

Elegant outpost of *Ladurée*'s mini-empire, with a conservatory at the back and a decadent Second Empire lounge upstairs. The famous *macarons* are out of this world, but they also do a good, if pricey, brunch.

LA PALETTE

43 rue de Seine Ⓜ Odéon. Mon–Sat 8am–2am. MAP PP.116–117, POCKET MAP B16

This venerable art-student hangout is now frequented more by art dealers, though it's still very relaxed, and the decor of paint-spattered palettes is superb. There's a roomy *terrasse* outside.

Restaurants

BRASSERIE LIPP

ALLARD

41 rue St-André-des-Arts Ⓜ Odéon. Ⓣ 01 43 26 48 23, Ⓦ restaurant-allard.fr. Daily noon–2.30pm & 7–11.30pm; sometimes closed in Aug. MAP PP.116–117, POCKET MAP C17

Proudly unreconstructed restaurant serving meaty, rich standards. If it wasn't for the almost exclusively international clientele, you could be dining in another century. Lunch *menu* €34, dinner around €80.

BRASSERIE LIPP

151 bd St-Germain Ⓜ St-Germain-des-Prés. Ⓣ 01 45 48 53 91, Ⓦ brasserielipp.fr. Daily noon–12.30am. MAP PP.116–117, POCKET MAP B17

One of the most celebrated of the classic Paris brasseries, the haunt of the successful and famous, *Lipp* has a wonderful 1900s wood-and-glass interior. Decent *plats*, including the famous *choucroute* (sauerkraut), start at €23, but exploring the *carte* gets expensive.

L'EPI DUPIN

11 rue Dupin Ⓜ Sèvres-Babylone. Ⓣ 01 42 22 64 56, Ⓦ epidupin.com. Mon 7–11pm, Tues–Fri noon–3pm & 7–11pm. MAP PP.116–117, POCKET MAP E9

This contemporary *bistrot* serves up imaginative seasonal food. There are two sittings – go for the second if you want to take your time. *Menus* at €39 and €52, or €28 at lunch.

LA FERRANDAISE

8 rue de Vaugirard Ⓜ St-Germain-des-Prés. Ⓣ 01 43 26 36 36, Ⓦ laferrandaise.com. Mon 7–10.30pm, Tues–Thurs noon–2.30pm & 7–10.30pm, Fri noon–2.30pm & 7–midnight, Sat 7–midnight. MAP PP.116–117, POCKET MAP C18

Arty photos of cows line the walls, and beef dominates the menu – though you'll also find dishes such as minced cod with ratatouille. Lunch *menu* €16; €37/€55 at dinner.

LA GRANDE CREMERIE

8 rue Grégoire de Tours Ⓜ Odéon. Ⓣ 01 43 26 09 09, Ⓦ lagrandecremerie.fr. Daily 7.30–11pm (apéritif from 6.30pm). MAP PP.116–117, POCKET MAP C17

They keep it simple but impeccable at this contemporary-rustic wine bar, serving the very best produce – white Italian ham with truffles, black pudding with toast – alongside natural and organic wines. The amazing food, friendly staff and warm space make this a godsend on this touristy stretch.

KITCHEN GALERIE BIS

25 rue des Grands-Augustins Ⓜ St-Michel. Ⓣ 01 46 33 00 85, Ⓦ zekitchengalerie.fr. Tues–Sat noon–2.15pm & 7.15–10.30pm. MAP PP.116–117, POCKET MAP C17

This sleek, modern restaurant offers innovative cooking, fusing Mediterranean cuisine with Asian flavours; a main course might be grilled mackerel with an apricot and cumin dressing. Go for the *menu découverte* and you'll be getting the chef's choices; at €66 it's a steal, particularly compared to prices in the area.

LAPEROUSE

51 quai des Grands Augustins Ⓜ St-Michel. ☎ 01 56 79 24 31, Ⓦ laperouse.com. Mon–Sat 11.30am–2.30pm & 7.30–10.30pm, Sat 7–11.30pm. MAP PP.116–117, POCKET MAP C16

The food is unexceptionally traditional, the prices inflated and the service patchy, but come for the experience: the eighteenth-century building on the Seine, the red plush seats, gilt panelling and tarnished mirrors. Above all, come for the private dining rooms (lunch from €45, dinner around €120).

SEMILLA

54 rue de Seine Ⓜ Mabillon. ☎ 01 43 54 34 50. Daily noon–3pm & 7–11pm. MAP PP.116–117, POCKET MAP B17

This stand-out modern *bistrot* serves up fantastically good food – an enticing mixture of fusion cuisine and updated French classics. Great-value lunch *menu* for €24 or expect to pay around €70 per person in the evening. Bookings taken up to 8.30pm or wait at the bar for a table.

Bars

LE 10

10 rue de l'Odéon Ⓜ Odéon. Daily 6pm–2am. MAP PP.116–117, POCKET MAP C18

Classic Art Deco-era posters line the walls of this small, dark, studenty bar. The vaulted cellar bar gets noisy in the small hours.

CASTOR CLUB

14 rue Hautefeuille Ⓜ Odéon. Tues–Sat 7pm–4am. MAP PP.116–117, POCKET MAP C17

An excellent and relatively laidback cocktail bar with speakeasy decor, serving good craft cocktails for around €13 (try the Chirac 95, made with Calvados) against a cool playlist of American country, rockabilly, soul and jazz.

CHEZ GEORGES

11 rue des Canettes Ⓜ Mabillon. Tues–Sat 2pm–2am; closed Aug. MAP PP.116–117, POCKET MAP B17

This delapidated wine bar, with its venerable zinc counter, is one of the few authentic addresses in an area ever-more dominated by theme pubs. The young, studenty crowd gets good-naturedly rowdy later on in the cellar bar.

PRESCRIPTION COCKTAIL CLUB

23 rue Mazarine Ⓜ Odéon. ☎ 09 50 35 72 87. Mon–Thurs & Sun 8pm–2am, Fri & Sat 8pm–4am. MAP PP.116–117, POCKET MAP C17

This trendy, exclusive cocktail bar hides a glamorously plush interior behind its artfully blank facade. Chic and restrained earlier in the evening, turning into a madhouse later on.

Club

LE MONTANA

28 rue Saint-Benoit Ⓜ St-Germain-des-Prés. Daily 11pm–5am. MAP PP.116–117, POCKET MAP B17

This small, exclusive and distinctly beautiful mini-club is achingly jet-set, and so celebrity-packed it doesn't need a publicly listed phone number. You'll have to look the part to get in, and feel the part to enjoy it. No entry fee, but expensive drinks.

LAPEROUSE

Montparnasse and southern Paris

Montparnasse divides the well-heeled opinion-formers of St-Germain and the 7e from the relatively anonymous populations to the south. Long a kind of borderland of theatres, cinemas and cafés, Montparnasse still trades on its association with the wild characters of the interwar years. The artistic and literary glitterati have mostly ended up in Montparnasse cemetery, but cafés favoured by the likes of Picasso are still going strong on boulevard du Montparnasse, and there are plentiful artistic attractions: from the intimate museums dedicated to sculptors Zadkine and Bourdelle, to the contemporary exhibits at the Fondation Cartier and Fondation Cartier-Bresson. Further south, the riverside offers some intriguing attractions: to the east, the cutting-edge Paris Rive Gauche, and to the west, the futuristic Parc André-Citroën.

TOUR MONTPARNASSE

33 av du Maine Ⓜ Montparnasse-Bienvenüe. ☎ 01 45 38 52 56, Ⓦ tourmontparnasse56.com. April–Sept daily 9.30am–11.30pm; Oct–March Sun–Thurs 9.30am–10.30pm, Fri & Sat 9.30am–11pm. €15. MAP P.126, POCKET MAP E11

At the station end of boulevard du Montparnasse, the 200-metre-high Tour Montparnasse skyscraper is one of the city's principal and most despised landmarks. That said, the 360° view from the top is better than the one from the Eiffel Tower, in that it includes the Eiffel Tower – and excludes the Tour Montparnasse. It also costs less to ascend, and queues are far shorter. The 56th-storey café-gallery offers a tremendous view westwards; sunset is the best time to visit.

THE TOUR MONTPARNASSE

JARDIN ATLANTIQUE

Access by lifts on rue Cdt. R. Mouchotte and bd Vaugirard, or by the stairs alongside platform #1 in Montparnasse station Ⓜ Montparnasse-Bienvenüe. Daily dawn–dusk. MAP P.126, POCKET MAP E11

Montparnasse station was once the great arrival and departure point for travellers heading across the Atlantic, a connection commemorated in the unexpected Jardin Atlantique, suspended above the

FOUNTAIN AT THE JARDIN ATLANTIQUE

train tracks behind the station. Hemmed in by cliff-like high-rise apartment blocks, the park is a fine example of Parisian flair, with fields of Atlantic-coast grasses, wave-like undulations in the lawns (to cover the irregularly placed concrete struts underneath) – and well-hidden ventilation holes that reveal sudden glimpses of TGV roofs and rail sleepers below.

MUSEE BOURDELLE

16–18 rue A. Bourdelle Ⓜ Montparnasse-Bienvenüe/Falguière. ☎ 01 49 54 73 73, Ⓦ bourdelle.paris.fr. Tues–Sun 10am–6pm. Free, €4–9 during temporary exhibitions. MAP P.126, POCKET MAP E10

One block northwest of the tower, the Musée Bourdelle has been built around the atmospheric atelier of the early twentieth-century sculptor. Rodin's pupil and Giacometti's teacher, Antoine Bourdelle created bronze and stone works that move from a naturalistic style – as in the series of Beethoven busts – towards a more geometric Modernism, seen in his better-known, monumental sculptures, some of which sit in the garden.

MUSEE ZADKINE

100bis rue d'Assas Ⓜ Vavin/RER Port-Royal. ☎ 01 55 42 77 20, Ⓦ zadkine.paris.fr. Tues–Sun 10am–6pm. Free; €7 during exhibitions. MAP P.126, POCKET MAP F10–11

The cottage-like home and garden studios of Russian-born Cubist sculptor Ossip Zadkine, where he lived from 1928 to 1967, are occupied by the tiny Musée Zadkine. A mixture of elongated figures and blockier works are displayed in the intimate rooms, while Cubist bronzes are scattered about the minuscule garden, sheltering under trees or emerging from clumps of bamboo.

FONDATION CARTIER POUR L'ART CONTEMPORAIN

261 bd Raspail Ⓜ Raspail. ☎ 01 42 18 56 50, Ⓦ fondation.cartier.fr. Tues 11am–10pm, Wed–Sun 11am–8pm. €10.50. MAP P.126, POCKET MAP F11–12

Rue Schoelcher and boulevard Raspail, on the east side of Montparnasse cemetery, have some interesting examples of twentieth-century architecture, from Art Nouveau to the translucent glass-and-steel facade of the Fondation Cartier pour l'Art Contemporain. Designed in 1994 by Jean Nouvel, the venue presents contemporary installations, videos, graffiti and multimedia – often by foreign artists little known in France – in high-quality temporary exhibitions that use the light-filled spaces to maximum advantage.

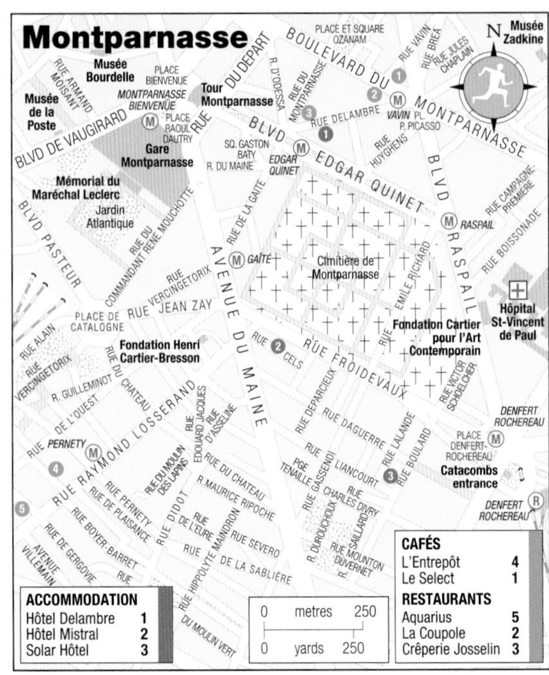

THE CATACOMBS

Place Denfert-Rochereau Ⓜ Denfert-Rochereau. ⓣ 01 43 22 47 63, Ⓦ catacombes.paris.fr. Tues–Sun 10am–8pm. €12. MAP P.126, POCKET MAP F12

For a surreal, somewhat chilling experience, head down into the catacombs below place Denfert-Rochereau, formerly place d'Enfer (Hell Square). Abandoned quarries stacked with millions of bones, cleared from overstocked charnel houses and cemeteries between 1785 and 1871, the catacombs are said to hold the remains of around six million Parisians, more than double the population of the city, not counting the suburbs. Lining the gloomy passageways, long thigh bones are stacked end-on, forming a wall to keep in the smaller bones and shards, which can be seen in dusty heaps behind. These femoral walls are further inset with gaping, hollow-eyed skulls, forming elaborate geometric patterns, while plaques carrying macabre quotations loom out of the gloom. It's a fascinating place, but note that there are a good couple of kilometres to walk, and it can quickly become claustrophobic. Book tickets online in advance to avoid long queues to get in.

FONDATION HENRI CARTIER-BRESSON

2 impasse Lebouis Ⓜ Gaîté. ⓣ 01 56 80 27 00, Ⓦ henricartierbresson.org. Tues, Thurs, Fri & Sun 1–6.30pm, Wed 1–8.30pm, Sat 11am–6.45pm; closed Aug. €7. MAP P.126, POCKET MAP E12

Old-fashioned networks of streets still exist in the Pernety and Plaisance *quartiers*, south of Montparnasse cemetery, where the slender steel-and-glass Fondation Henri

Cartier-Bresson is hidden away. The foundation houses the archive of the great Parisian photojournalist, and showcases the work of his contemporaries and of younger photographers.

MONTPARNASSE CEMETERY

Bd Edgar Quinet Ⓜ Raspail/Gaîté/Edgar Quinet. Mid-March to Nov 5 Mon–Fri 8am–6pm, Sat 8.30am–6pm, Sun 9am–6pm; Nov 6 to mid-March closes 5.30pm. Free. MAP P.126, POCKET MAP E11–F12

Second in size and celebrity to Père Lachaise, Montparnasse cemetery is an intriguing city of the dead, its ranks of miniature temples paying homage to illustrious names from Baudelaire to Beckett; pick up a free map at the entrance gate. The unembellished joint grave of Jean-Paul Sartre and Simone de Beauvoir lies right of the main entrance, while down avenue de l'Ouest, which follows the western wall, you'll find the tombs of Baudelaire, the painter Soutine, Dadaist Tristan Tzara and Ossip Zadkine. Across rue Emile-Richard, in the eastern section, lie car-maker André Citroën, Guy de Maupassant, César Franck, and the celebrated victim of French anti-Semitism at the end of the nineteenth century, Captain Dreyfus.

PARC ANDRE-CITROEN

Quai André-Citroën Ⓜ Balard. MAP PP.130–131

The riverfront south of the Eiffel Tower is a dull swathe, bristling with office blocks and miniature skyscrapers; it's brightened up at the southwestern extreme of the city limits by the Parc André-Citroën, the site of the old Citroën motor works. This is not a park for traditionalists: there is a central grassy area, but elsewhere concrete terraces and walled gardens with abstract themes define the Modernist space. Its best features are the huge glasshouses full of exotic-smelling shrubs, the capricious set of automated fountains – on hot days you'll see excitable teens dashing to and fro through its sudden spurts – and the tethered balloon (fine days only: 9am to roughly one hour before dusk; €12), which rises and sinks regularly on calm days (call ⓣ 01 44 26 20 00 to check conditions).

MONTPARNASSE CEMETERY FROM ABOVE

ALLEE DES CYGNES

ALLEE DES CYGNES

Ⓜ Bir-Hakeim. MAP PP.130–131, POCKET MAP A8–9

One of Paris's most charming walks leads down from the middle of the Pont de Bir-Hakeim along the tree-lined Allée des Cygnes, a narrow, mid-stream island built up on raised concrete embankments. Once you've taken in the views of the Eiffel Tower and both banks of the river, admired the passing coal barges and visited the curious small-scale version of the Statue of Liberty at the southern tip of the island, you might just share Samuel Beckett's opinion of the place – it was one of his favourite spots in Paris.

BUTTE-AUX-CAILLES

Ⓜ Corvisart/Place d'Italie. MAP P.129, POCKET MAP H12

Between boulevard Auguste-Blanqui and rue Bobillot, the lively hilltop quarter of Butte-aux-Cailles, with its little streets and cul-de-sacs of prewar houses and studios, is typical of pre-1960s Paris. The rue de la Butte-aux-Cailles itself is the animated heart of the area, lined with unpretentious, youthful and vaguely lefty bars and restaurants, most of which stay open late.

PARIS RIVE GAUCHE

Ⓜ Quai de la Gare/Bibliothèque François Mitterrand. MAP PP.130–131, POCKET MAP K11–L12

The easternmost edge of the 13ᵉ arrondissement, between the river and the Austerlitz train tracks, has been transformed as part of the Paris Rive Gauche development. The **Passerelle Simone de Beauvoir**, a footbridge crossing the Seine in a double-ribbon structure, sets the tone, while tethered barges have made the area a nightlife attraction. The floating swimming pool, **Piscine Josephine Baker**, is a wonderful place to do a few laps, while south of rue Tolbiac, **Les Frigos** warehouse (Ⓦ les-frigos.com), once used for cold-storage of produce destined for Les Halles, is now an anarchic studio space, with a bar-restaurant and occasional exhibitions.

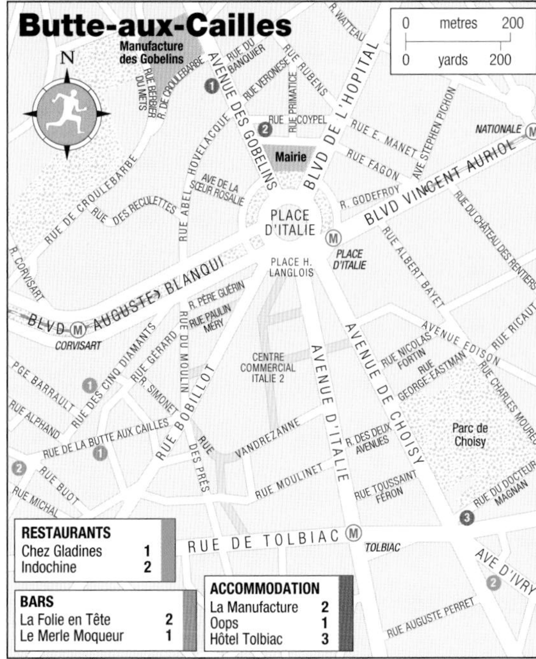

CITE DE LA MODE ET DU DESIGN

34 quai d'Austerlitz Ⓜ Austerlitz/Quai de la Gare. Ⓣ 01 76 77 25 30, Ⓦ citemodedesign.fr. MAP PP.130–131, POCKET MAP K11

The most recent Paris Rive Gauche development is the Docks en Seine complex, which houses the Cité de la Mode et du Design, a fashion institute, whose intrusive design of twisting, lime-green tubes is supposed to recall the sinuous shape of the river. It hosts occasional exhibitions, has a museum (see below), a number of shops and a restaurant, as well as two very popular clubs, rooftop *Nüba* and riverside *Wanderlust* (see p.133).

ART LUDIQUE-LE MUSEE

34 quai d'Austerlitz Ⓜ Austerlitz/Quai de la Gare. Ⓣ 01 45 70 09 49, Ⓦ artludique.com. Tues, Wed & Fri 11am–7pm, Thurs 11am–10pm, Sat & Sun 10am–8pm. €16.50. MAP PP.130–131, POCKET MAP K11

Art Ludique-Le Musée is entirely dedicated to the art of animation, manga, comics and video games. It puts on hugely popular exhibitions, which have recently focused on Aardman Animations and the Studio Ghibli.

CHINATOWN

Ⓜ Tolbiac. MAP PP.130–131

Paris's best Southeast Asian cuisine is to be found in Chinatown, home to several East Asian communities. Avenues de Choisy and d'Ivry are full of Vietnamese, Chinese, Thai, Cambodian and Laotian restaurants and food shops, as is **Les Olympiades**, a tattily futuristic pedestrian area seemingly suspended between tower blocks and accessed by escalators from rue Nationale, rue de Tolbiac and avenue d'Ivry.

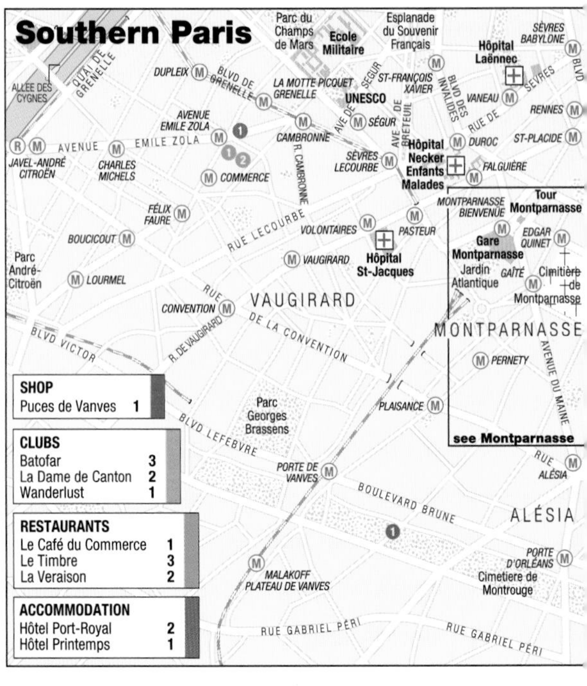

BIBLIOTHEQUE NATIONALE DE FRANCE

BIBLIOTHEQUE NATIONALE DE FRANCE

Quai de la Gare Ⓜ Quai de la Gare/ Bibliothèque François Mitterrand. Ⓣ 01 53 79 40 43, Ⓦ bnf.fr. Tues–Sat 10am–8pm, Sun 1–7pm. €3.50 for a reading room pass – over-16s only (bring ID). MAP PP.130–131, POCKET MAP L12

Architect Dominique Perrault's Bibliothèque Nationale de France dominates this modernized section of the riverbank with four enormous L-shaped towers – intended to look like open books – framing a sunken pine copse. Glass walls alongside the trees allow dappled light to filter through to the underground library spaces. It's worth wandering around inside to experience the structure at first hand, and to see the pair of wonderful globes that belonged to Louis XIV. There are regular, high-quality exhibitions (€9).

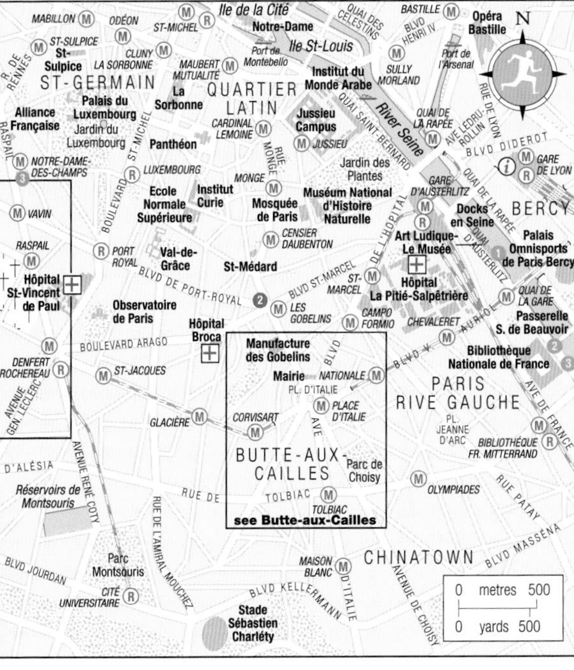

Shopping

PUCES DE VANVES

Av Georges-Lafenestre/av Marc-Sangnier Ⓜ Porte-de-Vanves. Marc-Sangnier Sat & Sun 7am–1pm, Georges-Lafenestre till 3pm. MAP PP.130–131

The city's best flea market for original finds, bric-a-brac and Parisian knick-knacks. It starts at daybreak and spreads along the pavements of avenues Marc-Sangnier and Georges-Lafenestre, petering out in place de la Porte-de-Vanves.

Cafés

L'ENTREPOT

7–9 rue Francis-de-Pressensé Ⓜ Pernety. Ⓦ lentrepot.fr. Mon–Sat noon–2.30pm & 7–11pm, Sun 11.45am–2.45pm & 7–11pm. MAP P.126, POCKET MAP E12

This is a lively, innovative arts cinema with a spacious, relaxed café and outdoor seating in the courtyard. Great Sunday brunch for €30), *plats du jour* for around €17–25, and frequent evening gigs.

LE SELECT

99 bd du Montparnasse Ⓜ Vavin. Daily 7pm–2am, Fri & Sat till 3am. MAP P.126, POCKET MAP F11

If you want to visit one of the great Montparnasse cafés, as frequented by Picasso, Matisse, Henry Miller and F. Scott Fitzgerald, make it this one. It's the least spoilt and most traditional of them all, and has the lowest prices – it's also conveniently located on the sunny side of the street. The food, however, can be disappointing.

Restaurants

AQUARIUS

40 rue de Gergovie Ⓜ Pernety/Plaisance. ☎ 01 45 41 36 88. Mon–Sat noon–2.30pm & 7–11pm. MAP P.126, POCKET MAP D12

The food is wholesome, if unspectacular, at this homely, welcoming and popular vegetarian restaurant. Nut roast, chilli and lasagne cost around €14.

LE CAFE DU COMMERCE

51 rue du Commerce Ⓜ Emile-Zola. ☎ 01 45 75 03 27, Ⓦ lecafeducommerce.com. Daily noon–3pm & 7pm–midnight. MAP PP.130–131, POCKET MAP B10

This huge, former workers' brasserie is a buzzing, dramatic place to eat, set on three lofty levels around a patio. Honest, high-quality meat is the speciality; expect to pay €16.50–22 for a *plat*. The lunch *menu* is a bargain at €16.

CHEZ GLADINES

30 rue des Cinq-Diamants Ⓜ Corvisart. ☎ 01 45 80 70 10, Ⓦ gladines.com. Daily noon–3pm & 7–11.45pm. MAP P.129, POCKET MAP H12

Cosy, welcoming and packed, this rickety corner *bistrot* serves hearty Basque and southwestern dishes – try mashed or fried potato with *magret de canard*. Around €20 for a (very) full meal. No credit cards.

LA COUPOLE

LA COUPOLE

102 bd du Montparnasse Ⓜ Vavin. ☎ 01 43 20 14 20, Ⓦ lacoupole-paris.com. Mon–Wed & Sun 8.30am–midnight, Thurs–Sat 8.30–1am. MAP P.126, POCKET MAP F11

The largest and loveliest of the old Montparnasse brasseries. Now part of the *Flo* chain, it remains a genuine institution, its Art Deco interior buzzing with atmosphere. Tasty food choices range from oysters to Welsh rarebit, with plenty of classics in between; *menus* at €31 and €39.

CREPERIE JOSSELIN

67 rue du Montparnasse Ⓜ Edgar Quinet/ Montparnasse. ☎ 01 43 20 93 50. Tues–Fri noon–3pm & 6–11pm, Sat noon–midnight, Sun noon–11pm; closed Aug. MAP P.126, POCKET MAP F11

Montparnasse is traditionally the Breton quarter of Paris (the station is on the direct line to northern France) and this crêperie couldn't be any more traditionally Breton, with its rustic decor and authentic buttery crêpes (€5–10), washed down with jugs of cider.

INDOCHINE

86 av de Choisy Ⓜ Tolbiac. ☎ 01 44 24 28 08. Mon, Tues & Thurs–Sun noon–3.30pm & 7–10.30pm. MAP P.129, POCKET MAP K12

This is a better-than-average Vietnamese option in the heart of Paris's Chinatown, with tasty *banh xeo* pancakes, zingy fresh *pho* and *bun bo hue* soups, plus vermicelli, stir fries and grilled specialities – you'll eat well for less than €20.

LE TIMBRE

3 rue Ste-Beuve Ⓜ Vavin/Notre-Dame-des-Champs. ☎ 01 45 49 10 40, Ⓦ restaurantletimbre.com. Tues–Sat noon–2pm & 7.30–10.30pm. MAP PP.130–131, POCKET MAP A19

"The Postage Stamp" deserves its name: operating from one minuscule corner of a tiny dining room, chef Charles Danet produces delicious modern and light French food on no-choice *prix-fixe menus*. You might have kale soup with egg followed by lamb sweetbread with white asparagus, rounded off with a heavenly chocolate mousse. Menus €26 at lunch, €34–49 at dinner.

LA VERAISON

64 rue de la Croix Nivert Ⓜ Commerce. Ⓣ 01 45 32 39 39, Ⓦ laveraison.com. Tues–Sat 7–10pm. MAP PP.130–131, POCKET MAP B10

The open kitchen at this terrific, contemporary neighbourhood *bistrot* turns out excellent modern French food – the likes of foie gras ravioli, beetroot gazpacho and duckling with sticky rice fritters – in a laidback space always brimming with happy locals.

Bars

LA FOLIE EN TETE

33 rue Butte-aux-Cailles Ⓜ Place-d'Italie/Corvisart. Ⓦ lafolieentete.wix.com/lesite. Mon–Sat 5pm–2am; happy hour 6–8pm. MAP P.129, POCKET MAP H12

The classic Butte-aux-Cailles bar: friendly and alternative, serving drinks and snacks in the day and playing a wide-ranging soundtrack, from world music to *chanson*, at night.

LE MERLE MOQUEUR

11 rue Butte-aux-Cailles Ⓜ Place-d'Italie/Corvisart. Daily 5pm–2am. MAP P.129, POCKET MAP H12

This narrow, distressed-chic bar – which saw the Parisian debut of Manu Chao – serves up flavoured rums and 1980s French rock to a young, noisy crowd.

LA FOLIE EN TETE

Clubs

BATOFAR

Quai François Mauriac Ⓜ Quai-de-la-Gare. Ⓣ 01 53 60 17 30, Ⓦ batofar.org. Opening times vary. MAP PP.130–131, POCKET MAP L12

Moored in front of the Bibliothèque Nationale, this lighthouse boat is a quirky space for electro, hip-hop and experimental funk. Entry €8–15.

LA DAME DE CANTON

Quai François Mauriac Ⓜ Quai-de-la-Gare. Ⓣ 01 53 61 08 49, Ⓦ damedecanton.com. Tues–Thurs 7pm–midnight, Fri & Sat 7pm–5am. MAP PP.130–131, POCKET MAP L12

Another kooky floating venue, *Batofar*'s neighbour is a beautiful Chinese junk that hosts relaxed but upbeat world music, *chanson* and DJ nights, along with edgy music hall and kids' shows.

WANDERLUST

36 Quai d'Austerlitz Ⓜ Gare d'Austerlitz. Ⓦ wanderlustparis.com. Opening times vary. MAP PP.130–131, POCKET MAP L11

This cool waterside club really comes into its own in summer when you can sip your cocktail on the vast rooftop terrace, looking out over the Seine, while a DJ plays an electro set.

Montmartre and northern Paris

One of Paris's most romantic quarters, Montmartre is famed for its association with artists like Renoir, Degas, Picasso and Toulouse-Lautrec. It long existed as a hilltop village outside the city walls, and today the steep streets around the Butte Montmartre, Paris's highest point, preserve an attractively village-like atmosphere – although the crown of the hill, around place du Tertre, is overrun with tourists. The Butte is topped by the church of Sacré-Coeur and its landmark bulbous white domes. At the foot of the Butte is Pigalle, once best known for its sleazy strip clubs but now rapidly gentrifying and full of trendy bars and shops. Much of the 9e arrondissement is genteel, with elegant townhouses. Rather more rough-edged is the neighbouring 10e, though this too is changing, as young, hip Parisians move in, attracted by the low rents. On the northern edge of the city, the mammoth St-Ouen market hawks everything from antiques to hand-me-downs.

METRO AT PLACE DES ABBESSES

BUTTE MONTMARTRE

Ⓜ Anvers/Abbesses. MAP PP.136–137, POCKET MAP G3–H3

Despite being one of the city's chief tourist attractions, the slopes of the Butte Montmartre manage to retain the quiet, almost secretive, air of their rural origins, charming streets offering lovely views back over the city. The quickest way up is by the funicular, which is part of the city's métro system, but it's more fun to walk up through the winding streets from Abbesses métro.

PLACE DES ABBESSES

Ⓜ Anvers/Abbesses. MAP PP.136–137, POCKET MAP G3

Shady place des Abbesses,

MUSEE DE L'EROTISME

featuring one of Paris's few complete surviving Guimard Art Nouveau métro entrances, is the hub of a lively neighbourhood. The streets immediately around the square are relatively chichi for Montmartre, filled with buzzing wine bars, laidback restaurants and little boutiques – good to explore if you're after one-off outfits and accessories, and great to hang out in of an evening. From here you can head up rue de la Vieuville, from where the stairs in rue Drevet lead to the minuscule place du Calvaire, which has a lovely view back over the city.

PLACE EMILE-GOUDEAU

Ⓜ Abbesses/Anvers. MAP PP.136–137, POCKET MAP G3

Halfway up steep, curving rue Ravignan is tiny place Emile-Goudeau, where Picasso, Braque and Juan Gris initiated the Cubist movement in an old piano factory known as the Bateau-Lavoir. The current building, a faithful reconstruction, is still occupied by studios. With its bench and little iron fountain, the *place* is a lovely spot to draw breath on your way up the Butte.

PLACE DU TERTRE

Ⓜ Abbesses. MAP PP.136–137, POCKET MAP G3

The bogus heart of Montmartre, the place du Tertre is best avoided: clotted with tour groups, overpriced restaurants, tacky souvenir stalls and jaded street artists. At the east end of the *place*, however, stands the serene church of **St-Pierre-de-Montmartre**, the oldest in Paris, along with St-Germain-des-Prés. Although much altered since it was built as a Benedictine convent in the twelfth century, the church retains its Romanesque and early Gothic character, with four ancient columns, probably leftovers from the Roman shrine that stood on the hill (which they knew as *mons mercurii* – Mercury's Hill).

MUSEE DE L'EROTISME

72 bd Clichy Ⓜ Blanche. Ⓣ 01 42 58 28 73, Ⓦ musee-erotisme.com. Daily 10am–2am. €10. MAP PP.136–137, POCKET MAP F3

Appropriately set among the sex shops and shows of Pigalle, the Musée de l'Erotisme explores different cultures' approaches to sex. Two floors brim with sacred and ethnographic art – displaying proud phalluses and well-practised positions from Asia, Africa and pre-Colombian Latin America, plus satirical European curiosities – and feature a fascinating history of Parisian brothels; the remaining five floors are filled with temporary exhibits.

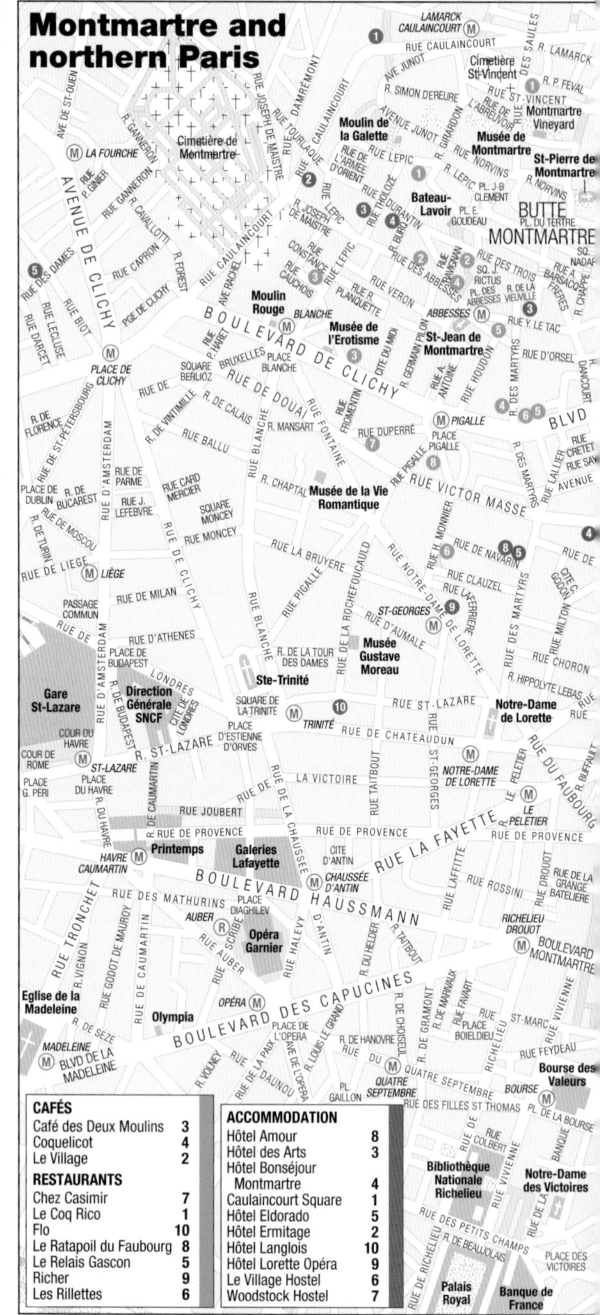
Montmartre and northern Paris
CAFÉS
Café des Deux Moulins 3
Coquelicot 4
Le Village 2
RESTAURANTS
Chez Casimir 7
Le Coq Rico 1
Flo 10
Le Ratapoil du Faubourg 8
Le Relais Gascon 5
Richer 9
Les Rillettes 6
ACCOMMODATION
Hôtel Amour 8
Hôtel des Arts 3
Hôtel Bonséjour Montmartre 4
Caulaincourt Square 1
Hôtel Eldorado 5
Hôtel Ermitage 2
Hôtel Langlois 10
Hôtel Lorette Opéra 9
Le Village Hostel 6
Woodstock Hostel 7
Cimetière de Montmartre
Cimetière St-Vincent
Montmartre Vineyard
Moulin de la Galette
Musée de Montmartre
St-Pierre de Montmartre
Bateau-Lavoir
BUTTE MONTMARTRE
Moulin Rouge
Musée de l'Erotisme
St-Jean de Montmartre
Musée de la Vie Romantique
Musée Gustave Moreau
Ste-Trinité
Notre-Dame de Lorette
Gare St-Lazare
Direction Générale SNCF
Printemps
Galeries Lafayette
Opéra Garnier
Olympia
Eglise de la Madeleine
Bourse des Valeurs
Bibliothèque Nationale Richelieu
Notre-Dame des Victoires
Palais Royal
Banque de France
BOULEVARD DE CLICHY
AVENUE DE CLICHY
BOULEVARD HAUSSMANN
BOULEVARD DES CAPUCINES
RUE LA FAYETTE
BOULEVARD MONTMARTRE
LA FOURCHE
PLACE DE CLICHY
BLANCHE
ABBESSES
PIGALLE
LIÈGE
ST-GEORGES
TRINITÉ
ST-LAZARE
HAVRE CAUMARTIN
CHAUSSÉE D'ANTIN
AUBER
OPÉRA
MADELEINE
QUATRE SEPTEMBRE
BOURSE
RICHELIEU DROUOT
NOTRE-DAME DE LORETTE
LE PELETIER
LAMARCK CAULAINCOURT

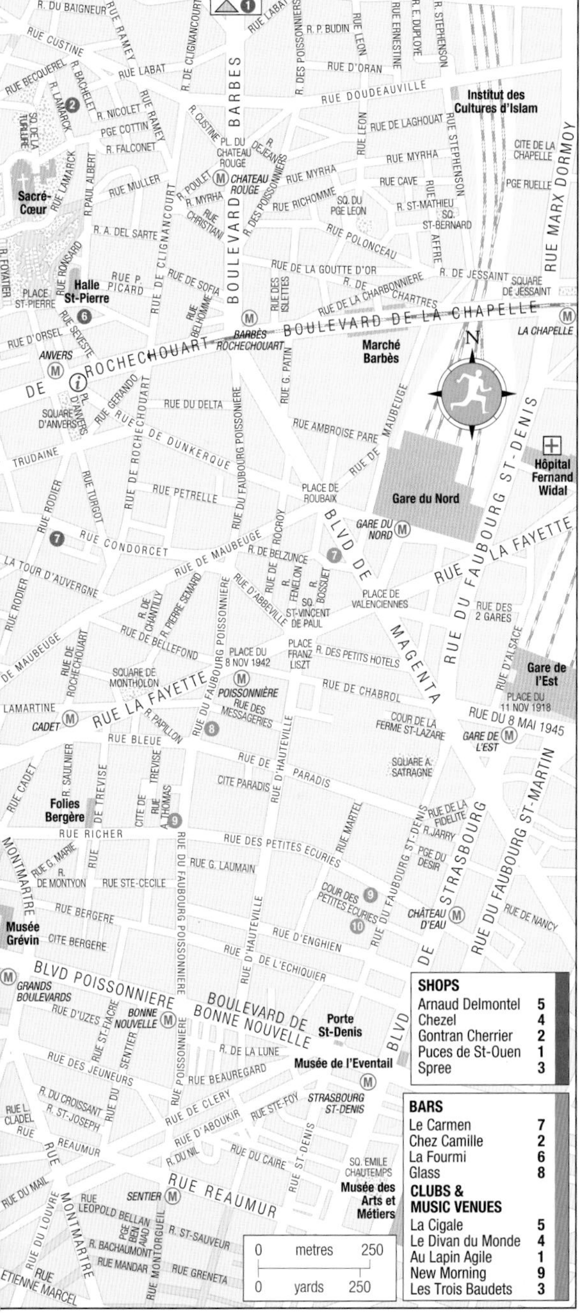
SHOPS
Arnaud Delmontel 5
Chezel 4
Gontran Cherrier 2
Puces de St-Ouen 1
Spree 3
BARS
Le Carmen 7
Chez Camille 2
La Fourmi 6
Glass 8
CLUBS & MUSIC VENUES
La Cigale 5
Le Divan du Monde 4
Au Lapin Agile 1
New Morning 9
Les Trois Baudets 3
0 metres 250
0 yards 250
Sacré-Cœur
Halle St-Pierre
Institut des Cultures d'Islam
Marché Barbès
Gare du Nord
Hôpital Fernand Widal
Gare de l'Est
Folies Bergère
Musée Grévin
Porte St-Denis
Musée de l'Eventail
Musée des Arts et Métiers
BOULEVARD BARBES
BOULEVARD DE LA CHAPELLE
BOULEVARD DE ROCHECHOUART
BLVD DE MAGENTA
RUE LA FAYETTE
RUE DU FAUBOURG ST-DENIS
RUE DU FAUBOURG ST-MARTIN
BLVD DE STRASBOURG
BLVD POISSONNIERE
BOULEVARD DE BONNE NOUVELLE
RUE REAUMUR
RUE MONTMARTRE
RUE MARX DORMOY

SACRE-COEUR

Ⓜ Anvers/Abbesses. Daily 6am–10.30pm. Free. Dome daily: May–Sept 8.30am–8pm, Oct–April 9am–5pm. €6. MAP PP.136–137, POCKET MAP G3

Crowning the Butte, Sacré-Coeur is a pastiche of Byzantine-style architecture, whose white tower and ice-cream-scoop dome has become an icon of the Paris skyline. Construction was started in the 1870s on the initiative of the Catholic Church to atone for the "crimes" of the revolutionary Commune, which first attempted to seize power from the heights of Montmartre. There's little to see in the soulless interior, but the view from the dome is fantastic – best enjoyed early in the morning or later in the afternoon if you don't want to look straight into the sun. **Square Willette**, at the foot of the monumental staircase, is named after the local artist who turned out on inauguration day to shout "Long live the devil!" Today the staircase acts as impromptu seating for visitors enjoying views, munching on picnics and tolerating the street entertainers; the crowds, and the guitar strumming, only increase as night falls.

MOULIN DE LA GALETTE

Rue Lepic Ⓜ Abbesses/Lamarck-Caulaincourt. MAP PP.136–137, POCKET MAP G3

One atmospheric way to get to the top of the Butte is to head up rue Tholozé, turning right below the wooden Moulin de la Galette into rue des Norvins. The *moulin* is one of two survivors of Montmartre's forty-odd windmills (the other sits on an adjacent street corner, on top of a restaurant confusingly given the same name), and was once a *guingette*, holding fashionable dances – as immortalized by Renoir in his *Bal du Moulin de la Galette*, which hangs in the Musée d'Orsay.

MUSEE DE MONTMARTRE

12 rue Cortot Ⓜ Lamarck-Caulaincourt. Ⓣ 01 49 25 89 37, Ⓦ museedemontmartre.fr. Daily 10am–6pm. €9.50. MAP PP.136–137, POCKET MAP G3

The intriguing little Musée de Montmartre, set in two old houses (the Maison du Bel Air and the recently renovated Hôtel Demarne) on a quiet street, recaptures something of the feel of the quarter's bohemian days, lining its period rooms with old posters, paintings and personal photos. The Maison du Bel Air was rented variously by Renoir,

SACRE-COEUR

MONTMARTRE CEMETERY

Dufy, Suzanne Valadon and her alcoholic son Utrillo. Valadon's studio was opened in 2014 for the first time to the public, and the three gardens have also been charmingly restored. You can walk round to the back of the museum to see the neat terraces of the tiny **Montmartre vineyard** – which produces some 1500 bottles a year. The streets leading off here are some of the quietest in Montmartre, and lovely for a romantic stroll.

MONTMARTRE CEMETERY

Entrance on av Rachel, underneath rue Caulaincourt Ⓜ Blanche/Place-de-Clichy. Mid-March to Nov 5 Mon–Fri 8am–6pm, Sat 8.30am–6pm, Sun 9am–6pm; Nov 6 to mid-March closes 5.30pm. Free. MAP PP.136–137, POCKET MAP F2–3

West of the Butte, the Montmartre cemetery is an intimate, melancholy place: tucked down below street level in the hollow of an old quarry, its steep tomb-dotted hills create a sombre ravine of the dead. The graves of Nijinsky, Zola, Stendhal, Berlioz, Degas, Feydeau, Offenbach and Truffaut, among others, are marked on a free map available at the entrance.

PIGALLE AND SOPI

Ⓜ Pigalle. MAP PP.136–137, POCKET MAP F3–H4

The southern slopes of Montmartre are bordered by the boulevards de Clichy and Rochechouart. At the Barbès end of bd Rochechouart crowds teem around the cheap Tati department stores and African street vendors hawk textiles, watches and trinkets. The area where the two roads meet, around **place Pigalle**, has long been associated with sleaze, with sex shops and shows, and streetwalkers vying for custom. The area is changing, however: the streets just south of place Pigalle have been rebranded SoPi ("South Pigalle") and are now some of the city's hippest. Most of the sleazy bars have closed and been replaced by trendy cocktail bars, bistros and organic grocers. Rues de Douai, Victor-Massé and Houdon sport a large number of electric guitar and hi-fi shops, while rue des Martyrs is one of Paris's most enjoyable gastro-streets, lined with fancy food and flower shops as it descends southwards from the Butte.

THE MOULIN ROUGE

82 bd de Clichy Ⓜ Blanche. Ⓣ 01 53 09 82 82, Ⓦ moulinrouge.fr. Shows at 9pm & 11pm. From €97. MAP PP.136–137, POCKET MAP F3

Though its environs have lost the glamour they once had, you can't help but be drawn towards the tatty red windmill, its windows filled with photos of beaming showgirls. When Toulouse-Lautrec immortalized the *Moulin Rouge* in his paintings, it was one of many such bawdy, populist cabarets in the area; nowadays, it survives on its reputation, offering expensive Vegas-style dinner-and-show deals.

MUSEE DE LA VIE ROMANTIQUE

16 rue Chaptal Ⓜ St-Georges/Blanche/Pigalle. Ⓣ 01 55 31 95 67, Ⓦ vie-romantique.paris.fr. Tues–Sun 10am–6pm. €7 for (all) temporary exhibitions, otherwise free. MAP PP.136–137, POCKET MAP F4

The Musée de la Vie Romantique evokes the era when this quarter was the home of Chopin, Delacroix, Dumas and other prominent figures in the Romantic movement. The bourgeois shuttered house, on a cobbled courtyard, once belonged to the painter Ary Scheffer; in addition to his sentimental portraits and the restored period interiors, you can see bits and pieces associated with his friend George Sand. The museum's *salon de thé* (mid-March to mid-Oct), located in the pretty garden, is a lovely place to unwind over a salad or quiche.

INSIDE THE MUSEE MOREAU

MUSEE MOREAU

14 rue de La Rochefoucauld Ⓜ Trinité. Ⓣ 01 48 74 38 50, Ⓦ musee-moreau.fr. Mon, Wed & Thurs 10am–12.45pm & 2–5.15pm, Fri–Sun 10am–5.15pm. €6. MAP PP.136–137, POCKET MAP F4

The little-visited **Gustave Moreau** museum, the ground floor of which was recently renovated and restored to its original decor, was conceived by the artist himself, to be carved out of the house he shared with his parents for many years – you can visit their tiny apartments, crammed with furniture and trinkets. Connected by a beautiful spiral staircase, the two huge, studio-like spaces are no less cluttered: Moreau's decadent canvases hang cheek by jowl, every surface crawling with figures and decorative swirls, or alive with deep colours and provocative symbolism, as in the museum's *pièce de résistance, Jupiter and Séméle.*

FAUBOURGS ST-DENIS AND ST-MARTIN

Ⓜ Château d'Eau. MAP PP.136–137, POCKET MAP J5

At the upper end of the 10ᵉ, the stations – the Gare du Nord and the Gare de l'Est – dominate, while to the south lies the fast-changing quarter of the faubourgs St-Denis and St-Martin, traditionally working class, but more and more popular with young

Parisian *bobos*, priced out of the more affluent areas of the city. A growing number of cutting-edge *bistrots*, chic boutiques, delis and cocktail bars is colonizing the streets between Château d'Eau and Cadet métros.

PORTE ST-DENIS AND PORTE ST-MARTIN

Ⓜ Strasbourg-St-Denis. MAP PP.136–137, POCKET MAP K11

The Porte St-Denis and Porte St-Martin are two triumphal arches, marooned by traffic, at either end of the boulevard St-Denis. The Porte St-Denis was erected to celebrate Louis XIV's victories on the Rhine and bear the bas-reliefs *The Crossing of the Rhine* and *The Capture of Maastricht*. Some 200m east, the more graceful Porte St-Martin was built two years later in celebration of further victories.

MUSEE DE L'EVENTAIL

2 bd de Strasbourg Ⓜ Strasbourg-St-Denis. Ⓣ 01 42 08 90 20, Ⓦ annehoguet.fr. Mon–Wed 2–6pm; closed Aug. €6.50. MAP PP.136–137, POCKET MAP J6

The fascination of the Musée de l'Eventail is that it's more working atelier than museum. In a small suite of period rooms in an ordinary Haussmann building, Anne Hoguet continues the family tradition of fan-making, working for customers from the worlds of haute couture and theatre. There is always an exhibition drawing on some of the museum's thousand-strong collection of fans, both historic and contemporary.

MARCHE BARBES

Boulevard de la Chapelle Ⓜ Barbès-Rochechouart. Wed 8am–1pm, Sat 7am–3pm. MAP PP.136–137, POCKET MAP H3

After World War I, when large numbers of North Africans were first imported to replenish the ranks of Frenchmen dying in the trenches, the swathe of Paris north of the Gare du Nord gradually became an immigrant ghetto. Today, while the *quartier* remains poor, it is a vibrant place, home to a host of mini-communities, predominantly West African and Congolese, but with pockets of South Asian, Haitian, Turkish and other ethnicities as well. Countless shops sell ethnic music and fabrics, but to get a feel for the place, head to the twice-weekly Marché Barbès, heaving with African groceries, exotic fish and and halal meat.

INSTITUT DES CULTURES D'ISLAM

56 rue Stephenson Ⓜ La Chapelle/Marx Dormoy. Ⓣ 01 53 09 99 84, Ⓦ institut-cultures-islam.org. Tues–Thurs, Sat & Sun 10am–9pm, Fri 4–9pm. Free. MAP PP.136–137, POCKET MAP J3

Opened in 2013, the Institut des Cultures d'Islam stages exhibitions of contemporary art from the Islamic world. These are usually fascinating and thought-provoking, with recent exhibitions including Syrian artists responding to the current war and chaos in their country, and women artists depicting domestic life in the Middle East and Iran.

PORTE ST-DENIS

ITEMS FOR SALE AT THE PUCES DE ST-OUEN

Shops

ARNAUD DELMONTEL

39 rue des Martyrs Ⓜ St-Georges. Ⓦ arnaud-delmontel.com. Mon & Wed–Sun 7am–8.30pm. MAP PP.136–137, POCKET MAP G4

Exquisite Parisian patisserie with a funky twist, its *bavaroises*, *macarons* and tarts decorated in fresh candy colours. The award-winning bread is outstanding, too.

CHEZEL

59 rue Condorcet Ⓜ Pigalle. Tues–Fri noon–7.30pm, Sat 11.30am–7.30pm. MAP PP.136–137, POCKET MAP G4

One of the best of the three or four (the others come and go) little vintage fashion shops on this street. Prices from €30 to easily five times that for a classic – some serious designer wear finds its way here.

GONTRAN CHERRIER

22 rue Caulaincourt Ⓜ Abbesses. Ⓦ gontrancherrierboulanger.com. Mon, Tues & Thurs–Sat 7.30am–8pm, Sun 8am–8pm. MAP PP.136–137, POCKET MAP F3.

Gontran Cherrier bakes some of the most creative bread in Paris and disciples will trek across the city for his squid-ink buns filled with gravadlax, thin-crusted savoury tarts and signature sweet pastries.

PUCES DE ST-OUEN

Ⓜ Porte de Clignancourt. Officially (many stands closed Mon) Sat–Mon 9am–6.30pm – unofficially, from 5am. MAP PP.136–137, POCKET MAP H1

Spreading beyond the *périphérique* at the northern edge of the city, between the Porte de St-Ouen and the Porte de Clignancourt, the **puces de St-Ouen** claims to be the largest flea market in the world, though nowadays it's predominantly a proper – and pricey – antiques market. Mainly selling furniture, with all sorts of fashionable junk like old café-bar counters, telephones, traffic lights, jukeboxes and the like, it offers many quirky treasures. Of the twelve or so individual markets, you could concentrate on Marché **Dauphine**, good for movie posters, *chanson* and jazz records, comics and books, and Marché **Vernaison** for curios and bric-a-brac. Under the flyover of the *périphérique*, vendors hawk counterfeit clothing, sunglasses and pirated DVDs, while cup-and-ball scam merchants try their luck.

SPREE

16 rue de la Vieuville Ⓜ Abbesses. Ⓦ spree.fr. Tues–Sat 11am–7.30pm, Mon & Sun 3–7pm. MAP PP.136–137, POCKET MAP G3

This funky, feminine clothing store/gallery led by designers such as Vanessa Bruno, Isabel Marant and Christian Wijnants is typical of the trendy Abbesses scene. It also stocks vintage pieces, accessories, furniture and beauty products.

Cafés

CAFE DES DEUX MOULINS

15 rue Lepic Ⓜ Blanche. Daily 7.30–2am.. MAP PP.136–137, POCKET MAP F3

Once a must-see for *Amélie* fans (she waited tables here in the film), this comfortably shabby retro diner/café is now a down-to-earth neighbourhood hangout once more – burly *ouvriers* in the morning, hipsters in the evening – serving breakfasts, brunches and standard *plats* at good prices.

COQUELICOT

24 rue des Abbesses Ⓜ Abbesses. Ⓣ 01 46 06 18 77. Tues–Fri 8am–5.30pm, Sat & Sun 8am–6.30pm. MAP PP.136–137, POCKET MAP G3.

This award-winning bakery doubles as a charming café that is a hugely popular lunch or brunch spot (book ahead for the latter). Sit down with your chosen sandwich or *tarte*, or pick from the extensive menu.

LE VILLAGE

36 rue des Abbesses Ⓜ Abbesses. Daily 7am–2am. MAP PP.136–137, POCKET MAP G3.

A friendly café-bar with a teeny *terrasse* that extends across the pavement after dark. The interior is a retro delight – gleaming ceramic wall tiles, huge mirrors and a zinc bar. Equally good for a morning coffee, a light lunch of *croques* or salads, or an evening cognac – and perfect for watching the world go by.

Restaurants

CHEZ CASIMIR

6 rue de Belzunce Ⓜ Gare-du-Nord. Ⓣ 01 48 78 28 80. Mon–Fri noon–2pm & 7.30–10.30pm, Sat & Sun 10am–7pm. MAP PP.136–137, POCKET MAP H4

This no-frills corner *bistrot*, in a quiet spot a stone's throw from the Gare du Nord, is a gem: traditional but imaginative French cuisine at bargain prices (around €30), with a fine brunch at weekends.

LE COQ RICO

98 rue Lepic Ⓜ Abbesses/Blanche. Ⓣ 01 42 59 82 89, Ⓦ lecoqrico.com. Daily noon–2.30pm & 7–11pm. MAP PP.136–137, POCKET MAP G3

It's all about the birds at Antoine Westermann's chic, relatively formal Montmartre outfit, from the huge rôtisserie that turns out moist whole grilled chickens to the duck rillettes, roast pigeon and poultry soups. Mains €22–45.

FLO

7 cour des Petites-Ecuries Ⓜ Château-d'Eau. Ⓣ 01 47 70 13 59, Ⓦ brasserieflo-paris.com. Tues–Sat noon–3pm & 7pm–midnight, Sun & Mon noon–3pm & 7–11pm. MAP PP.136–137, POCKET MAP J5

This dark and splendid old-time Alsatian brasserie is so beautiful that even the stroppy service and the crammed-in tourist/business clientele can't spoil the experience. Hearty brasserie food, with lots of fish and seafood – and butter in everything. *Menus* from €29.

FLO

LE RATAPOIL DU FAUBOURG

72 rue du Faubourg Poissonière Ⓜ Poissonière. ⓣ 01 42 46 30 53, ⓦ ratapoildufaubourg.fr. Mon–Fri noon–2.30pm & 7.30–11pm, Sat 7.30–11pm. MAP PP.136–137, POCKET MAP H5

One of the new breed of accomplished restaurants populating the 10ᵉ, *Ratapoil* is a modern *bistrot* serving unfussy contemporary country food – red mullet tartare, mussels, roast pigeon with morels. At dinner (*menus* €30–60) you can choose to share small dishes or go for more traditional mains. Don't miss the salted-caramel pudding.

LE RELAIS GASCON

6 rue des Abbesses & 13 rue de Joseph Maistre Ⓜ Abbesses. ⓣ 01 42 58 58 22. Mon–Thurs 10.30am–midnight, Fri–Sun 10:30am–12.30am (food from noon). MAP PP.136–137, POCKET MAP G3

This noisy two-storey restaurant (upstairs is cosier) provides a welcome blast of Gascon heartiness. Enormous hot salads start at €13.50, and there are good-value *plats* and lunch *menus*.

RICHER

2 rue Richer Ⓜ Poissonière/Bonne Nouvelle. ⓦ lericher.com. Daily 8am–midnight; full meals served noon–2.30pm & 7.30–10.30pm. MAP PP.136–137, POCKET MAP H5

This light, modern dining room – a fresh update on the traditional all-day Parisian brasserie – offers coffee, wine and tapas all day long. It's the short seasonal menu that's really worth coming for, though, using fresh ingredients in innovative ways – perhaps steamed hake with beetroot puree, horseradish and Thai basil. Mains around €18. No reservations.

LES RILLETTES

33 rue de Navarin Ⓜ St-Georges/Pigalle. ⓣ 01 48 74 02 90. Tues–Sat 7–11pm. MAP PP.136–137, POCKET MAP G4

The husband-and-wife team

LA FOURMI

who run this charming small restaurant create a wonderful, warm-hearted atmosphere. This is delicious country cooking, featuring dishes largely from the Auvergne, such as sausage cooked in a hay pot and black pork with red peppers. Mains from €20.

Bars

LE CARMEN

34 rue Duperré Ⓜ Pigalle. ⓣ 01 45 26 50 00, ⓦ le-carmen.fr. Daily midnight–6am. MAP PP.136–137, POCKET MAP G4

This astonishingly beautiful cocktail bar occupies the grand, high-ceilinged reception rooms of Georges Bizet's old house. You'll feel like you're at the ball from *La Traviata*, except for the fact that the music is provided by edgy DJs, and everyone's drinking designer cocktails.

CHEZ CAMILLE

8 rue Ravignan Ⓜ Abbesses. Tues–Sat 6pm–1.30am, Sun 6pm–midnight. MAP PP.136–137, POCKET MAP G3

With an effortlessly stylish decor – creamy walls, ceiling fans, a few old mirrors, mismatched seating – this tiny bar pulls a local crowd of all ages who could just as easily be enjoying a quiet chat as dancing to Elvis or raï.

LA FOURMI

74 rue des Martyrs Ⓜ Pigalle/Abbesses. Mon–Thurs 9am–2am, Fri & Sat 9am–4am, Sun 10am–2am. MAP PP.136–137, POCKET MAP G4

Artfully distressed, high-ceilinged café-bar full of Parisian bohos sipping coffee and cocktails. Light meals available during the day. DJs at weekends.

GLASS

7 rue Frochot Ⓜ Pigalle. Ⓦ quixotic-projects .com. Mon–Thurs & Sun 7pm–4am, Fri & Sat 7pm–5am. MAP PP.136–137, POCKET MAP G4

Don't be put off by the grotty surroundings; this little bar is at the heart of the "SoPi" phenomenon, a hub of cool in this gentrifying neighbourhood. The whisky-based cocktails (€10), organic hot dogs and craft beers hit the spot with the young, up-for-it crowd.

Clubs and music venues

LA CIGALE

120 bd de Rochechouart Ⓜ Pigalle. Ⓣ 01 49 25 81 75, Ⓦ lacigale.fr. MAP PP.136–137, POCKET MAP G4

This historic 1400-seater Pigalle theatre, which once played host to the likes of Mistinguett and Maurice Chevalier, is a leading venue for rock and indie acts from France and continental Europe.

LE DIVAN DU MONDE

75 rue des Martyrs Ⓜ Anvers. Ⓣ 01 40 05 06 99, Ⓦ divandumonde.com. MAP PP.136–137, POCKET MAP G4

A youthful venue in a former café whose regulars once included Toulouse-Lautrec, with an exciting programme ranging from poetry slams to swing nights to Congolese rumba.

AU LAPIN AGILE

22 rue des Saules Ⓜ Lamarck-Caulaincourt. Ⓣ 01 46 06 85 87, Ⓦ au-lapin-agile.com. Tues–Sun 9pm–1am. MAP PP.136–137, POCKET MAP G2

Painted and patronized by Picasso and other leading lights of the Montmartre scene, this legendary club – in a shuttered building hidden in a pretty garden – still hosts cabaret, poetry and *chanson* nights (€28). Touristy crowd, but authentic musicians.

NEW MORNING

7–9 rue des Petites-Ecuries Ⓜ Chateau. d'Eau. Ⓣ 01 45 23 51 41, Ⓦ newmorning.com. MAP PP.136–137, POCKET MAP J5

One of the most exciting venues in Paris, mixed and buzzing, and *the* place to catch international names in jazz and world music. It's usually standing room only.

LES TROIS BAUDETS

64 bd de Clichy Ⓜ Blanche/Pigalle. Ⓣ 01 42 62 33 33, Ⓦ lestroisbaudets.com. MAP PP.136–137, POCKET MAP F3

This historic pocket theatre was refitted in 2009, and has found a proud place on the *chanson* scene. Specializes in young, upcoming French performers. Tickets around €10–17.

PERFORMER AT NEW MORNING

Northeastern Paris

Northeastern Paris, comprising the Canal St-Martin, Belleville, Ménilmontant and La Villette, is one of the most diverse and vibrant parts of the city, home to sizeable ethnic populations, as well as students and artists. The area's most popular attractions are Père-Lachaise cemetery, the final resting place of numerous famous artists and writers; the leafy Canal St-Martin, with its trendy cafés and bars; and the vast, postmodern Parc de la Villette. Some of the city's best nightlife is concentrated on rues Oberkampf and Jean-Pierre Timbaud, while two attractive parks, the Buttes-Chaumont and Parc de Belleville, reward visitors with fine views over the city.

PLACE DE LA REPUBLIQUE

Ⓜ République. MAP P.148, POCKET MAP G13

The place de la République (or Répu, as it's affectionately known by locals) is one of the city's largest squares and was recently given a major makeoever, with fountains and more benches and trees added. By long-standing tradition, rallies and demonstrations often end at the place de la République. At the centre of the square stands an enormous bronze statue of Marianne, the female symbol of the Republic, holding an olive branch in one hand, and a tablet inscribed with the words "Droits de l'Homme" in the other. The statue still bears graffiti from the huge crowds that packed the square in January 2015 in the wake of the Charlie Hebdo massacres, and again in November of that year after terrorist attacks on the city left 130 people dead, turning it into a sort of unofficial memorial.

In the summer an open-air "games kiosk", l'R de Jeux (mid-June to mid-Sept Tues–Sun 2–8pm), sets up on the eastern side of the square, with some six hundred toys and games for both adults and children, including construction

PLACE DE LA REPUBLIQUE

kits, scooters and board games, any of which you can borrow for free (bring ID).

CANAL ST-MARTIN

MAP P.148, POCKET MAP K4–6

Built in 1825 to enable river traffic to shortcut the great western loop of the Seine around Paris, the Canal St-Martin possesses a great deal of charm, especially along its southern reaches: plane trees line the cobbled *quais,* and elegant, high-arched footbridges punctuate the spaces between the locks, from where you can still watch the odd barge slowly rising or sinking to the next level. In the last decade or so the area has been colonized by the new arts and media intelligentsia, bringing in their wake trendy bars, cafés and boutiques. The area is particularly lively on Sunday afternoons when the *quais* are closed to traffic; pedestrians, cyclists and rollerbladers take over the streets, and people hang out along the canal's edge.

ROTONDE DE LA VILLETTE

Ⓜ Stalingrad/Jaurès. Ⓦ larotonde.com. MAP P.148, POCKET MAP K3

The Canal St-Martin goes underground at the busy **place de la Bataille de Stalingrad**, dominated by the Neoclassical Rotonde de la Villette, a handsome stone rotunda fronted with a portico, inspired by Palladio's Villa La Rotonda in Vicenza. This was one of the toll houses designed by the architect Ledoux as part of Louis XVI's scheme to tax all goods entering the city. At that time, every road out of Paris had a customs post, or *barrière*, linked by a 6m-high wall, known as "Le Mur des Fermiers-Généraux" – a major irritant in the run-up to the Revolution. Cleaned and restored, the *rotonde* is used for exhibitions and has a restaurant and wine bar. Backing the toll house is an elegant aerial stretch of métro, supported by Neoclassical iron-and-stone pillars. Note that the area has a dodgy reputation at night, as it's a known haunt of drug dealers.

BASSIN DE LA VILLETTE

Ⓜ Stalingrad/Riquet/Laumière. MAP P.148, POCKET MAP L3

Beyond the Rotonde de la Villette the canal widens out into the Bassin de la Villette, built in 1808. The recobbled docks area bears few traces of its days as France's premier port, its dockside buildings now offering canal boat trips (see box, p.187) and housing a multiplex cinema, the **MK2** (see p.188), which has screens on both banks, linked by shuttle boat. On Sundays and public holidays people stroll along the *quais*, jog, cycle, play boules, fish or take a rowing boat out in the dock; in August, as part of the **Paris Plages** scheme (see p.192), you can rent canoes and pedaloes. Continuing regeneration has seen the arrival of new bars, restaurants and the *St Christopher's* hostel (see p.179), housed in a converted boat hangar.

THE CANAL ST-MARTIN

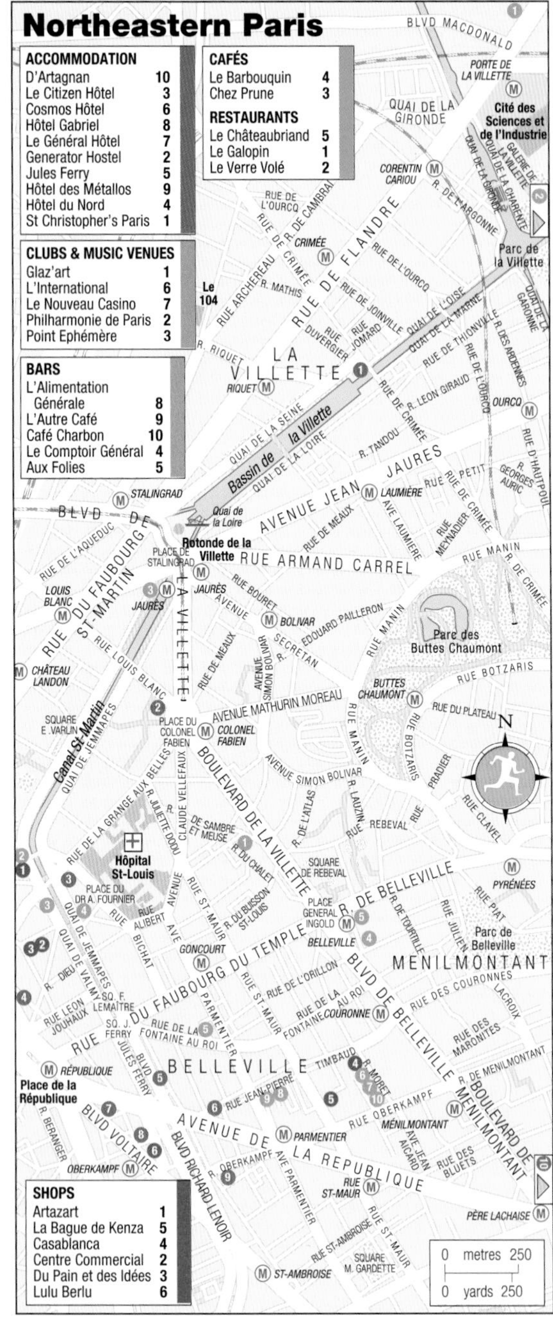
Northeastern Paris
ACCOMMODATION
D'Artagnan 10
Le Citizen Hôtel 3
Cosmos Hôtel 6
Hôtel Gabriel 8
Le Général Hôtel 7
Generator Hostel 2
Jules Ferry 5
Hôtel des Métallos 9
Hôtel du Nord 4
St Christopher's Paris 1
CAFÉS
Le Barbouquin 4
Chez Prune 3
RESTAURANTS
Le Châteaubriand 5
Le Galopin 1
Le Verre Volé 2
CLUBS & MUSIC VENUES
Glaz'art 1
L'International 6
Le Nouveau Casino 7
Philharmonie de Paris 2
Point Ephémère 3
BARS
L'Alimentation Générale 8
L'Autre Café 9
Café Charbon 10
Le Comptoir Général 4
Aux Folies 5
SHOPS
Artazart 1
La Bague de Kenza 5
Casablanca 4
Centre Commercial 2
Du Pain et des Idées 3
Lulu Berlu 6
BLVD MACDONALD
PORTE DE LA VILLETTE
Cité des Sciences et de l'Industrie
QUAI DE LA GIRONDE
CORENTIN CARIOU
Parc de la Villette
LA VILLETTE
Le 104
RIQUET
Bassin de la Villette
STALINGRAD
Rotonde de la Villette
AVENUE JEAN JAURES
RUE ARMAND CARREL
JAURÈS
LOUIS BLANC
BOLIVAR
LAUMIÈRE
OURCQ
CRIMÉE
Parc des Buttes Chaumont
BUTTES CHAUMONT
RUE BOTZARIS
CHÂTEAU LANDON
Canal St-Martin
PLACE DU COLONEL FABIEN
COLONEL FABIEN
AVENUE MATHURIN MOREAU
BOULEVARD DE LA VILLETTE
Hôpital St-Louis
PYRÉNÉES
Parc de Belleville
MENILMONTANT
BELLEVILLE
GONCOURT
RUE DU FAUBOURG DU TEMPLE
COURONNE
RÉPUBLIQUE
Place de la République
BLVD VOLTAIRE
AVENUE DE LA REPUBLIQUE
PARMENTIER
MÉNILMONTANT
BOULEVARD DE MENILMONTANT
OBERKAMPF
RUE ST-MAUR
PÈRE LACHAISE
ST-AMBROISE
BLVD RICHARD LENOIR
0 metres 250
0 yards 250

THE GEODE

LE 104

104 rue d'Aubervilliers Ⓜ Ricquet. ⓣ 01 53 35 50 00, Ⓦ 104.fr. Tues–Fri noon–7pm, Sat & Sun 11am–7pm; free entry to the main hall. MAP P.148, POCKET MAP K2–L2

Located in one of the poorest parts of the 19^{e}, in a former grand nineteenth-century funeral parlour, Le 104 is a huge arts centre, with an impressive glass-roofed central hall (*nef curial*) and numerous artists' studios. It hosts exhibitions and installations, dance and theatre, with an emphasis on the experimental and cutting-edge. The complex also houses a good bookshop, a charity shop, a café and restaurant.

PARC DE LA VILLETTE

Ⓜ Porte-de-Pantin/Porte-de-la-Villette. ⓣ 01 40 03 75 75, Ⓦ lavillette.com. Daily 6am–1am. Free. MAP P.148, POCKET MAP M2

Built in 1986 on the site of what was once Paris's largest abattoir and meat market, the Parc de la Villette's landscaped grounds include a state-of-the-art science museum, the brand-new Philharmonie concert hall, a superb music museum, a series of themed gardens and a number of jarring, bright-red "follies". The effect of these disparate elements can be quite disorienting – all in line with the creators' aim of eschewing meaning and "deconstructing" the whole into its parts. All very well, but on a practical level you'll probably want to pick up a map at the information centre at the southern entrance to help you make sense of it all.

The extensive park grounds contain twelve themed gardens, aimed mainly at children. In the Jardin des Miroirs, for example, steel monoliths hidden among the trees and scrub cast strange reflections, while, predictably, dune-like shapes, sails and windmills make up the Jardin des Dunes (for under-13s and accompanying adults). Also popular with children is the eighty-metre-long Dragon Slide.

In front of the Cité des Sciences floats the Géode (hourly shows: Tues–Sat 10.30am–8.30pm, Mon hours vary; €12; Ⓦ lageode.fr), a bubble of reflecting steel that looks as though it's been dropped from an intergalactic boules game into a pool of water. Inside is a screen for Omnimax films, not noted for their plots, but a great visual experience.

CITE DES SCIENCES ET DE L'INDUSTRIE

Parc de la Villette Ⓜ Porte-de-la-Villette. Ⓦ cite-sciences.fr. Tues–Sat 10am–6pm, Sun 10am–7pm. €9. Planetarium shows hourly 11am–5pm; 35min; €3. Cité des Enfants Ⓣ 08 92 69 70 72; Tues–Sun; check online for times of sessions; €9. MAP P.148, POCKET MAP M1

The Cité des Sciences et de l'Industrie is one of the world's finest science museums, set in a huge building four times the size of the Pompidou Centre. An excellent programme of temporary exhibitions complements the permanent exhibition, called Explora, covering subjects such as sound, robotics, energy, light, ecology, maths, medicine, space and language. The Cité has a special section for children called the Cité des Enfants, with areas for 2- to 7-year-olds and 5- to 12-year-olds; all children must be accompanied by an adult and a session lasts ninety minutes (book online). Among the engaging activities, children can play with water and construct buildings on a miniature construction site.

PERE-LACHAISE CEMETERY

MUSEE DE LA MUSIQUE

Philharmonie 2, Parc de la Villette Ⓜ Porte-de-Pantin. Ⓣ 01 44 84 45 00, Ⓦ philharmoniedeparis.fr. Tues–Sat noon–6pm, Sun 10am–6pm. €7; under-26s free. POCKET MAP M3

The Musée de la Musique presents the history of music from the end of the Renaissance to the present day, both visually, exhibiting some 1000 instruments and artefacts, and aurally, via excellent audio-guides (available in English, with special ones for children; free), which narrate the history of the instruments, accompanied by extracts of music. Among the exquisite instruments on display are ornately carved theorbos and viol da gambas, a piano that belonged to Chopin and guitars once played by Jacques Brel and Django Reinhardt.

PERE-LACHAISE CEMETERY

Main entrance on bd de Ménilmontant Ⓜ Père-Lachaise/Philippe Auguste. Mon–Fri 8am–5.30pm, Sat 8.30am–5.30pm, Sun 9am–5.30pm. Free. POCKET MAP A20/21–B20/21

Final resting place of a host of French and foreign notables, Père-Lachaise covers some 116 acres, making it one of the world's largest cemeteries. It's surely also one of the most atmospheric – an eerily beautiful haven, with terraced slopes and magnificent old trees spreading their branches over the moss-grown tombs. Free maps are available at the entrance, but it's worth buying a more detailed one, as some of the graves are tricky to track down; you can buy maps near the main entrance.

Among the most visited graves is that of Chopin (Division 11), often attended by Poles bearing red-and-white wreaths and flowers. Fans also flock to the grave of ex-Doors singer Jim Morrison (Division 6), who died in Paris aged 27.

One of the most impressive of the individual tombs is Oscar Wilde's (Division 89), topped with a sculpture by Jacob Epstein of a mysterious Pharaonic winged messenger. *Femme fatale* Colette's tomb, close to the main entrance in Division 4, is very plain, though always covered in flowers, while Marcel Proust lies in his family's conventional black marble tomb (Division 85).

On a more sombre note, in Division 97 you'll find memorials to the victims of the Nazi concentration camps and to executed Resistance fighters.

PARC DES BUTTES-CHAUMONT

Ⓜ Buttes-Chaumont/Botzaris. MAP P.148, POCKET MAP L5–M4

The Parc des Buttes-Chaumont was constructed under Haussmann in the 1860s to camouflage what until then had been a desolate warren of disused quarries, rubbish dumps and shacks. Out of this rather unlikely setting, a fairy-tale-like park was created – there's a grotto with a cascade and artificial stalactites, and a picturesque lake from which a huge rock rises up, topped with a delicate Corinthian temple. From the temple you get fine views of the Sacré-Coeur and beyond, and you can also go boating on the lake in summer.

BELLEVILLE

Ⓜ Belleville/Pyrénées. MAP P.148, POCKET MAP K6–L6

Absorbed into Paris in the 1860s and subsequently built up with high-rise blocks to house migrants from rural areas and the ex-colonies, Belleville might not exactly be

THE PARC DE BELLEVILLE

"belle", but it's worth seeing this side of the city. The main street, rue de Belleville, abounds with Vietnamese, Thai and Chinese shops and restaurants, which spill south along boulevard de Belleville and rue du Faubourg-du-Temple. African and Oriental fruits, spices, music and fabrics attract shoppers to the boulevard de Belleville market on Tuesday and Friday mornings. From the Parc de Belleville, with its terraces and waterfalls, you get great views across the city, especially at sunset.

MENILMONTANT

Ⓜ Ménilmontant. MAP P.148, POCKET MAP M5–M6

Ménilmontant has a similar history to that of Belleville, and aligns itself along one straight, steep, long street, the rue de Ménilmontant and its lower extension, rue Oberkampf. Although run-down in parts, its popularity with students and artists has brought a cutting-edge vitality to the area. Alternative shops and trendy bars and restaurants have sprung up among the grocers and cheap hardware stores, especially along rue Oberkampf and rue Jean-Pierre Timbaud, one of the city's premier after-dark hangouts.

Shops

ARTAZART

83 quai de Valmy Ⓜ Jacques-Bonsergent. Ⓦ artazart.com. Mon–Fri 10.30am–7.30pm, Sat 11am–7.30pm, Sun 1.30–7.30pm. MAP P.148, POCKET MAP K5

One of the many attractive shops on the Canal St-Martin, this one sells books, magazines and gifts devoted to contemporary graphic art, design and photography, and there are regular book signings, exhibitions and events too.

LA BAGUE DE KENZA

106 rue St-Maur Ⓜ St-Maur. Ⓦ labaguedekenza.com. Mon–Thurs, Sat & Sun 9am–9pm, Fri 1.30–9pm. MAP P.148, POCKET MAP L6

An Algerian pâtisserie full of enticing cakes made of dates, oranges, pistachios, figs, almonds and other tasty ingredients. A little *salon de thé* is attached too.

CASABLANCA

17 rue Moret Ⓜ Ménilmontant. Ⓦ casablanca-vintage.fr. Mon–Sat 2–7pm. MAP P.148, POCKET MAP L6

Cool vintage store, with lots of Thirties, Forties and mid-century gear and a particularly good line in natty men's suits. A visiting barber offers vintage-style haircuts.

LA BAGUE DE KENZA

CENTRE COMMERCIAL

2 rue de Marseille Ⓜ Jacques-Bonsergent. Ⓦ centrecommercial.cc. Mon 1–7.30pm, Tues–Sat 11am–8pm, Sun 2–7pm. MAP P.148, POCKET MAP K6

This pioneering concept store is concerned with the environment and fair trade, stocking ecofriendly French designers such as Valentine Gauthier and Veja, plus a decent selection of lesser-known labels for both men and women.

DU PAIN ET DES IDEES

34 rue Yves Toudic Ⓜ Jacques-Bonsergent. Ⓦ dupainetdesidees.com. Mon–Fri 6.45am–8pm. MAP P.148, POCKET MAP K6

Named best bakery in Paris by *Gault et Millau* in recent years, and a visit quickly reveals why: heavenly baguettes, brioches and the signature *pain des amis*, a nutty flatbread.

LULU BERLU

2 rue Grand Prieuré Ⓜ Oberkampf. Ⓦ luluberlu.com. Mon–Sat 11am–7pm. MAP P.148, POCKET MAP H14

This shop is crammed with twentieth-century toys and curios, most with their original packaging. There's a particularly good collection of 1970–90s favourites, including *Doctor Who*, *Star Wars*, *Planet of the Apes* and *Batman* pieces, plus a good range of new toys.

Cafés

LE BARBOUQUIN

3 rue Ramponeau Ⓜ Belleville. Mon–Fri 9am–7pm, Sat & Sun 10am–7pm. MAP P.148, POCKET MAP L6

Sitting on the corner of rue Dénoyez, a backstreet famous for its street art, *Le Barbouquin* is a welcoming bookshop-café where you can pluck one of the secondhand English or French books off the shelf, settle in an armchair and sip a coffee, mint-and-ginger tea or fresh juice; light food includes savoury tarts and wraps.

CHEZ PRUNE

36 rue Beaurepaire Ⓜ Jacques-Bonsergent. Ⓣ 01 42 41 30 47. Mon–Sat 8am–2am, Sun 10am–2am. MAP P.148, POCKET MAP K5

Named after the owner's grandmother (a bust of whom can be found inside), *Chez Prune* is popular with an artsy crowd and is friendly and laidback, with pleasant outdoor seating overlooking the canal. Lunchtime dishes around €14; evening snacks like platters of cheese or charcuterie around €11; beer €3.

Restaurants

LE CHATEAUBRIAND

129 av Parmentier Ⓜ Goncourt. Ⓣ 01 43 57 45 95. Tues–Sat 7.30–10.30pm. Bookings taken 3–7.30pm up to 3 weeks in advance. MAP P.148, POCKET MAP H13

Innovative Basque chef, Inaki Aizpitarte, has helped change the face of the Paris dining scene with this avant-garde *bistrot*, one of the city's finest addresses and regularly rated among the fifty best restaurants in the world. The multi-course tasting menu changes daily and is a culinary adventure, featuring the likes of mackerel ceviche with pear sorbet, and oyster soup with red fruits and beetroot. At €70 a head for a no-choice menu, this is extremely good value for what you get. Second sitting is at 9.30pm, for which no reservations are taken – just turn up and be prepared to queue.

LE GALOPIN

34 rue Sainte-Marthe Ⓜ Belleville/Goncourt. Ⓣ 01 42 06 05 03, Ⓦ le-galopin.com. Mon–Wed 7.30–11pm, Thurs & Fri noon–2pm & 7.30–11pm. MAP P.148, POCKET MAP L5

With its pared-down decor of bare brick walls and simple wooden chairs, this neighbourhood place epitomizes the neo-*bistrot* scene, offering a seven-course no-choice dinner *menu* of small, delicate plates (€54). At lunch there's a three-course *menu* for €32. Mains might include cauliflower soup with salmon roe, squid with peppers and pork jus or seabass with celery and butternut squash.

LE VERRE VOLE

67 rue de Lancry Ⓜ Jacques-Bonsergent. Ⓣ 01 48 03 17 34. Daily 12.30–2pm & 7.30–10.30pm. MAP P.148, POCKET MAP K5

This wine shop doubles as a simple, cool venue for amazing food, with an appreciative local crowd filling the formica tables crammed into the small space. The short menu lists beautifully executed modern and traditional dishes (from €25) along with cheaper, simpler offerings such as sausage with lentils. There's a great wine selection – you pay the over-the-counter price plus €7 corkage fee.

CHEZ PRUNE

Bars

L'ALIMENTATION GENERALE

64 rue Jean-Pierre Timbaud Ⓜ Parmentier. Ⓦ alimentation-generale.net. Wed, Thurs & Sun 7pm–2am, Fri & Sat 7pm–5am. MAP P.148, POCKET MAP L6

One of Oberkampf's hottest nightlife spots, with a global line-up of live music ranging from Afro-rock to Italian folk. On Fri and Sat nights a DJ takes over later on and there's room for dancing. There's usually a cover charge of €10 that includes the first drink.

L'AUTRE CAFE

62 rue Jean-Pierre Timbaud Ⓜ Parmentier Daily 8am–2am. MAP P.148, POCKET MAP L6

Amid the heaving throng of bars on this popular nightlife stretch, this high-ceilinged *fin-de-siècle* café-bar-restaurant stands slightly apart, perhaps because it seems to welcome all comers and has no trace of pretension, and yet still has a great vibe. Drinks are reasonably priced, and the food isn't bad either, especially if you stick to the blackboard specials (around €10).

CAFE CHARBON

CAFE CHARBON

109 rue Oberkampf Ⓜ Saint-Maur/ Parmentier. Sun–Thurs 9am–2am, Fri & Sat 9am–4am. MAP P.148, POCKET MAP L6

The place that pioneered the rise of the Oberkampf bar scene in the mid-90s is still going strong and continues to draw in a fashionable crowd. Part of its allure is the attractively restored twentieth-century decor, with comfy booths and dangling lights. The long happy hour (daily 5–8pm) helps too.

LE COMPTOIR GENERAL

80 quai de Jemmapes Ⓜ Goncourt/ République. Ⓦ lecomptoirgeneral.com. Daily 11am–2am. MAP P.148, POCKET MAP K5

Tucked away like a secret off the Canal St-Martin, this is a super-cool bar, with an exotic atmosphere and a quirky decor of chandeliers, red carpets, tropical plants and little nooks full of African souvenirs and vintage objects. The great cocktails, friendly staff and impeccably cool playlist – from The Velvet Underground to soukous – keeps the lively, mixed crowd happy. Occasional live African music. Donation for entry requested.

AUX FOLIES

8 rue de Belleville Ⓜ Belleville- Ⓦ aux-folies-belleville.fr. Daily 7pm–2am. MAP P.148, POCKET MAP L5

Once a *café-théâtre* where Edith Piaf and Maurice Chevalier sang, *Aux Folies* offers a slice of Belleville life; its outside terrace and long brass bar, with mirrored tiles, pinball machine and broken window panes held together with sticking tape, are packed day and night with a cosmopolitan crowd, enjoying beer, cocktails and mint tea.

Clubs

GLAZ'ART

7–15 av de la Porte de la Villette Ⓜ Porte de la Villette. ⓣ 01 40 36 55 65, ⓦ glazart.com. Times vary, but weekend club nights usually 11pm–5am. MAP P.148, POCKET MAP M1

An alternative-leaning venue, serious about its music, with live acts and DJ sets from punk to jungle. A trek from the centre, but it's spacious and in summer there's a glorious outdoor "beach". Entry €13–20.

LE NOUVEAU CASINO

109 rue Oberkampf Ⓜ Parmentier. ⓣ 01 43 57 57 40, ⓦ nouveaucasino.net. Fri & Sat midnight–5am. MAP P.148, POCKET MAP L6

Right behind *Café Charbon* (see opposite) lies this excellent venue. An experimental line-up of gigs from 8pm makes way for a relaxed, dancey crowd later on, with music ranging from electro-pop or house to rock. Entry from €9.

Music venues

L'INTERNATIONAL

5 rue Moret Ⓜ Ménilmontant. ⓦ linternational.fr. Tues–Sat 6pm–2am. MAP P.148, POCKET MAP L6

With two stages and at least two free gigs a night, this friendly *café-concert* is a staple on the Oberkampf scene, showcasing the best new, indie and edgy acts – mostly French, but not exclusively – in all genres, from rap to electro.

PHILHARMONIE DE PARIS

221 av Jean-Jaurès Ⓜ Porte-de-Pantin. ⓦ philharmoniedeparis.fr. MAP P.148, POCKET MAP M2

The Philharmonie de Paris is the city's long-awaited new concert hall, opened in 2015. Designed by Jean Nouvel, this state-of-the-art hall, seating up to 2400, is a massive grey building with a ramp that zigzags its way up the facade and gives access to the panoramic rooftop. The interior is creamy-warm and soft, with curved balconies dipping down towards the stage. The acoustics are excellent and you never feel far away from the action, even on the top level. The Orchestre de Paris and the Ensemble InterContemporain have taken up residence here, promising some exciting music-making.

HAIM AT LE NOUVEAU CASINO

POINT EPHEMERE

200 quai de Valmy Ⓜ Jaurès/Louis Blanc. ⓣ 01 40 34 02 48, ⓦ pointephemere.org. Mon–Sat 12.30pm–2am, Sun 1–10pm (later if there's a concert). MAP P.148, POCKET MAP K4

A great, energetic atmosphere pervades this creative space for music, dance and visual arts, set in a former canal boathouse. Bands play rock, indie, jazz and more, while the rotating art exhibitions run from the quotidian to the abstract. In the warmer months you can take your drinks outside and sit on the banks of the canal.

The Bois de Boulogne and western Paris

The Bois de Boulogne, with its trees, lakes, cycling trails and beautiful floral displays, is a favourite Parisian retreat from the city. It runs all the way down the west side of the well-manicured 16e arrondissement. The area is mainly residential with few specific sights, the chief exceptions being the Musée Marmottan, with its dazzling collection of late Monets, and the spectacular new Fondation Louis Vuitton contemporary art centre. The most rewarding areas for exploration are the old villages of Auteuil and Passy, which were incorporated into the city in the late nineteenth century. They soon became desirable districts, and well-to-do Parisians commissioned houses here. As a result, the area is rich in fine examples of architecture, notably by Hector Guimard and Le Corbusier. Further west bristle the gleaming skyscrapers of the purpose-built commercial district of La Défense, dominated by the enormous Grande Arche.

BOIS DE BOULOGNE

Ⓜ Porte Maillot/Porte Dauphine. MAP P.159, POCKET MAP A5

The Bois de Boulogne was designed by Baron Haussmann and supposedly modelled on London's Hyde Park – though it's a very French interpretation. The "bois" of the name is somewhat deceptive, but the extensive parklands (just under nine square kilometres) do

BOIS DE BOULOGNE

RIDE AT THE JARDIN D'ACCLIMATATION

contain some remnants of the once great Forêt de Rouvray. As its location would suggest, the Bois was once the playground of the wealthy. It also gained a reputation as the site of the sex trade and its associated crime; the same holds true today and you should avoid it at night. By day, however, the park is an extremely pleasant spot for a stroll. The best, and wildest, part for walking is towards the southwest corner. Vélib' bikes are available for rent at the entrance to the Jardin d'Acclimatation and you can go boating on the Lac Inférieur.

PARC DE BAGATELLE

Bois de Boulogne Ⓜ Porte Maillot. Daily 9.30am to dusk. €6. MAP P.159

The Parc de Bagatelle, within the Bois de Boulogne, comprises a range of garden styles from French and English to Japanese. Its most famous feature is the stunning rose garden, at its best in June, while in other parts of the garden there are beautiful displays of tulips, hyacinths and daffodils in early April, irises in May, and waterlilies in early August. In June and July the park's orangery is the attractive setting for the prestigious Chopin Festival (Ⓦ frederic-chopin.com).

THE JARDIN D'ACCLIMATATION

Bois de Boulogne Ⓜ Porte Maillot. Ⓣ 01 40 67 90 82, Ⓦ jardindacclimatation.fr. Daily: April–Sept 10am–7pm; Oct–March 10am–6pm. €3 or €5.90 including return train ride from métro; rides from €2.90. MAP P.159

The children's Jardin d'Acclimatation is an action-packed funfair, zoo and amusement park all rolled into one. The fun starts at the Porte-Maillot métro stop: a little train runs from here to the Jardin (every 15min 11am–6pm). The park's many attractions include bumper cars, donkey rides, sea lions, bears and monkeys, a huge trampoline and a magical mini-canal ride (*la rivière enchantée*).

FONDATION LOUIS VUITTON

Av du Mahatma Gandhi Ⓜ Porte Maillot/Les Sablons. Ⓦ fondationlouisvuitton.fr. Opening hours vary. €14 (includes access to the Jardin d'Acclimatation). MAP P.159

A new, Frank Gehry-designed contemporary art centre, the Fondation Louis Vuitton, opened inside the Jardin d'Acclimatation in autumn 2014. Designed to house the collection of the richest man in France, Bernard Arnault, Gehry's huge, dramatic structure, dubbed "the cloud of glass", comprises twelve glass "sails" made up of 3600 glass panels, and sits surrounded by a moat of water. Evoking a ship buffeted by the wind (or possibly a giant insect), the glass sails jut out at odd angles, revealing the dazzling-white inner walls.

Inside, escalators take you down to the moat level (or "grotto") with its striking Olafur Eliasson installation of coloured glass, mirror and sound, while stairways spiral up to roof terraces revealing unexpected vistas of the Eiffel Tower and La Défense. There are eleven galleries, an auditorium, a restaurant and a shop. The permanent collection, shown in themed exhibitions, includes choice works by Rothko, Jeff Koons, Takashi Murakami, Richard Serra and Jean-Michel Basquiat. A shuttle bus runs to the Fondation (every 10–15min; €1) from avenue Friedland, just off place Charles de Gaulle.

VILLA LA ROCHE

Square du Dr-Blanche Ⓜ Jasmin. Ⓣ 01 42 88 75 72, Ⓦ fondationlecorbusier.fr. Mon 1.30–6pm, Tues–Sat 10am–6pm; closed Aug. €8. POCKET MAP A7

Le Corbusier's first private houses, dating to 1923, were the adjoining Villa Jeanneret and the Villa La Roche. The latter is in strictly cubist style, with windows in bands, the only extravagance being a curved frontage. It may look commonplace now from the outside, but at the time it was built it was in great contrast to anything that had gone before. The interior is appropriately decorated with Cubist paintings.

MAISON DE BALZAC

47 rue Raynouard Ⓜ Passy. Ⓣ 01 55 74 41 80. Tues–Sun 10am–6pm. Free. MAP P.159

The Maison de Balzac is a summery little house with pale green shutters, tucked away down some steps that lead through a shady, rose-filled garden – a delightful place to dally on wrought-iron seats, surrounded by busts of the writer. Balzac wrote some of his best-known works here, including *La Cousine Bette* and *Le Cousin Pons*. The museum preserves his study, while other exhibits include a complex family tree of around a thousand of the characters that feature in his *Comédie Humaine*.

FONDATION LOUIS VUITTON

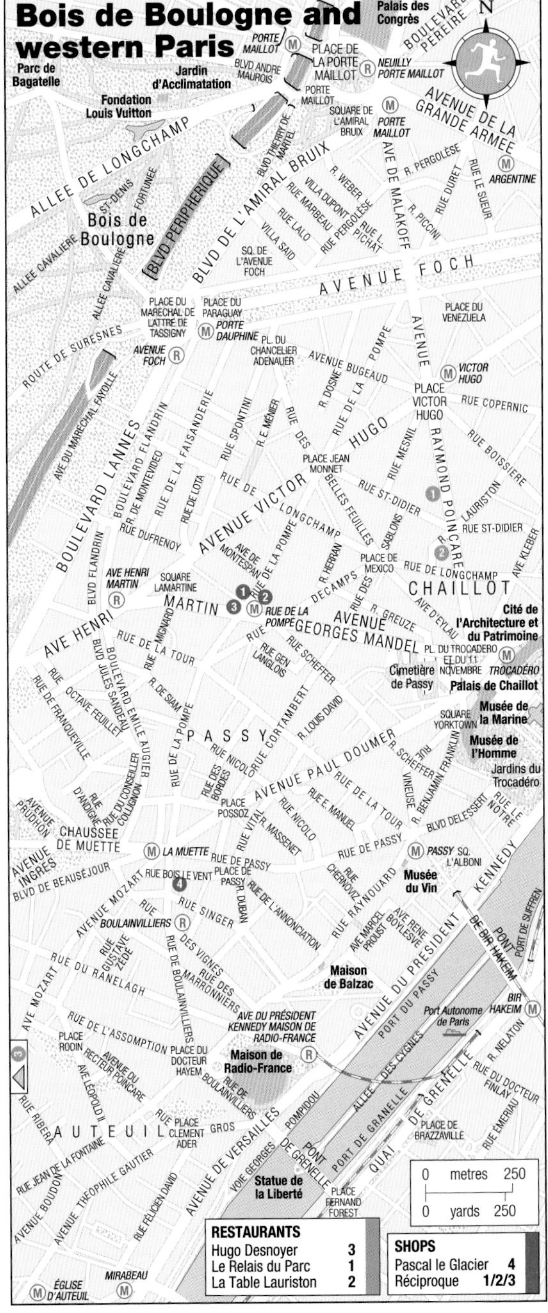
Bois de Boulogne and western Paris
Parc de Bagatelle
Jardin d'Acclimatation
Fondation Louis Vuitton
Palais des Congrès
PORTE MAILLOT
PLACE DE LA PORTE MAILLOT
BLVD ANDRE MAUROIS
NEUILLY PORTE MAILLOT
PORTE MAILLOT
SQUARE DE L'AMIRAL BRUIX
PORTE MAILLOT
BOULEVARD PEREIRE
AVENUE DE LA GRANDE ARMEE
ARGENTINE
ALLEE DE LONGCHAMP
Bois de Boulogne
BLVD PERIPHERIQUE
BLVD DE L'AMIRAL BRUIX
BLVD THIERRY DE MARTEL
AVE DE MALAKOFF
R. PERGOLÈSE
RUE DURET
RUE LE SUEUR
R. WEBER
VILLA DUPONT
RUE MARBEAU
RUE LALO
VILLA SAID
RUE PERGOLÈSE
RUE L. PICHAT
R. PICCINI
SQ. DE L'AVENUE FOCH
AVENUE FOCH
ALLEE CAVALIERE
ROUTE DE SURESNES
PLACE DU MARECHAL DE LATTRE DE TASSIGNY
PLACE DU PARAGUAY
PORTE DAUPHINE
PL. DU CHANCELIER ADENAUER
AVENUE FOCH
PLACE DU VENEZUELA
AVENUE BUGEAUD
RUE DE LA POMPE
AVENUE RAYMOND POINCARE
VICTOR HUGO
PLACE VICTOR HUGO
RUE COPERNIC
AVE DU MARECHAL FAYOLLE
BOULEVARD LANNES
BOULEVARD FLANDRIN
R. DE MONTEVIDEO
RUE DE LA FAISANDERIE
RUE DE LOTA
RUE SPONTINI
R. E. MÉNIER
R. DOSNE
RUE DES BELLES FEUILLES
AVENUE VICTOR HUGO
PLACE JEAN MONNET
RUE MESNIL
RUE BOISSIERE
RUE DE LONGCHAMP
RUE ST-DIDIER
LAURISTON
RUE DUFRENOY
AVE DE MONTESPAN
RUE DE LA POMPE
R. HERRAN
SABLONS
PLACE DE MEXICO
RUE DE LONGCHAMP
AVE KLEBER
BLVD FLANDRIN
AVE HENRI MARTIN
SQUARE LAMARTINE
DECAMPS
R. GREUZE
CHAILLOT
AVE D'EYLAU
Cité de l'Architecture et du Patrimoine
RUE DE LA POMPE
AVENUE GEORGES MANDEL
PL. DU TROCADERO ET DU 11 NOVEMBRE
TROCADÉRO
Cimetière de Passy
Palais de Chaillot
AVE HENRI MARTIN
RUE DE LA TOUR
RUE MIGNARD
BLVD JULES SANDEAU
BOULEVARD EMILE AUGIER
RUE GEN LANGLOIS
RUE SCHEFFER
RUE OCTAVE FEUILLET
RUE DE FRANQUEVILLE
R. DE SIAM
RUE CORTAMBERT
R. LOUIS DAVID
SQUARE YORKTOWN
Musée de la Marine
Musée de l'Homme
Jardins du Trocadéro
PASSY
RUE DE LA POMPE
RUE NICOLO
RUE DES BORDES
AVENUE PAUL DOUMER
R. SCHEFFER
RUE BENJAMIN FRANKLIN
VINEUSE
RUE DE LA TOUR
RUE LE NOTRE
BLVD DELESSERT
RUE DU CONSEILLER COLLIGNON
RUE D'ANDIGNE
AVENUE PRUDHON
CHAUSSEE DE MUETTE
PLACE POSSOZ
RUE VITAL
R. MASSENET
RUE E. MANUEL
RUE NICOLO
LA MUETTE
RUE DE PASSY
RUE DE PASSY
PASSY
SQ. L'ALBONI
AVENUE INGRES
BLVD DE BEAUSÉJOUR
AVENUE MOZART
RUE BOIS LE VENT
PLACE DE PASSY
R. DUBAN
RUE DE L'ANNONCIATION
RUE CHERNOVIZ
RUE RAYNOUARD
Musée du Vin
KENNEDY
PONT DE BIR HAKEIM
PORT DE SUFFREN
RUE SINGER
BOULAINVILLIERS
AVE MARCEL PROUST
AVE RENE BOYLESVE
AVENUE DU PRESIDENT KENNEDY
RUE GUSTAVE ZEDE
RUE DE BOULAINVILLIERS
RUE DES VIGNES
RUE DES MARRONNIERS
Maison de Balzac
RUE DU RANELAGH
AVE MOZART
AVE DU PRÉSIDENT KENNEDY MAISON DE RADIO-FRANCE
PORT DU PASSY
BIR HAKEIM
Port Autonome de Paris
ALLEE DES CYGNES
R. NELATON
RUE DE L'ASSOMPTION
PLACE RODIN
RUE DU RECTEUR POINCARE
AVE LÉOPOLD II
PLACE DU DOCTEUR HAYEM
Maison de Radio-France
RUE DE BOULAINVILLIERS
RUE DU DOCTEUR FINLAY
RUE RIBERA
AUTEUIL
RUE JEAN DE LA FONTAINE
PLACE CLEMENT ADER
GROS
AVENUE DE VERSAILLES
POMPIDOU
PONT DE GRENELLE
PORT DE GRENELLE
QUAI DE GRENELLE
PLACE DE BRAZZAVILLE
RUE EMERIAU
AVENUE BOUDON
AVENUE THEOPHILE GAUTIER
RUE FÉLICIEN DAVID
VOIE GEORGES
Statue de la Liberté
PLACE FERNAND FOREST
0 metres 250
0 yards 250
RESTAURANTS
Hugo Desnoyer 3
Le Relais du Parc 1
La Table Lauriston 2
SHOPS
Pascal le Glacier 4
Réciproque 1/2/3
MIRABEAU
ÉGLISE D'AUTEUIL

AUTEUIL

Ⓜ Michel-Ange-Auteuil. MAP P.159

The Auteuil district has become an integral part of the city, and yet even now the atmosphere in its streets is decidedly village-like. You'll find a number of attractive *villas* (leafy lanes of old houses) in these parts, fronted with English-style gardens, not to mention some fine Art Nouveau buildings by Hector Guimard – there's a concentration on rue de la Fontaine, such as Castel Béranger at no. 14, with exuberant decoration and shapes in the windows, roofline and chimney.

MUSEE MARMOTTAN

2 rue Louis-Boilly Ⓜ Muette. ☎ 01 44 96 50 33, Ⓦ marmottan.fr. Tues–Sun 10am–6pm, Thurs till 9pm. €11. POCKET MAP A7

The Musée Marmottan is best known for its excellent collection of Monet paintings. One of the highlights is *Impression, soleil levant*, a canvas from 1872 of a misty Le Havre morning, and whose title the critics usurped to give the Impressionist movement its name. There's also a selection of works from Monet's last years at Giverny, including several *Nymphéas* (Waterlilies) and *Le Pont Japonais*. The collection also features some of his contemporaries – Manet, Renoir and Berthe Morisot – and a room full of beautiful medieval illuminated manuscripts.

LA DEFENSE

Ⓜ/RER Grande-Arche-de-la-Défense/ Esplanade de la Défense. POCKET MAP A4

An impressive complex of gleaming skyscrapers, La Défense is Paris's prestige business district. Its most popular attraction is the huge Grande Arche. Apartment blocks and big businesses loom between the arch and the river, while avant-garde sculptures by artists such as Joan Miró relieve the jungle of concrete and glass. Landmark buildings include the sleek Tour EDF, the Tour Majunga, with its radically "flowing" effect, and the Tour First, which, at 231m, is France's tallest skyscraper.

THE GRANDE ARCHE AT LA DEFENSE

GRANDE ARCHE DE LA DEFENSE

Ⓜ/RER Grande-Arche-de-la-Défense ☎ 01 49 07 27 27, Ⓦ www.grandearche.com. Daily 10am–7pm. €10. POCKET MAP A4

The Grande Arche de la Défense, built in 1989 for the bicentenary of the Revolution, is an astounding 112-metre-high structure clad in white marble, standing 6km out and at a slight angle from the Arc de Triomphe, completing the western axis of this monumental east–west vista. There are excellent views of the city from the steps that lead up to the base of the arch and also from the roof, which is reached via a glass elevator. For the most dramatic approach to the arch get off the métro a stop early at Esplanade-de-la-Défense, and walk along Esplanade de Général de Gaulle.

Shops

PASCAL LE GLACIER

17 rue Bois-le-Vent Ⓜ Muette. Tues–Sat 10.30am–7pm; closed Aug. MAP P.159, POCKET MAP A8

Exquisite home-made sorbets – as well as delicious ice creams – made with Evian water and fresh fruits, in more than fifty seasonal flavours, such as sanguino orange, mango, white peach, raspberry, pear, and even rhubarb.

RECIPROQUE

89, 92, 93–97, 101 rue de la Pompe Ⓜ Pompe. Ⓦ reciproque.fr. Tues–Sat 11am–7pm. MAP P.159, POCKET MAP A7

Specialists in secondhand haute couture, with labels such as Christian Lacroix, Moschino and Manolo Blahnik. Women's design at nos. 93–95 and 101; suits, coats and accessories for men at no. 92; gifts and jewellery at no. 89.

Restaurants

HUGO DESNOYER

28 rue du Dr-Blanche Ⓜ Jasmin. Ⓣ 01 46 47 83 00, Ⓦ hugodesnoyer.com. Shop Tues–Sat 8.30am–7.30pm; food served 11am–3pm. MAP P.159, POCKET MAP A8

A carnivore's dream: a few tables in one of Paris's best butcher's shops where you can dine on the finest cuts, mainly veal and beef, prepared simply and to perfection. It's not cheap, though – reckon on around €65 a head.

LE RELAIS DU PARC

59 av Raymond Poincaré Ⓜ Victor Hugo. Ⓣ 01 44 05 66 10. Mon–Fri noon–2.30pm & 7–10.30pm, Sun brunch 12.30–3pm. MAP P.159, POCKET MAP A6

As you might expect from a chef who formerly worked at *Guy Savoy*, Stéphane Duchiron's cuisine is refined and sophisticated; starters might include courgette stuffed with rock fish, chickpeas and aubergine puree, mains perfectly cooked roast lamb or hake en croûte, and desserts a crispy millefeuille. In the summer, meals are served outdoors in a lovely garden. Lunch *menu* from €29, dinner tasting menu €72, à la carte mains around €30.

LA TABLE LAURISTON

129 rue Lauriston Ⓜ Trocadéro. Ⓣ 01 47 27 00 07, Ⓦ latablelauriston.com. Mon–Fri noon–2.30pm & 7.30–10.30pm; closed Aug. MAP P.159, POCKET MAP A7

The staid, well-heeled crowd in this relaxed neighbourhood restaurant enjoy well-executed *cuisine bourgeoise*: Burgundy snails, Basque octopus salad and Chateaubriand with morels are typical. You'll easily spend €50–60 per person.

RECIPROQUE

Day-trips

Even if you're on a weekend break, one or two major sights may tempt you beyond the city limits. It's worth making an effort to get out to the château de Versailles, the ultimate French royal palace, awesome in its size and magnificence, and boasting exquisite gardens that are free to visit. Also enchanting is the château of Chantilly, with its gorgeous setting and wonderful art collection, while a trip to Monet's beautiful gardens at Giverny is equally enticing.

VERSAILLES

Twenty kilometres southwest of Paris, the royal town of Versailles is renowned for Louis XIV's extraordinary **Château de Versailles**. With 700 rooms, 67 staircases and 352 fireplaces alone, Versailles is, without doubt, the apotheosis of French regal indulgence. It's not advisable, or indeed possible, to see the whole behemoth in one day – if you can, avoid the unbearable morning crowds by heading for the grounds and Marie Antoinette's estate first, moving on to the palace proper in the relative peace of late afternoon.

THE PETIT TRIANON GARDENS AT VERSAILLES

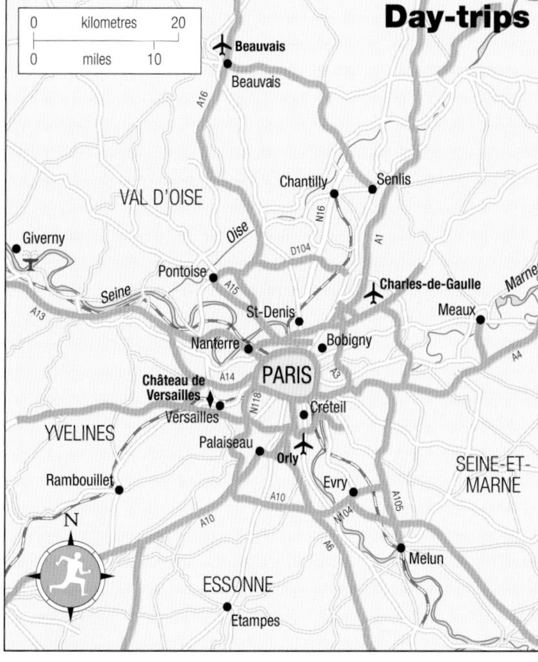

Versailles practicalities

To **get to Versailles**, take the RER line C5 from Champs de Mars or another Left Bank station to Versailles-Rive Gauche; it's a thirty-minute journey, and the palace is less than ten minutes' walk from the station.

Tickets for the **château** cost €15, including audioguide, while admission to Marie-Antoinette's estate is €10. Queues can be nightmarish, so by far the best option is to buy the one-day **Passeport Versailles** at www.chateauversailles.fr (€18, or €25 during the Grandes Eaux Musicales fountain show, ie April–Oct Sat and Sun) in advance. It's available online (print at home) from branches of Fnac (see p.79), in the tourist office at Versailles (on the way to the palace), and, in Paris, at the Carrousel du Louvre (see p.191). You can also buy the Passeport at the château itself up until 3pm on the day, though this of course means queuing with everyone else. Ticket-holders walk straight in through the gate marked "A".

Guided tours (Tues–Sun 9am–5pm; prices vary), many of which are expertly conducted in English, take you into some of the wings and private apartments that you don't otherwise get to see. You can book online or just turn up on the day, but arrive early to guarantee a place; they're well worth it. The more specialized 90min "themed tours" have to be booked by phone (01 30 83 78 00); they focus on subjects such as music and women, and are usually in French.

CHATEAU DE VERSAILLES PARK

CHATEAU DE VERSAILLES

01 30 83 78 00, chateauversailles.fr. April–Sept Tues–Sun 9am–6.30pm; Oct–March Tues–Sun 9am–5.30pm

Driven by envy of his finance minister's château at Vaux-le-Vicomte, the young Louis XIV recruited the same design team – architect Le Vau, painter Le Brun and gardener Le Nôtre – to create a **palace** a hundred times bigger. Construction began in 1664 and lasted virtually until Louis XIV's death in 1715. Second only to God, and the head of an immensely powerful state, Louis was an institution rather than a private individual. His risings and sittings, comings and goings, were minutely regulated and rigidly encased in ceremony, attendance at which was an honour much sought after by courtiers. Versailles was the headquarters of every arm of the state, and the entire court of around 3500 nobles lived in the palace (in a state of squalor, according to contemporary accounts).

Following the king's death, the château was abandoned for a few years before being reoccupied by Louis XV in 1722. It remained a residence of the royal family until the Revolution of 1789, when the furniture was sold and the pictures dispatched to the Louvre. Thereafter, Versailles fell into ruin until Louis-Philippe established his giant museum of French Glory here – it still exists, though most is mothballed. In 1871, during the Paris Commune, the château became the seat of the nationalist government, and the French parliament continued to meet in Louis XV's opera building until 1879.

Without a guide you can visit the **State Apartments**, used for the king's official business. A procession of gilded drawing rooms leads to the dazzling **Galerie des Glaces** (Hall of Mirrors), where the Treaty of Versailles was signed after World War I. More fabulously rich rooms, this time belonging to the **queen's apartments**, line the northern wing, beginning with the queen's bedchamber, which has been restored exactly as it was in its last refit of 1787, with hardly a surface unadorned with gold leaf or pretty floral decoration.

THE DOMAINE DE MARIE-ANTOINETTE

Daily: April–Oct Tues–Sun noon–6.30pm; Nov–March noon–5.30pm

Hidden away in the northern reaches of the park is the Domaine de Marie-Antoinette, the young queen's country retreat, where she found relief from the stifling etiquette of the court. Here she commissioned some dozen or so buildings, sparing no expense and imposing her own style and tastes throughout (and gaining herself a reputation for extravagance that did her no favours).

The centrepiece is the elegant Neoclassical **Petit Trianon** palace, built by Gabriel in the 1760s for Louis XV's mistress, Mme de Pompadour, and given to Marie-Antoinette by her husband Louis XVI as a wedding gift. The airy, sunlit interior provides a lovely contrast to the stuffy pomp of the Versailles palace proper, and boasts an intriguing *cabinet des glaces montantes*, a pale-blue salon fitted with sliding mirrors that could be moved to conceal the windows, creating a more intimate space. West of the palace, in the formal Jardin français, is the Queen's Theatre where Marie-Antoinette would regularly perform, often as a maid or shepherdess, before the king and members of her inner circle.

On the other side of the palace lies the bucolic **Jardin anglais**, with its little winding stream, grassy banks and artificial grotto, and the enchanting, if bizarre, **Hameau de la Reine**, an olde-worlde play village and farm (now restocked with real animals) where the queen indulged her fashionable Rousseau-inspired fantasy of returning to the "natural" life.

The Italianate **Grand Trianon** palace, designed by Hardouin-Mansart in 1687 as a country retreat for Louis XIV, was refurbished in Empire style by Napoleon, who stayed here intermittently between 1805 and 1813.

VERSAILLES PARK & GARDEN

April–Oct 7am–8.30pm; Nov–March 8am–6pm

You could spend a whole day exploring the lovely **park** (free, except when *spectacles* are on), with its symmetrical gardens, grand vistas, statuary, fountains and pools; trails of varying length are detailed on notice boards. Take a picnic, or stop at one of the tearooms, cafés or more formal restaurants dotted around the grounds. Baroque music is played in the garden (Tues spring & summer; €8), and on weekends the fountains dance to the music (€9; ⓦ chateauversailles-spectacles.fr).

Distances in the park are considerable. A *petit train* shuttles between the terrace in front of the château and the Trianons (€3.75; every 15min–1hr). You could also rent a buggy (driving licence needed), a bike or a rowing boat.

THE MARBLE COURT AT THE CHATEAU DE VERSAILLES

CHANTILLY

People mostly visit **Chantilly**, a small town 40km north of Paris, to watch horses race and to see Italian art in the romantic château. The horses are hard to miss: scores of thoroughbreds can be seen thundering along the forest rides of a morning, and two of the season's classiest flat races are held here – the Jockey Club and the Prix de Diane.

CHATEAU DE CHANTILLY

03 44 27 31 80, domainedechantilly.com. Daily except Tues: château April–Oct 10am–6pm (grounds 8pm); Nov–March 10.30am–5pm (grounds 6pm). Château, grounds, horse museum & horse show €17; grounds only €8; various other tickets available (see website)

Dating mostly from the late nineteenth century, the Château de Chantilly replaced a palace destroyed in the Revolution, which had been built for the Grand Condé, Louis XIV's famous general. It's a beautiful structure, surrounded by what's more a lake than a moat, looking out over formal gardens. Inside, in the **Musée Condé**, is a superb collection of Classical art, featuring works by Botticelli, Piero di Cosimo, Raphael, Delacroix, Poussin and Van Dyck.

Don't miss the **Cabinet des Livres**, which displays a perfect facsimile of the fabulous *Les Très Riches Heures du Duc de Berry*, the most celebrated of all the medieval Books of Hours, and the museum's single greatest treasure. The illuminated pages illustrating the months of the year with representative scenes from contemporary (early 1400s) rural life – such as harvesting and ploughing – are richly coloured and drawn.

You can also visit the **private apartments** of the Princes de Condé, with their superb furnishings and exquisite wood panelling, and take a separate guided tour (€3) of the apartments of the Petit Château, which belonged to the château's last private owners, the Duc and Duchess d'Aumale.

Just down the drive from the château is the colossal eighteenth-century stable block (Grandes Ecuries), housing the **Musée du Cheval**, which boasts fifteen rooms and more than two hundred objects and artworks devoted to the horse and its history. Check the website for the regular equestrian shows.

Trains run from the Gare du Nord to Chantilly every hour or so (25min). There are free

CHATEAU DE CHANTILLY

MONET'S GARDENS AT GIVERNY

buses to the town centre (line #15) from Chantilly station; get off by the Grandes Ecuries and walk 500m to the château gates. Alternatively, it's a 30min walk along a signposted path; turn right outside the station, then left along the avenue des Aigles.

MONET'S GARDENS AT GIVERNY

84 rue Claude Monet ⓣ 02 32 51 28 21, ⓦ fondation-monet.com. April–Oct daily 9.30am–6pm. €9.50

Claude Monet's gardens are in **Giverny**, Normandy – 65km from Paris, but well worth the trip. Monet lived in Giverny from 1883 till his death in 1926, painting and repainting the effects of the changing seasonal light on the gardens he laid out between his house and the river. Every month from spring to autumn has its own appeal, but May and June, when the rhododendrons flower round the lily pond and the wisteria bursts into colour over the famous Japanese bridge, are the prettiest months to visit.

Monet's house stands at the top of the gardens, an idyllic pastel-pink building with green shutters. Inside, the rooms are all painted different colours, exactly as they were when Monet lived here, and the painter's original collection of Japanese prints, including wonderful works by Hokusai and Hiroshige, still hangs on the walls.

Trains run to Vernon from Paris-St-Lazare (4–5 daily; 45min), from where there's a bus to Giverny (check website for times), or take a taxi or walk (1hr).

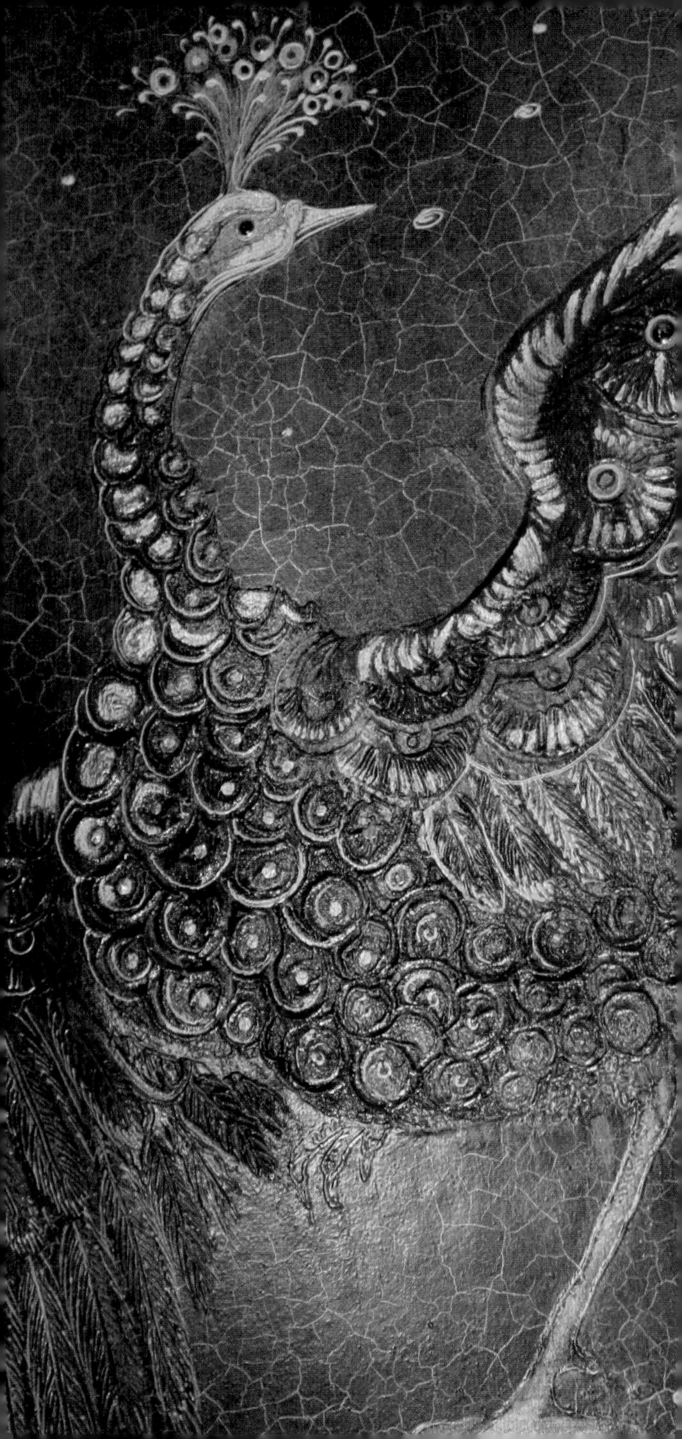

ACCOMMODATION

Hotels

Paris is extremely well supplied with hotels. The ones reviewed here are all classics, places that offer something special – a great location, unusually elegant decor or a warm welcome. The grandest establishments are mostly found in the Champs-Elysées area, while the trendy Marais quarter is a good bet for something elegant but relatively relaxed. You'll find more homely, old-fashioned hotels around the Quartier Latin, St-Germain and the Eiffel Tower quarter.

Most hotels offer two categories of room: at the bottom end of the scale this means choosing between an en-suite bathroom or shared facilities, while more expensive places may charge a premium rate for larger or more luxurious rooms. Prices aren't exorbitant, by European standards, but then rooms can be surprisingly small for the money. Many hotels offer lower rates than those publicly advertised; the reviews below show the lowest rate you're likely to get for a double room. Continental breakfast is normally an extra €6 to €12 per person.

The Islands

HOTEL DU JEU DE PAUME > **54 rue St-Louis-en-l'Ile Ⓜ Pont-Marie. Ⓣ 01 43 26 14 26, Ⓦ jeudepaumehotel.com.** MAP PP.36–37, POCKET MAP F17. This quiet, charming boutique hotel occupies the site of a tennis court built for Louis XIII in 1634 ("jeu de paume" is "real tennis"). The wood-beam court is now a breakfast room, from which a glass lift whisks you up to the 28 rooms, decorated in contemporary style. **€295**

HOTEL DE LUTECE > **65 rue St-Louis-en-l'Ile Ⓜ Pont-Mairie. Ⓣ 01 43 26 23 52, Ⓦ paris-hotel-lutece.com.** MAP PP.36–37, POCKET MAP E17. This slender seventeenth-century townhouse, located on the most desirable island in France, has a cosy old-world charm and is run by helpful and friendly staff. The rooms are small, but comfy and characterful, with wood beams and fresh contemporary decor in shades of terracotta and cream. **€127**

Booking accommodation

It's wise to reserve your accommodation as early as possible. All receptionists speak some English – but it's worth bearing in mind that more and more places offer online booking as well. If you book by phone you may be asked for just a credit card number, or sometimes for written or faxed confirmation. The tourist office can make bookings for you for free – either in person at one of their offices (see p.191 for addresses) or online at Ⓦ www.parisinfo.com; many hotels on the site offer discounted rates.

The Champs-Elysées and Tuileries

HOTEL D'ALBION > 15 rue de Penthièvre Ⓜ Miromesnil. Ⓣ 01 42 65 84 15, Ⓦ hotelalbion .net. MAP PP.46–47, POCKET MAP E5. This small, family-run hotel occupies a nineteenth-century townhouse set around a quiet courtyard garden. Just a 10min walk from the Champs-Elysées, it represents excellent value for the area. Most of the vibrantly decorated rooms have a view over the garden. **€95**

HOTEL LE BRISTOL > 112 rue du Faubourg St-Honoré Ⓜ Miromesnil. Ⓣ 01 53 43 43 00, Ⓦ lebristolparis .com. MAP PP.46–47, POCKET MAP D5. This is among the city's most luxurious hotels, and yet it manages to retain a discreet and warm ambience. Gobelins tapestries adorn the walls and some rooms have private roof gardens. A sumptuously designed new wing has been added of late, and there's also a garden, swimming pool, health club and gourmet restaurant to enjoy. **€850**

HOTEL LANCASTER > 7 rue de Berri Ⓜ George V. Ⓣ 01 40 76 40 76, Ⓦ hotel-lancaster.com. MAP PP.46–47, POCKET MAP C5. Once the *pied-à-terre* for old-world celebs such as Greta Garbo and Marlene Dietrich, this elegantly restored nineteenth-century townhouse is still a favourite hideout for those fleeing the paparazzi. Rooms retain original features and are resplendent with Louis XVI and Rococo antiques, but with a touch of contemporary chic thrown in too. There's also a superlative restaurant and zen-style interior garden. **€350**

HOTEL LE LAVOISIER > 21 rue Lavoisier Ⓜ St Augustin. Ⓣ 01 53 30 06 06, Ⓦ hotellavoisier .com. MAP PP.46–47, POCKET MAP E5. A stylish boutique hotel in a Haussmann-era townhouse, on a quiet side-street around 15min walk from the Champs-Elysées. The good-sized rooms have painted wooden floors and high ceilings and are charmingly decorated. Wi-fi access costs €5 per device per stay. **€144**

HOTEL DE LA TREMOILLE > 14 rue de la Trémoille Ⓜ Alma-Marceau. Ⓣ 01 56 52 14 00, Ⓦ tremoille.com. MAP PP.46–47, POCKET MAP C6. A swanky five-star boasting understated rooms with harmonious decor and shimmering black-and-white bathrooms; room service is delivered through a specially designed hatch to avoid disturbing guests. There's also a spa and gym. **€325**

Eiffel Tower area

HOTEL DU CHAMPS-DE-MARS > 7 rue du Champs-de-Mars Ⓜ École-Militaire. Ⓣ 01 45 51 52 30, Ⓦ hotelduchampdemars.com. MAP PP.54–55, POCKET MAP C8. A well-run hotel with cosy, colourful and excellent-value rooms. The location – a nice neighbourhood lying just off the lively rue Cler market – is terrific. There's free wi-fi too. **€155**

HOTEL DU PALAIS BOURBON > 49 rue de Bourgogne Ⓜ Varenne. Ⓣ 01 44 11 30 70, Ⓦ bourbon-paris-hotel .com. MAP PP.54–55, POCKET MAP E8. This handsome old building on a quiet street in the hushed, posh district near the Musée Rodin offers spacious, prettily furnished rooms, with plenty of period detail. Homely family rooms (€230) are also available. Breakfast is included in the price. **€187**

The Grands Boulevards and *passages*

HOTEL BRIGHTON > 218 rue de Rivoli Ⓜ Tuileries. Ⓣ 01 47 03 61 61, Ⓦ paris-hotel-brighton.com. MAP PP.66–67, POCKET MAP A14. An elegant hotel dating back to the late nineteenth century. The "classic" rooms with internal views are fine, but the "superior" rooms are far preferable, particularly those that offer magnificent views down over the Tuileries gardens. **€249**

HOTEL CHOPIN > 46 passage Jouffroy, entrance on bd Montmartre, near rue du Faubourg-Montmartre Ⓜ Grands-Boulevards. Ⓣ 01 47 70 58 10, Ⓦ hotelchopin-paris-opera.com. MAP PP.66–67, POCKET MAP G5. A charming, quiet hotel set in an atmospheric period building hidden away at the end of a picturesque 1850s *passage*. Rooms are pleasantly furnished, though the cheaper ones are on the small side and a little dark. **€75**

HOTEL CRAYON > 25 rue de Bouloi Ⓜ Louvre-Rivoli. Ⓣ 01 42 36 54 19, Ⓦ hotelcrayon.com. MAP PP.66–67, POCKET MAP C14. Colourful, artist-owned hotel with a guesthouse feel. The 26 small, funky rooms are all different, with vibrant colour-blocking, and are scattered with mismatched vintage and retro furniture. Check online for deals. *Hôtel Crayon Rouge*, 150m away at 42 rue Croix des Petits Champs, is similar. **€186**

HOTEL MANSART > 5 rue des Capucines Ⓜ Opéra/Madeleine. Ⓣ 01 42 61 50 28, Ⓦ paris-hotel-mansart.com. MAP PP.66–67, POCKET MAP A13. This gracious hotel is just a stone's throw from the *Ritz*, but offers rooms that are a fraction of the price; and while they're not quite in the luxury bracket they're very agreeably decorated in Louis XIV style. It's worth asking to see a few rooms, as three in the standard class have balconies and some have huge bathrooms. The more expensive rooms look out onto place Vendôme. **€225**

RELAIS ST HONORE > 308 rue St-Honoré Ⓜ Tuileries. Ⓣ 01 42 96 06 06, Ⓦ hotel-relais-saint-honore.com. MAP PP.66–67, POCKET MAP B14. A snug little hotel run by friendly and obliging staff, and set in a stylishly renovated seventeenth-century townhouse. The pretty wood-beamed rooms are done out in warm colours and rich fabrics. Some have mezzanine areas and there's a suite suitable for families. **€240**

HOTEL THERESE > 5–7 rue Thérèse Ⓜ Palais Royal-Musée du Louvre. Ⓣ 01 42 96 10 01, Ⓦ hoteltherese.com. MAP PP.66–67, POCKET MAP B14. A very attractive boutique hotel, on a quiet street within easy walking distance of the Louvre, offering more expensive "traditional" rooms, pared-down and stylish with dark wood fittings, and "classic" rooms, smaller but good value. Book in advance as it's very popular. **€200**

HOTEL VIVIENNE > 40 rue Vivienne Ⓜ Grands-Boulevards/Bourse. Ⓣ 01 42 33 13 26, Ⓦ hotel-vivienne.com. MAP PP.66–67, POCKET MAP G6. Ideally located for the Opéra Garnier and the Grands Boulevards, this is a friendly place, with good-sized rooms done up in nice woods and prints. The cheaper doubles have shower only and shared toilet. **€90**

Beaubourg and Les Halles

RELAIS DU LOUVRE > 19 rue des Prêtres St-Germain l'Auxerrois Ⓜ Palais Royal-Musée du Louvre. Ⓣ 01 40 41 96 42, Ⓦ relaisdulouvre.com. MAP P.78, POCKET MAP C15. This discreet hotel is set on a quiet backstreet opposite the church of St-Germain l'Auxerrois. The decor is traditional, with rich fabrics, Turkish rugs and reassuringly solid furniture. The hotel's relaxed atmosphere and charming service attract a clientele who come back every year. **€128**

The Marais

HOTEL DU BOURG TIBOURG > 19 rue du Bourg-Tibourg Ⓜ Hôtel-de-Ville. Ⓣ 01 42 78 47 39, Ⓦ bourgtibourg.com. MAP PP.84–85, POCKET MAP F16. Oriental meets medieval, with a dash of Second Empire, at this sumptuously designed, and perennially fashionable, boutique hotel. Tiny rooms are packed with rich velvets, silks and drapes. The hotel would make a perfect romantic hideaway. **€261**

HOTEL DE LA BRETONNERIE > 22 rue Ste-Croix de la Bretonnerie Ⓜ Hôtel-de-Ville. Ⓣ 01 48 87 77 63, Ⓦ hotelparismaraisbretonnerie.com. MAP PP.84–85, POCKET MAP F16. A charming place on a lively Marais street; the rooms are decorated with quality fabrics, oak furniture, and, in some cases, four-poster beds. The beamed attic rooms on the fourth floor are particularly appealing. Front-facing rooms may suffer from street noise at night. **€129**

HOTEL CARON DE BEAUMARCHAIS > 12 rue Vieille-du-Temple Ⓜ Hôtel-de-Ville. Ⓣ 01 42 72 34 12, Ⓦ carondebeaumarchais.com. MAP PP.84–85, POCKET MAP F16. Named after the eighteenth-century French playwright Beaumarchais, this pretty hotel has only nineteen rooms. Everything – down to the original engravings and Louis XVI-style furniture, not to mention the pianoforte in the foyer – evokes the refined tastes of high-society pre-Revolutionary Paris. Rooms overlooking the courtyard are small but cosy while those on the street are more spacious, some with balconies, others with chandeliers. **€115**

HOTEL JULES ET JIM > 11 rue des Gravilliers Ⓜ Arts-et-Métiers. Ⓣ 01 44 54 13 13, Ⓦ hoteljulesetjim.com. MAP PP.84–85, POCKET MAP F14. Very cool, contemporary hotel, with lots of hip design features – check out the reception desk made of books – and 23 quiet, swish rooms. There's a good bar opening onto the cobbled courtyard (it closes at 11pm to avoid disturbing guests in courtyard rooms), and really welcoming staff. **€240**

HOTEL DE NICE > 42 bis rue de Rivoli Ⓜ Hôtel-de-Ville. Ⓣ 01 42 78 55 29, Ⓦ hoteldenice.com. MAP PP.84–85, POCKET MAP F16. A delightful old-world charm pervades this six-storey establishment, its pretty rooms hung with old prints and furnished with deep-coloured fabrics. Double-glazing helps to block out the traffic on rue de Rivoli. **€100**

HOTEL PAVILLON DE LA REINE > 28 pl des Vosges Ⓜ Bastille. Ⓣ 01 40 29 19 19, Ⓦ pavillon-de-la-reine.com. MAP PP.84–85, POCKET MAP G16. A perfect honeymoon hideaway in a beautiful ivy-covered mansion off the adorable place des Vosges, it preserves an intimate ambience, with friendly, personable staff. **€297**

HOTEL DU PETIT MOULIN > 29–31 rue du Poitou Ⓜ St-Sébastien-Froissart/Filles-du-Calvaire. Ⓣ 01 42 74 10 10, Ⓦ hotelpetitmoulinparis.com. MAP PP.84–85, POCKET MAP G15. This glamorous boutique hotel is set in an old bakery and was designed top to bottom by Christian Lacroix. The designer's *joie de vivre* reigns in the seventeen rooms, with a fusion of styles from elegant Baroque to Sixties kitsch: pinks and lime greens vie with *toile de Jouy* prints, and pod chairs sit by antique dressing tables. **€198**

HOTEL DE LA PLACE DES VOSGES > 12 rue de Birague Ⓜ Bastille. Ⓣ 01 42 72 60 46, Ⓦ hotelplacedesvosges.com. MAP PP.84–85, POCKET MAP G17. A charming, well-priced hotel in a glorious building, dating back to 1605, very near the beautiful place des Vosges. Rooms are contemporary in style, and small, but some have wooden floors, stone walls and wooden beams. **€90**

HOTEL ST-LOUIS MARAIS > 1 rue Charles-V Ⓜ Sully-Morland. Ⓣ 01 48 87 87 04, Ⓦ saintlouismarais.com. MAP PP.84–85, POCKET MAP G17. Originally forming part of the seventeenth-century Célestins convent, this characterful, quiet place retains its period feel, with stone walls, exposed beams and tiled floors. The standard rooms have private showers, while superior ones have bathtubs; all have flat-screen TVs. The cheaper doubles are very small. **€175**

Bastille

MAMA SHELTER > 109 rue de Bagnolet Ⓜ Alexandre-Dumas. Ⓣ 01 43 48 48 48, Ⓦ mamashelter.com. MAP P.98, POCKET MAP C21. The endless focus on hip and cool branding – "Mama says" this, "Mama says" that – can be a bit wearing, but the youthful *Mama Shelter*, owned by Club Med founders and designed by Philippe Starck, actually offers surprisingly good rates and can be a lot of fun. Free in-room movies and iMacs are standard, while a bar-restaurant (live music at weekends), sun terrace and top-notch service complete the package. €89

HOTEL MARAIS BASTILLE > 36 bd Richard-Lenoir Ⓜ Bréguet-Sabin/Bastille. Ⓣ 01 48 05 75 00, Ⓦ maraisbastille.com. MAP P.98, POCKET MAP H16. Part of the Best Western chain, this 37-room hotel has a swish, contemporary interior. The public spaces are a bit overdesigned, but the rooms, while small, are comfy and clean, done out in soothing hues with splashes of paintbox-bright colour and modern bathrooms. €169

HOTEL DE LA PORTE DOREE > 273 av Daumesnil Ⓜ Porte-Dorée. Ⓣ 01 43 07 56 97, Ⓦ hoteldelaportedoree.com. MAP P.98, POCKET MAP M11. A welcoming, family-friendly hotel tastefully refurbished by an American–French family. Preserves period features such as ceiling mouldings and fireplaces, and many of the furnishings are antique, but all rooms have private shower or bath, TV and comfy beds. €132

The Quartier Latin

HOTEL DU COMMERCE > 14 rue de la Montagne-Ste-Geneviève Ⓜ Maubert-Mutualité. Ⓣ 01 43 54 89 69, Ⓦ commerceparishotelcom. MAP PP.106–107, POCKET MAP D18. This budget hotel is good value if you want to stay very centrally yet without breaking the bank. While some of the rooms are small and occasionally noisy, all are very clean and the beds are comfy. Prices range from washbasin-only cheapies to simple en-suites. No credit cards. €68

LES DEGRES DE NOTRE DAME > 10 rue des Grands Degrés Ⓜ St-Michel/Maubert-Mutualité. Ⓣ 01 55 42 88 88, Ⓦ www.lesdegreshotel.com. MAP PP.106–107, POCKET MAP E17. This charming, superbly idiosyncratic hotel has just ten rooms. The building is ancient and the rooms all very different, with prices corresponding to size. Unique, personal touches are everywhere: hand-painted murals, antique mirrors and curious nooks. Perhaps the loveliest room of all is under the roof, with its own stairs. Breakfast included. €98

ESMERALDA > 4 rue St-Julien-le-Pauvre Ⓜ St-Michel/Maubert-Mutualité. Ⓣ 01 43 54 19 20, Ⓦ hotel-esmeralda.fr. MAP PP.106–107, POCKET MAP D17. Dozing in an ancient house on square Viviani, this rickety old hotel offers a deeply old-fashioned feel, with cosily unmodernized en-suite rooms done up in worn red velvet or faded florals. A few rooms have superb views of Notre-Dame. €125

FAMILIA HOTEL > 11 rue des Ecoles Ⓜ Cardinal-Lemoine/Maubert-Mutualité/Jussieu. Ⓣ 01 43 54 55 27, Ⓦ familiahotel.com. MAP PP.106–107, POCKET MAP E18. Friendly, family-run hotel in the heart of the *quartier*. Rooms are small but attractive, with beams and *toile de Jouy* wallpaper; some have views of Notre-Dame, others have balconies. €80

HOTEL DES GRANDES ECOLES > 75 rue du Cardinal-Lemoine Ⓜ Cardinal-Lemoine. Ⓣ 01 43 26 79 23, Ⓦ hotel-grandes-ecoles.com. MAP PP.106–107, POCKET MAP E19. Follow the cobbled alleyway to a large, peaceful garden and this tranquil hotel, with its pretty, old-fashioned rooms. Reservations are taken three months in advance, on the 15th of the month; don't be even a day late. €135

HOTEL MARIGNAN > 13 rue du Sommerard Ⓜ Maubert-Mutualité.

01 43 54 63 81, hotel-marignan.com. MAP PP.106–107, POCKET MAP D18. Great-value place, totally sympathetic to the needs of rucksack-toting foreigners, with free wi-fi, laundry, ironing and kitchen facilities, a library of guidebooks – and rooms for up to five people. The cheapest share bathrooms with one other room. **€91**

HOTEL RESIDENCE HENRI IV > 50 rue des Bernardins Maubert-Mutualité. 01 44 41 31 81, residencehenri4.com. MAP PP.106–107, POCKET MAP E18. Set back from the busy rue des Ecoles on a cul-de-sac, this hotel is discreet and elegant, featuring classically styled rooms. Some have period features like fireplaces, and all have miniature kitchenettes. **€120**

SELECT HOTEL > 51 place de la Sorbonne Cluny-Sorbonne. 01 46 34 14 80, selecthotel.fr. MAP PP.106–107, POCKET MAP C18. Situated right on the *place*, this hotel has had the full designer makeover, with exposed stone walls, leather and recessed wood trim much in evidence. **€125**

St-Germain

HOTEL DU DANUBE > 58 rue Jacob St-Germain-des-Prés. 01 42 60 34 70, hoteldanube .fr. MAP PP.116–117, POCKET MAP B16. An elegant, very friendly hotel set right in the heart of St-Germain. The standard rooms are small and attractively decorated, but the *supérieures* are the ones to go for: unusually large, each with a pair of handsome, tall windows. It's very popular, so be sure to book well in advance. **€180**

GRAND HOTEL DES BALCONS > 3 rue Casimir-Delavigne Odéon. 01 46 34 78 50, www.balcons.com. MAP PP.116–117, POCKET MAP C18. Although it has been somewhat modernized, this appealing, comfortable hotel has retained a few Art Deco motifs in its rooms. It's fair value, and in a lovely location near the Odéon and Luxembourg gardens. Other than those on the fifth floor, the balconies in question are small, decorative affairs. **€98**

HOTEL DES MARRONNIERS > 21 rue Jacob St-Germain-des-Prés. 01 43 25 30 60, hotel-marronniers.com. MAP PP.116–117, POCKET MAP B16. A charming, old-fashioned hotel, with tiny rooms swathed in deep velvet curtains and expensive fabric wall-coverings. The breakfast room gives onto a pleasant pebbled courtyard garden. **€195**

HOTEL MICHELET-ODEON > 6 place de l'Odéon Odéon. 01 53 10 05 60, hotelmicheletodeon.com. MAP PP.116–117, POCKET MAP C18. A bargain for a hotel so close to the Jardin du Luxembourg. Rooms are clean, quiet and unusually attractive (especially those facing onto the *place*) and some are unusually large for the price. **€100**

HOTEL DE NESLE > 7 rue de Nesle St-Michel. 01 43 54 62 41, hoteldenesleparis.com. MAP PP.116–117, POCKET MAP C16. Eccentric and sometimes chaotic hotel whose rooms are decorated with cartoon historical murals that you'll either love or hate. Rooms are tiny, but inexpensive for the amazingly central location. **€85**

RELAIS CHRISTINE > 3 rue Christine Odéon/St Michel. 01 40 51 60 80, relais-christine.com. MAP PP.116–117, POCKET MAP C17. Deeply elegant, romantic four-star in a sixteenth-century former convent set around a deliciously hidden courtyard. It's well worth paying the 20 percent premium for one of the *supérieure* rooms. **€425**

RELAIS SAINT-SULPICE > 3 rue Garancière St-Sulpice/St-Germain-des-Prés. 01 46 33 99 00, relais-saint-sulpice.com. MAP PP.116–117, POCKET MAP B18. Set in an aristocratic townhouse immediately behind St-Sulpice's apse, this is a discreetly classy small hotel with well-furnished rooms painted in cheerful Provençal colours. The sauna is a nice touch. **€183**

HOTEL DE L'UNIVERSITE > 22 rue de l'Universite Ⓜ Rue-du-Bac. Ⓣ 01 42 61 09 39, Ⓦ hoteluniversite.com. MAP PP.116–117, POCKET MAP A16. Cosy, quiet boutique three-star with antique details, including beamed ceilings and fireplaces in the larger, slightly pricier rooms. **€205**

Montparnasse and southern Paris

HOTEL DELAMBRE > 35 rue Delambre Ⓜ Edgar-Quinet. Ⓣ 01 43 20 66 31, Ⓦ delambre-paris-hotel.com. MAP P.126, POCKET MAP F11. Beyond the appealing turquoise and gold exterior you'll find the odd colourful flourish in this reliable choice on the northern edge of Montparnasse towards St-Germain. Above all, though, the *Delambre* stands out for its friendly service and spotless, comfortable en-suite rooms, some of which have little balconies. **€89**

LA MANUFACTURE > 8 rue Philippe de Champagne Ⓜ Place d'Italie. Ⓣ 01 45 35 45 25, Ⓦ hotel-la-manufacture.com. MAP P.129, POCKET MAP J12. Even the smallest rooms of the sixty-odd choices at this comfortable, welcoming hotel are attractive, trimmed in bright colours, with wood flooring; some have large bathrooms, some have balconies, and others look onto the handsome *mairie*. **€95**

HOTEL MISTRAL > 24 rue de Cels Ⓜ Pernety/Alésia. Ⓣ 01 43 20 25 43, Ⓦ hotel-mistral-paris.com. MAP P.126, POCKET MAP E12. Welcoming, cosy and pleasantly refurbished hotel on a very quiet street, with a little courtyard garden, where breakfast is served in warmer weather. **143**

HOTEL PORT-ROYAL > 8 bd Port-Royal Ⓜ Gobelins. Ⓣ 01 43 31 70 06, Ⓦ port-royal-hotel.fr. MAP PP.130–131, POCKET MAP H12. A friendly, good-value one-star that has been in the same family since the 1930s. En-suite doubles, though small, are attractive and very clean (€95); those with shared bath are considerably cheaper. It's in a quiet, residential area at the rue Mouffetard end of the boulevard, near the métro and the Quartier Latin. No credit cards. **€68**

HOTEL PRINTEMPS > 31 rue du Commerce Ⓜ La Motte-Picquet-Grenelle/Émile-Zola. Ⓣ 01 45 79 83 36. MAP PP.130–131, POCKET MAP B10. The cheap furnishings, thin walls and ageing decor don't prevent this being a reasonable backpacker choice: benefits include its lively and safe neighbourhood location, cheery welcome and low prices. The nicer rooms have small balconies. **€50**

HOTEL TOLBIAC > 122 rue de Tolbiac Ⓜ Tolbiac/Place d'Italie. Ⓣ 01 44 24 25 54, Ⓦ hotel-tolbiac.com. MAP P.129, POCKET MAP K12. Situated on a noisy junction, this big, friendly budget hotel has a bright colour scheme, free internet and wi-fi, and good prices. Both en suites (from €75) and doubles with shared facilities are available. **€58**

SOLAR HOTEL > 22 rue Boulard Ⓜ Denfert-Rochereau. Ⓣ 01 43 21 08 20, Ⓦ solarhotel.fr. MAP P.126, POCKET MAP F12. Set on an old-fashioned Montparnasse street, this budget hotel has an original and friendly spirit – there are paintings by local artists on the walls, cultural events in the back garden and the hotel strives to be ecological, with low-energy fittings, organic breakfasts and free bike rental. Don't be put off by the exterior: rooms are basic, but comfortable and bright, with a/c, TV and free wi-fi. Breakfast included in the price. **€89**

Montmartre and northern Paris

HOTEL AMOUR > 8 rue Navarin Ⓜ Pigalle. Ⓣ 01 48 78 31 80, Ⓦ hotelamourparis.fr. MAP PP.136–137, POCKET MAP G4. This designer hotel is aimed squarely at an achingly cool clientele, with old parquet, new paintwork and a deliberately boho Pigalle porn theme. Every room is decorated differrently – one is all black with disco balls above the bed – but none has phone or TV, and all have iPod speakers. There's also a spacious dining area and a vodka bar. **€250**

HOTEL DES ARTS > 5 rue Tholozé Ⓜ Abbesses/Blanche. Ⓣ 01 46 06 30 52, Ⓦ arts-hotel-paris.com. MAP PP.136–137, POCKET MAP G3. Manages that rare combination of homeliness and efficiency, with courteous staff and a welcoming feel. Rooms are fairly small but well maintained, quiet and very comfortable, with dashes of colour and style – and the topmost "superior" ones have Eiffel Tower views. €95

HOTEL BONSEJOUR MONTMARTRE > 11 rue Burq Ⓜ Abbesses. Ⓣ 01 42 54 22 53, Ⓦ hotel-bonsejour-montmartre.fr. MAP PP.136–137, POCKET MAP G3. The location is a dream – on a quiet, untouristy street on the slopes of Montmartre, footsteps away from great neighbourhood bars and restaurants – and the simple, old-fashioned, clean rooms (with shower, WC down the hall) are a serious bargain. Ask for the corner rooms 23, 33, 43 or 53, which have balconies. €69

CAULAINCOURT SQUARE > 2 sq Caulaincourt, by 63 rue Caulaincourt Ⓜ Lamarck-Caulaincourt. Ⓣ 01 46 06 46 06, Ⓦ caulaincourt.com. MAP PP.136–137, POCKET MAP G2. Describing itself as a boutique hostel, the lively and friendly *Caulaincourt Square*, on the heights of Montmartre, offers both dorm rooms (from €27) and en-suite doubles (from €72). Rooms are small and faintly shabby but decent enough, and breakfast is free. €72

HOTEL ELDORADO > 18 rue des Dames Ⓜ Place de Clichy. Ⓣ 01 45 22 35 21, Ⓦ eldoradohotel.fr. MAP PP.136–137, POCKET MAP E3. Idiosyncratic hotel in the bohemian Batignolles village, with its own little restaurant and a flower-filled courtyard garden. The small rooms are worn in places, but charmingly decorated, with bright colours offsetting vintage furnishings and the old hotel fittings that are fast disappearing from Paris. The cheapest rooms have washbasin only and shared bathrooms. €60

HOTEL ERMITAGE > 24 rue Lamarck Ⓜ Anvers. Ⓣ 01 42 64 79 22, Ⓦ ermitagesacrecoeur.fr. MAP PP.136–137, POCKET MAP H3. One of the highest-altitude hotels in Paris, this discreet and charming family-run place has a deliciously old-fashioned feel, its rooms decorated with antique objets d'art and lots of florals. Just a stone's throw from the Sacre-Coeur, but it's best to approach via the Anvers metro and the *funiculaire* to avoid the steep climb. They also offer apartments. €135

HOTEL LANGLOIS > 63 rue St-Lazare Ⓜ Trinité. Ⓣ 01 48 74 78 24, Ⓦ hotel-langlois.com. MAP PP.136–137, POCKET MAP F5. Despite having all the facilities of a three-star, this genteel hotel has barely changed in the last century, with antique furnishings and some handsome rooms. €185

HOTEL LORETTE OPERA > 36 rue Notre-Dame de Lorette Ⓜ St-Georges. Ⓣ 01 42 85 18 81, Ⓦ astotel.com. MAP PP.136–137, POCKET MAP G4. With its handsome location by elegant place Georges, this welcoming hotel feels refreshingly unlike a chain, though it is part of the Astotel group and staff are very professional. The warm, moderately stylish rooms are all a good size. €107

Northeastern Paris

LE CITIZEN HOTEL > 96 quai de Jemmapes Ⓜ Jacques Bonsergent. Ⓣ 01 83 62 55 50, Ⓦ lecitizenhotel.com. MAP P.148, POCKET MAP K5. The *Citizen* is an ecofriendly design hotel with only twelve rooms. The Zen-style decor of light wood and pale tones makes for nice, airy rooms, all of which have windows overlooking the Canal St-Martin. The cheaper rooms are compact, the more expensive are twice as big. €219

COSMOS HOTEL > 35 rue Jean-Pierre Timbaud Ⓜ Parmentier. Ⓣ 01 43 57 25 88, Ⓦ cosmos-hotel-paris.com. MAP P.148, POCKET MAP H14. Contemporary budget hotel, excellently located for the bars and cafés of Oberkampf, offering clean, minimalist en-suite rooms. The styling is a little bland, the fittings occasionally a bit rough around the edges and the bathrooms are minuscule, but beds are super-comfortable and it's a welcoming base. The larger doubles (€82) are worth the extra for a longer stay. €72

HOTEL GABRIEL > 25 rue du Grand-Prieuré Ⓜ Oberkampf. Ⓣ 01 47 00 13 38, Ⓦ hotelgabrielparis.com. MAP P.148, POCKET MAP H14. Beyond the unremarkable exterior is an elegant and tranquil hotel that combines an old-fashioned feel with modern design. Rooms are tiny but swish, with lots of cool contemporary furnishings and good bathrooms. Breakfast is included and can be eaten in your room. **€119**

LE GENERAL HOTEL > 5–7 rue Rampon Ⓜ République. Ⓣ 01 47 00 41 57, Ⓦ legeneralhotel.com. MAP P.148, POCKET MAP G14. This cool boutique hotel, run by helpful staff, is a lesson in restrained modern design. The bright rooms have spotless bathrooms and rosewood furnishings. Facilities include a sauna and fitness centre, and the breakfast area turns into a bar in the evenings. **€150**

HOTEL DES METALLOS > 50 rue de la Folie Mericourt Ⓜ Oberkampf. Ⓣ 01 43 38 73 63, Ⓦ hoteldesmetallos.com. MAP P.148. POCKET MAP H14. While it might not quite live up to its description as a "design" hotel, the uncluttered, neutral decor of this modern, ecoconscious place has a certain simple appeal. There are excellent online discounts available too, making it very good value for the area. **€89**

HOTEL DU NORD > 47 rue Albert Thomas Ⓜ Jacques Bonsergent/ Republique. Ⓣ 01 42 01 92 10, Ⓦ hoteldunord-leparivelo.com. MAP P.148, POCKET MAP G13. A pretty ivy-strewn entrance leads into a cosy reception and 23 simple en-suite rooms. The cheaper ones look onto the courtyard and are smaller and darker. Ten bicyles are available for guests to use for free. **€86**

Hostels

Hostels are an obvious choice for a tight budget, but won't necessarily be cheaper than sharing a room in a budget hotel. Many take advance bookings, including the two main hostel groups: FUAJ (Ⓦ www.fuaj.fr), which is part of Hostelling International; and MIJE (Ⓦ www.mije.com), which runs three excellent hostels in historic buildings in the Marais. Independent hostels tend to be noisier places, often with bars attached.

D'ARTAGNAN > 80 rue Vitruve Ⓜ Porte de Bagnolet. Ⓣ 01 40 32 34 56, Ⓦ fuaj.org. MAP P.148, POCKET MAP C21. This colourful, modern HI hostel is the largest in France with 440 beds and facilities including a small cinema, restaurant and bar, internet access and a swimming pool nearby. Guests have to vacate the rooms between 11am and 3pm for cleaning. It's very popular, so get here early or book online or by phone on the central reservations number: Ⓣ 01 44 89 87 27. Doubles and rooms for three to five are a few euros more per head than the dorm price. **Dorm beds from €27.40**

BVJ LOUVRE > 20 rue Jean-Jacques-Rousseau Ⓜ Louvre/ Châtelet-Les-Halles. Ⓣ 01 53 00 90 90, Ⓦ bvjhotel.com. MAP PP.66–67, POCKET MAP C14. With 200 beds, the *BVJ Louvre* attracts an international studenty crowd, though dorms (sleeping eight) have a slightly institutional feel. Single rooms are available. **Dorm beds €30, twins €70**

BVJ PARIS QUARTIER LATIN > 44 rue des Bernardins Ⓜ Maubert-Mutualité. Ⓣ 01 43 29 34 80, Ⓦ bvjhotel.com. MAP PP.106–107, POCKET MAP E18. Spick-and-span hostel in a good location. Single rooms (€49) and dorm beds are good value; for double rooms (€70) you can do better elsewhere. **Dorm beds €30**

LE FAUCONNIER > 11 rue du Fauconnier Ⓜ St-Paul/Pont Marie. Ⓣ 01 42 74 23 45, Ⓦ mije.com. MAP PP.84–85, POCKET MAP F17. MIJE hostel in a superbly renovated seventeenth-century building. Dorms sleep three to eight, and there are some single (€55) and double rooms too (€82), with en-suite showers. **Dorm beds €33.50**

LE FOURCY > 6 rue de Fourcy Ⓜ St Paul. Ⓣ 01 42 74 23 45. MAP PP.84–85, POCKET MAP F17. Another excellent MIJE hostel (same prices and deal as *Le Fauconnier*, see above). Housed in a beautiful mansion, this place has a small garden and an inexpensive restaurant. Doubles and triples also available.

GENERATOR HOSTEL > 9–11 place du Colonel Fabien Ⓜ Colonel-Fabien. Ⓣ 01 70 98 84 00, Ⓦ generatorhostels.com. MAP P.148, POCKET MAP K4. New, well-run hostel right by the métro, with spotless dorms (four- to ten-bed, with one eight-bed women-only option) and private bathrooms. Facilities are excellent, with good bedding, lots of storage space, a friendly bar and a handy café. **Dorm beds €40.50**

JULES FERRY > 8 bd Jules-Ferry Ⓜ République. Ⓣ 01 43 57 55 60, Ⓦ fuaj.fr. MAP P.148, POCKET MAP H13. Fairly central HI hostel, in a lively area at the foot of the Belleville hill. Difficult to get a place, but they can help find a bed elsewhere. Two to four people in each room. **Dorm beds from €21**

MAUBUISSON > 12 rue des Barres Ⓜ Pont Marie/Hôtel de Ville. Ⓣ 01 42 74 23 45. MAP PP.84–85, POCKET MAP F16. A MIJE hostel in a magnificent medieval building on a quiet street. Shared use of the restaurant at *Le Fourcy* (see above). Dorms only, sleeping four. **Dorm beds €33.50**

OOPS > 50 ave des Gobelins Ⓜ Gobelins. Ⓣ 01 47 07 47 00, Ⓦ oops-paris.com. MAP P.129, POCKET MAP J12. This "design hostel" is brightly decorated with funky patterns. All dorms are en suite, there's free wi-fi, a/c and a basic breakfast, and it's open 24 hours. Private doubles from €70. Unexceptional location, but it's just a couple of métro stops south of the Quartier Latin. **Dorm beds from €27**

ST CHRISTOPHER'S PARIS > 68–74 Quai de la Seine Ⓜ Crimée/Laumière. Ⓣ 01 40 34 34 40, Ⓦ st-christophers.co.uk/paris-hostels. MAP P.148, POCKET MAP L3. Massive hostel overlooking the waters of the Bassin de la Villette – some way from the centre. Rooms sleep six to eight and are pleasant in a functional, cabin-like way, but there's a great bar, inexpensive restaurant, and free internet access. As well as dorms there are also twins and doubles available. **Dorm beds from €22.90**

LE VILLAGE HOSTEL > 20 rue d'Orsel Ⓜ Anvers. Ⓣ 01 42 64 22 02, Ⓦ villagehostel.fr. MAP PP.136–137, POCKET MAP H3. Attractive independent hostel in a handsome building, with good facilities and a view of Sacré-Coeur from the terrace. Breakfast included. Small discounts in winter. **Dorm beds from €32**

WOODSTOCK HOSTEL > 48 rue Rodier Ⓜ Anvers/St-Georges. Ⓣ 01 48 78 87 76, Ⓦ woodstock.fr. MAP PP.136–137, POCKET MAP H4. A reliable hostel with its own bar, set in a great location on a pretty street near Montmartre. Breakfast included. **Dorm beds €28**

YOUNG AND HAPPY HOSTEL > 80 rue Mouffetard Ⓜ Monge/Censier-Daubenton. Ⓣ 01 47 07 47 07, Ⓦ youngandhappy.fr. MAP PP.106–107, POCKET MAP H11. Noisy, basic and studenty independent hostel in a lively, touristy location. Dorms, with shower, sleep four, and there are a few doubles (from €32 per person). Lockout 11am–4pm. **Dorm beds from €24.95**

EAU DE PARFUM
L'HEURE BLEUE
GUERLAIN

ESSENTIALS

Arrival

It's easy to get from both of Paris's main airports to the city centre using the efficient public transport links. The budget airline airport, Beauvais, is served by buses. If you're arriving by train, of course, it's easier still: just get on the métro.

By air

The two main Paris **airports** that deal with international flights are Roissy-Charles de Gaulle and Orly, both well connected to the centre. Information on them can be found on Ⓦ parisaeroport .fr. A third airport, Beauvais, is used by Ryanair. Bear in mind that you can buy a Paris Visite card at the airports which will cover multiple journeys to and within the city (see p.185).

ROISSY-CHARLES DE GAULLE AIRPORT

Roissy-Charles de Gaulle Airport, usually referred to as Charles de Gaulle and abbreviated to CDG, is 23km northeast of the city. The airport has two main terminals linked by a shuttle bus.

The cheapest way to get to the centre of Paris – if you book well in advance – is on the easyBus shuttle (every 30–45min 4.30am–12.30am; 45min–1hr; from €3.95; Ⓦ easybus .co.uk) to the Palais Royal in the 1[er]. Places must be booked in advance online. Otherwise, the easiest and quickest way to reach the city centre is by the **Roissyrail** train link, on RER line B, which takes thirty minutes (every 15min 5am–midnight; €10 one way). You can pick it up direct at CDG 2, but from CDG 1 you have to get a shuttle bus (*navette*) to the RER station first. The train is fast to Gare du Nord, then stops at Châtelet-Les Halles, St-Michel and Denfert-Rochereau, all of which have métro stations for onward travel. Ordinary commuter trains also run on this line, but make more stops and have fewer facilities for luggage storage.

Various **bus companies** provide services from the airport direct to a number of city-centre locations, though may take longer than Roissy-rail. The **Roissybus**, for instance, connects CDG 1 and CDG 2 with the Opéra-Garnier (corner of rues Auber and Scribe; Ⓜ Opéra/RER Auber); it runs every fifteen to thirty minutes from 5.45am to 12.30am, costs €11 one-way and takes around 1hr 15min. There are also two buses run by Le Bus Direct (Ⓦ lebusdirect.com): one stops outside Charles-de-Gaulle-Etoile RER/ métro and the other at the Gare de Lyon before terminating near the Gare Montparnasse. Timings are similar to the Roissybus, but tickets are more expensive at €29 return.

A more useful alternative is the **minibus door-to-door service**, Paris Blue, which costs from €39 for two people, with one piece of luggage each. It operates round-the-clock but bookings must be made at least 24 hours in advance on Ⓣ 01 30 11 13 00 or via Ⓦ paris-blue-airport-shuttle.fr.

Taxis into central Paris from CDG cost from around €50 on the meter and should take between fifty minutes and an hour. Note that if your flight gets in after midnight your only means of transport is a taxi, minibus service or the Noctilien bus #N143.

ORLY AIRPORT

Orly Airport (Ⓦ parisaeroport .fr), 14km south of Paris, has two terminals, Orly Sud (south; for international flights) and Orly Ouest (west; for domestic flights), linked by shuttle bus but easily walkable.

The easiest way into the centre is the **Orlyval**, a fast train shuttle link to RER station Antony, from where you can pick up RER line B trains to the central RER/métro stations Denfert-Rochereau, St-Michel and Châtelet-Les Halles; it runs every four to seven minutes from 6am to 11pm (€12.05 one way including shuttle; 35min to Châtelet; ⓦ orlyval.com). Two other services are also worth considering: the **Orlybus**, which runs to Denfert-Rochereau RER/métro station in the 14e (every 15–20min 6am–midnight; 30min; €7.70 one way); and tram T7, which runs to métro Villejuif-Louis-Aragon, on métro line 7 (every 8–15min 5.30am–12.30am; 45min; €1.80).

Taxis take about 35 minutes to the city centre and cost around €40.

BEAUVAIS AIRPORT

Beauvais Airport (ⓣ 08 92 68 20 66, ⓦ aeroportbeauvais.com) is a fair distance from Paris – some 80km northwest – and is used by Ryanair. Coaches (€17 one way, €15.90 if bought online) shuttle between the airport and Porte Maillot, at the northwestern edge of Paris, where you can pick up métro line 1 to the centre. Coaches take about an hour, and leave between fifteen and thirty minutes after the flight has arrived and about three hours before the flight departs on the way back. Tickets can be bought via the airport's website, at Arrivals or from the Pershing bus station, near the Porte Maillot terminal.

By rail

Eurostar (ⓣ 03432 186 186, ⓦ eurostar.com) trains terminate at the **Gare du Nord** in the northeast of the city – a bustling convergence of international, long-distance and suburban trains, the métro and several bus routes. Coming off the train, turn left for the métro and the RER, immediately right and through the side door for taxis (roughly €10–15 to the centre). The Eurostar offices and check-in point for departures are both located on the mezzanine level, above the main station entrance.

Gare du Nord is also the arrival point for trains from Calais and northern European countries, such as Belgium. Paris has five other mainline train stations, part of the national SNCF network: the **Gare de l'Est** serves eastern France and central and eastern Europe; the **Gare St-Lazare** serves the Normandy coast and Dieppe; the **Gare de Lyon** serves Italy, Switzerland and TGV trains to southeast France. South of the river, the **Gare Montparnasse** is the terminus for Chartres, Brittany, the Atlantic coast and TGV lines to southwest France and the Loire Valley; the **Gare d'Austerlitz** runs ordinary trains to the Loire Valley and the Dordogne. The motorail station, **Gare de Paris-Bercy**, is down the tracks from the Gare de Lyon on boulevard de Bercy.

For **information** on national train services and reservations phone ⓣ 36 35 (within France only), or consult: ⓦ sncf.com. For information on suburban lines call ⓣ 36 58 or look up ⓦ transilien.com. You can buy **tickets** at any train station, at travel agents and online at the SNCF website.

By road

If arriving by bus – international or domestic – you'll almost certainly arrive at the main **Gare Routière**, at the eastern edge of the city; métro Gallieni (line 3) links it to the centre. If you're driving in yourself, don't travel straight across the city. Use the ring road – the **boulevard périphérique** – to get around to the nearest *porte*: it's quicker, except at rush hour, and easier to navigate.

Getting around

While walking is undoubtedly the best way to discover Paris, the city's integrated **public transport system** of bus, métro, tram and trains – the RATP (Régie Autonome des Transports Parisiens; Ⓦ ratp.fr) – is reasonably priced, fast and meticulously signposted. You'll find a métro map at the front of this book; alternatively, free métro and bus maps of varying sizes and detail are available at most stations, bus terminals and tourist offices: the largest and most useful is the *Grand Plan de Paris numéro 2*, which overlays the métro, RER and bus routes on a map of the city so you can see exactly how transport lines and streets match up. If you just want a handy pocket-sized métro/bus map ask for the *Petit Plan de Paris* or the smaller *Paris Plan de Poche*. You can download a useful searchable interactive online version at Ⓦ ratp.fr.

Tickets and passes

For a short stay, it's worth buying a **carnet** of ten tickets, available from any station or *tabac* (€14.10, as opposed to €1.80 for an individual ticket, or €2 when bought on buses). The RATP is divided into **five zones**, and the métro system itself more or less fits into zones 1 and 2. The same tickets are valid for the buses (including the night bus), métro and, within the city limits and immediate suburbs (zones 1 and 2), the RER express rail lines, which also extend far out into the Ile de France. Only one ticket is ever needed on the métro system, and within zones 1 and 2 for any RER or bus journey, but you can't switch between buses or between bus and métro/RER on the same ticket. Children under 4 travel free and from ages 4 to 10 at half-price. Don't buy from the touts who hang round the main stations – you may pay well over the odds, quite often for a used ticket – and be sure to keep your ticket until the end of

Touring Paris by public transport

A good way to take in the sights is to hop on a **bus**. Bus #20 (wheelchair accessible) from the Gare de Lyon follows the Grands Boulevards and does a loop through the 1er and 2e arrondissements. Bus #24 (also wheelchair accessible) between Porte de Bercy and Gare St-Lazare follows the left bank of the Seine. Bus #29 is one of the best routes for taking in the city: it ventures from the Gare St-Lazare past the Opéra Garnier, the Bourse and the Centre Pompidou, through the Marais and past Bastille to the Gare de Lyon. For La Voie Triomphale, take a trip on bus #73 between La Défense and the Musée d'Orsay, while bus #63 drives a scenic route along the Seine on the Rive Gauche, then crosses the river and heads up to Trocadéro, where there are wonderful views of the Eiffel Tower. Many more bus journeys – outside rush hours – are worthwhile trips in themselves: get hold of the *Grand Plan de Paris* from a métro station and check out the routes of buses #38, #48, #64, #67, #68, #69, #82, #87 and #95.

The **métro**, surprisingly, can also provide some scenery: the overground line on the southern route between Charles-de-Gaulle-Etoile and Nation (line 6) gives you views of the Eiffel Tower, the Ile des Cygnes, the Invalides, the new Bibliothèque Nationale and the Finance Ministry.

the journey as you'll be fined on the spot if you can't produce one.

If you're doing a fair number of journeys for just one day, it might be worth getting a **Mobilis day-pass** (€7 for zones 1 and 2; €9.30 zones 1–3), which offers unlimited access to the métro, buses, trams and, depending on which zones you choose, the RER – note that the Mobilis pass is not valid to or from the airports.

Other possibilities are the **Paris Visite** passes (Ⓦ ratp.fr), one-, two-, three- and five-day visitors' passes at €12.30, €20, €27.30 and €39.30 for Paris and close suburbs, or €25.85, €39.30, €51.10 and €67.40 to include the airports, Versailles and Disneyland Paris (make sure you buy this one when you arrive at Roissy-Charles de Gaulle or Orly to get maximum value). A half-price child's version is also available. You can buy them from métro and RER stations, tourist offices and online from Ⓦ helloparis.co.uk or Ⓦ parismetro.com. Paris Visite passes become valid on the first day you use them and entitle you to unlimited travel (in the zones you have chosen) on bus, métro, trams, RER, SNCF, the Montmartrobus around Montmartre and the Montmartre funicular between the hours of 5.30am and 1.30am; they also allow you discounts at certain monuments, museums and tours, including day-tickets to Disneyland Paris. If you're going to Paris by Eurostar, you could save time by buying passes from the info point at the St Pancras International Eurostar terminal.

The métro and RER

The **métro**, combined with the **RER** (Réseau Express Régional) suburban express lines, is the simplest way of moving around the city. The métro runs from 5.20am to 1.20am, RER trains from 4.45am to 1.30am. Stations (abbreviated: Ⓜ Concorde, RER Luxembourg, etc) are evenly spaced and you'll rarely find yourself more than 500m from one in the centre, though the interchanges can involve a lot of legwork, including many stairs. Every station has a big plan of the network outside the entrance and several inside, as well as a map of the local area. The métro lines are colour-coded and designated by numbers for the métro and by letters for the RER, although they are signposted within the system with the names of the terminus stations: for example, travelling from Montparnasse to Châtelet, you follow the sign "Direction Porte-de-Clignancourt"; from Gare d'Austerlitz to Grenelle on line 10 you follow "Direction Boulogne–Pont-de-St-Cloud". The numerous interchanges (*correspondances*) make it possible to travel all over the city in a more or less straight line. For RER journeys beyond the city, make sure that the station you want is illuminated on the platform display board.

Buses and trams

The city's **buses** (7am–8.30pm, with some continuing to 1.30am) are easy to use, and allow you to see much more than on the métro. However, many lines don't operate on Sundays and holidays – log onto Ⓦ ratp.fr for a map of the most useful tourist routes.

Bus stops display the name of the stop, the numbers of the buses that stop there, a map showing all the stops on the route, and the times of the first and last services. As with all forms of transport you can buy a single ticket (€1.80, or €2 from the driver), or a pre-purchased carnet ticket or pass (see p.184); insert it into one of the machines on board to validate. Press the red button to request a stop.

On Sunday afternoons and holidays from mid-April to mid-September, a special **Balabus service** (not to be confused with Batobus, see opposite) passes all the major tourist sights between the Grande Arche de la Défense and Gare de Lyon (every 15–20min 1.30–9pm). Bus stops are marked "Balabus", and you'll need one to three bus tickets, depending on the length of your journey. Paris Visite and Mobilis passes are also valid.

Night buses (Noctilien; vianavigo.com) ply 47 routes at least every hour from 12.30am to 5.30am between place du Châtelet and the suburbs. Details of routes are available online.

Paris's **trams** are mostly concentrated in the outer reaches of the city; however, the T3a line, from Pont du Garigliano in the west to Porte de Vincennes in the east, is useful for getting from west to east in the south of the city (see ratp.fr for maps and schedules). Tram stops are marked by a large "T".

Taxis

Taxi charges are fairly reasonable, though considerably more if you call one out; there's a pick-up charge of €3.83. The minimum charge for a journey is €7, and you'll pay €1 for each piece of luggage. Waiting time costs from €32.05 an hour. Drivers don't have to take more than three passengers (they don't like people sitting in the front); if a fourth passenger is accepted, €4 will be added to the fare. A **tip** of ten percent is expected.

Waiting at a **taxi rank** (*arrêt taxi*) is usually more effective than hailing one from the street. If the large green light on top of the vehicle is lit up, the taxi is free. Taxis can be rather thin on the ground at lunchtime and after 7pm, when you might prefer to call one out – the main firms are all on one number (01 45 30 30 30).

Cycling

Parisians have taken enthusiastically to Velib' (velib.paris), the self-service bike scheme set up in 2007. Thousands of sleek, modern – and heavy – bicycles are stationed at around 1500 locations around the city; you simply pick one up at one rack, or *borne*, ride to your destination, and drop it off again. The scheme hasn't been without its problems, mainly owing to vandalism and theft, but it's certainly popular and widely admired.

Passes – one-day €1.70, weekly €8 – are sold online up to two weeks in advance and from meters at each *borne*; plug in your credit card details (which will also secure a €150 deposit, not cashed unless you damage the bike). The first thirty minutes on top of the cost of the pass are free, but after that costs mount; €1 for the next half-hour, €2 for the next, and €4 for every further half-hour. Helmets are not provided. There are between twelve and twenty bike stands at each *borne*, which are around 300m apart. Maps of the network are displayed at the *bornes*, and available to print in advance from their website. Incidentally, if you're caught running a red light while cycling in Paris, you'll be fined €100 on the spot.

Boats

One of the most enjoyable ways to get around Paris is on the **Batobus** (08 25 05 01 01, batobus.com), which operates all year round, apart from January, stopping at nine points along the Seine, including the Eiffel Tower and the Jardin des Plantes. Boats run every fifteen to thirty minutes (Feb, March, Nov and Dec 10.30am–4.30pm; March to May,

Boat trips

Most tourists are keen to take a **boat trip** on the Seine. The faithful old Bateaux-Mouches (bateaux-mouches.fr) is the best-known operator. Leaving from the Embarcadère du Pont de l'Alma on the Right Bank in the 8e (Alma-Marceau), the rides last 1hr 10min, cost €13.50 (€5.50 for children and over-65s) and take you past the major Seine-side sights, such as Notre-Dame and the Louvre. From April to September boats leave every 30–45 minutes from 10.15am to 7pm, then every 20 minutes from 7 to 11pm; winter departures are less frequent, and a minimum of fifty passengers is needed. Barge trips on Paris's canal are also possible and are a great way to discover a less well-known area of the city. Trips are run by Canauxrama (canauxrama.com) and Paris Canal (pariscanal.com).

Sept and Oct 10am–7pm; June–Aug 10am–9.30pm). The total journey time for a round-trip is around ninety minutes and you can hop on and off as many times as you like – a day-pass costs €17, two consecutive days €19 (kids half-price).

Driving

Travelling **by car** – in the daytime at least – is hardly worth it because of the difficulty of finding parking spaces. You're better off locating a motel-style place on the edge of the city and using public transport. If you're determined to use the pay-and-display parking system you must buy a **Paris Carte** (like a phonecard) worth €15–40 from a *tabac*, then look for the blue "P" signs alongside grey parking meters. Put the card in the meter and it automatically deducts from the value on the card – it costs €2.40–4 an hour depending on location, for a maximum of two hours. Alternatively, make for an underground **car park**; these cost up to €2.50 per hour, or around €25 for 24 hours.

If you want to rent a car in Paris your cheapest option is the city's pioneering electric car rental scheme, **Autolib'** (autolib.eu), operating on the same model as Velib' (see opposite). Some three thousand cars are available to rent from numerous stands all over the city. Cars can be picked up at one station and deposited at another. As with Velib', you need to buy a subscription card first, either online or from one of the thirty subscription kiosks in the city. You can either subscribe for a year (€120) or just "pay as you go": you pay €1 to book, the first twenty minutes are free and each subsequent half-hour costs €9. The scheme is open to anyone with a driving licence over the age of 18, and you don't have to have been driving for 2 years to be eligible.

Directory A–Z

Addresses

Paris is divided into twenty districts, or arrondissements. The first arrondissement, or "1er", is centred on the Louvre, in the heart of the city. The rest wind outward in a clockwise direction like a snail's shell: the 2e, 3e and 4e are central; the 5e, 6e and 7e lie on the inner part of the left (south) bank; while the 8e–20e make up the outer districts. Parisian addresses often quote the arrondissement, along with the nearest métro station(s), too.

Banks and exchange

All **ATM**s – *distributeurs* or *points argent* – give instructions in French or English. You can also use credit cards for (interest-paying) cash advances at banks and ATMs. On the whole, the best **exchange rates** are offered by banks, though there's always a commission charge. Certainly be very wary of bureaux de change, as they can really rip you off. Standard banking hours are Monday to Friday from 9am to 4 or 5pm. A few banks close for lunch; some are open on Saturday 9am to noon; all are closed on Sunday and public holidays. Money-exchange bureaux stay open until 6 or 7pm, tend not to close for lunch and may even open on Sundays.

Cinemas

Paris has a world-renowned concentration of cinemas, and moviegoers can choose from around three hundred films showing in any one week. Tickets rarely need to be purchased in advance and are good value at around €9. Among the more interesting cinemas in the city are: **Le Louxor**, 170 bd de Magenta (Barbès-Rochechouart), a 1920s cinema with wonderfully restored neo-Egyptian decor; **Le Grand Rex**, 1 bd Poissonnière (Bonne Nouvelle), a famously kitsch Art Deco cinema showing blockbusters (usually dubbed); **Max Linder Panorama**, 24 bd Poissonnière (Bonne Nouvelle), a 1930s cinema showing films in the original format, with state-of-the-art sound; **La Pagode**, 57bis rue de Babylone (François-Xavier), a reproduction Japanese pagoda and the most beautiful of the city's cinemas; the **MK2** cinema (Stalingrad), showing a mix of art-house and blockbuster films, but perhaps most appealing for its setting on the banks of the Bassin de la Villette; and the cluster of inventive cinemas at the junction of rue Champollion and rue des Ecoles, **Reflet Medicis**, **La Filmothèque** and **Le Champo** (Cluny-La Sorbonne), which offer up rare screenings and classics. The **Cinémathèque Française**, 51 rue de Bercy (cinematheque.fr; Bercy), shows dozens of films every week, including lots of art-house fare, and costs just €6.50.

Crime

Petty theft sometimes occurs on the métro, at train stations and at tourist hotspots such as Les Halles and around rue de la Huchette, in the Quartier Latin. Serious crime against tourists is rare. To report thefts, you have to make your way to the *commissariat de police* in the arrondissement where the theft took place. The Préfecture de Police de Paris is at 7 boulevard du Palais (01 53 73 53 73). For rape crisis (SOS Viol) call 08 00 05 95 95.

Embassies and consulates

Australia, 4 rue Jean-Rey, 15e (Bir-Hakeim) 01 40 59 33 00, france.embassy.gov.au; **Canada**, 35 av Montaigne, 8e (Franklin-D.-Roosevelt) 01 44 43 29 00, canadainternational.gc.ca; **Ireland**, 4 rue Rude,

16e (Charles-de-Gaulle-Etoile) 01 44 17 67 00, embassyofireland.fr; **New Zealand**, 103 rue de Grenelle, 7e (Solferino) 01 45 01 43 43; **South Africa**, 59 quai d'Orsay, 7e; (Invalides) 01 53 59 23 23, www.afriquesud.net; **UK**, 35 rue du Faubourg-St-Honoré, 8e (Concorde) 01 44 51 31 00, ukinfrance.fco.gov.uk; **US**, 2 av Gabriel, 1er (Concorde) 01 43 12 22 22, france.usembassy.gov.

LGBT travellers

Paris has a vibrant, upfront gay community, and full-on prejudice or hostility is rare. Legally, France is liberal as regards homosexuality, with legal consent starting at 16 and laws protecting gay couples' rights. The Centre Gai Lesbien Bi et Trans, 63 rue Beaubourg, 3e, 01 43 57 21 47, centrelgbtparis.org (Tues–Sat 3.30–8pm; Arts-et-Métiers), is a useful port of call for information and advice. Useful contacts and listings can be found in the excellent glossy monthly magazine, *Têtu* (tetu.com).

Health

Pharmacies can give good advice on minor complaints, offer appropriate medicines and recommend a doctor. Most are open roughly 8am–8pm; details of the nearest one open at night are posted in all pharmacies. You can find a good English-speaking chemist at Swann, 6 rue Castiglione, 1er (01 42 60 72 96). Pharmacies open at night include Dérhy/Pharmacie des Champs-Elysées, 84 avenue des Champs-Elysées, 8e (01 45 62 02 41; 24hr; George-V); Pharmacie des Halles, 10 bd Sébastopol, 4e (01 42 72 03 23; Mon–Sat 9am–midnight, Sun 9am–10pm; Châtelet). British citizens with a European Health Insurance Card (available from post offices) can take advantage of French health services. Non-EU citizens are strongly advised to take out travel insurance.

Emergency numbers

Ambulance 15; police 17; fire 18.

Internet

Though most hotels have free wi-fi, US and UK visitors will find that in general access in cafés and bars is not as widespread as in their home countries. Your best bet is to follow the *bobo* (bourgeois-bohemian) trail – to the Marais, Montmartre and the Canal St-Martin, for example. More conveniently, you can connect to the city's free wi-fi network from more than 300 parks, museums and libraries; these are all clearly marked with a "Paris Wi-Fi" logo, and the municipal website, paris.fr/wifi, lists all the hotspots.

Lost property

The **lost property office** (Bureau des Objets Trouvés) is at the Préfecture de Police, 36 rue des Morillons, 15e; 08 21 00 25 25 (Mon–Thurs 8.30am–5pm, Fri 8.30am–4.30pm; Convention). For property lost on public transport, phone the RATP on 32 46. If you lose your passport, report it at a police station, then your embassy (see opposite).

Museum/monument passes

The cost of entrance tickets to **museums and monuments** can add up, but with a little pre-planning you can sightsee relatively cheaply. The permanent collections at all municipal museums are free all year round, while all national museums (including the Louvre and Musée d'Orsay) are free on the first Sunday of the month – see the tourist office website, parisinfo.com, for a full list – and to under-18s.

Elsewhere, the cut-off age for free admission varies between 18, 12 and 4. Reduced admission is often available for 18- to 26-year-olds and for those over 60 or 65 (regardless of whether you are still working or not); you'll need to carry your passport or ID card with you as proof of age. Some discounts (often around one-third off) are available for students with an ISIC Card (International Student Identity Card; Ⓦ isic.org); this is usually the only card accepted for student admissions.

If you're planning to visit a great many museums in a short time it might be worth buying the **Paris Museum Pass** (€48 for 2 consecutive days, €62 for 4 consecutive days, €74 for 6 consecutive days; Ⓦ parismuseumpass.com). Available online and from tourist offices and participating museums, it's valid for 35 or so of the most important museums and monuments including the Pompidou Centre, the Louvre and the Château de Versailles, and allows you to bypass ticket queues (though not the security checkpoints); it often doesn't cover the cost of special exhibitions. The Paris Visite multi-day transport pass (see p.185) also offers discounts on a number of museum admissions.

Opening hours

Most shops, businesses, information services, museums and banks in Paris stay open all day. The exceptions are the smaller shops and enterprises, which may close for lunch some time between 12.30pm and 2pm. Basic **hours of business** are from 8 or 9am to 6.30 or 7.30pm Monday to Saturday for the big shops, and Tuesday to Saturday for smaller shops (some of the smaller shops may open on Monday afternoon). You can always find boulangeries and food shops that stay open on days when others close – on Sunday normally until noon. Shops are also open on Sunday afternoons in the Marais, on the Champs-Elysées and in other major tourist zones.

Restaurants, **bars** and **cafés** often close on Sunday or Monday, and quite a few restaurants also close on Saturdays, especially at midday. It's common for bars and cafés to stay open to 2am, and even extend hours on a Friday and Saturday night, closing earlier on Sunday. Restaurants won't usually serve after 10pm, though some brasseries cater for night owls and serve meals till the early hours. Many restaurants and shops take a holiday between the middle of July and the end of August, and over Easter and Christmas.

Post

French post offices (la Poste) – look for bright yellow-and-blue signs – are generally open Mon–Fri 8am–7pm, Sat 8am–noon. However, Paris's main office, temporarily at 16 rue Etienne Marcel (Ⓜ Etienne-Marcel) while the main building in rue du Louvre undergoes major renovation, is open 24 hours for all postal services (but not banking). The easiest place to buy ordinary stamps (*timbres*) is at a tobacconist (*tabac*). Postcards (*cartes postales*) and letters (*lettres*) up to 20g cost €1 for the UK and EU, and €1.25 for North America, Asia and Oceania. For anything heavier, most post offices now have yellow *guichets automatiques* which weigh your letter or package and give you the correct stamps.

Racism

Paris has an unfortunate reputation for racism, but harassment of tourists is unlikely to be a problem. That said, there are reports of unpleasant incidents such as restaurants claiming to be fully booked, or shopkeepers with a suspicious eye, and travellers of North African or Arab appearance may be unlucky enough to encounter outright hostility or excessive police interest.

Telephones

Most foreign mobile/cell phones automatically connect to a local provider as soon as you reach France. Make sure you know what your provider's call charges are in advance, as these can be extortionate. Data roaming charges, however, once very high, were recently massively reduced, and by June 2017 are set to be abolished completely. France operates on the European GSM standard, so US cell phones won't work unless you've got a tri-band phone. Prepaid phonecards (*télécartes*) for use in phone booths or hotel phones are also available; these are sold in post offices, *tabacs* and newsstands. For calling within Paris, you'll always need to dial the regional code first – ⓣ 01. Local calls are inexpensive, especially off-peak, though hotel phones usually carry a significant mark-up. Domestic and international off-peak rates run at weekends and weekdays from 7pm to 8am. The number for French directory enquiries and operator assistance is ⓣ 12.

Time

Paris, and all of France, is in the Central European Time Zone (GMT+1): one hour ahead of the UK, six hours ahead of Eastern Standard Time and nine hours ahead of Pacific Standard Time. In France, and all of the EU, Daylight Saving Time (+1hr) lasts from the last Sunday of March through to the last Sunday of October, so for one week in late March and/or early April North American clocks lag an extra hour behind.

Tipping

Service is almost always included in restaurant bills, so you don't need to leave more than small change. Taxi drivers and hairdressers expect around ten percent. You should tip only at the most expensive hotels; in other cases you're probably tipping the proprietor.

Tourist information

At Paris's **tourist offices** (ⓦ parisinfo.com) you can pick up maps and information, book accommodation and buy travel passes and the Paris Museum Pass (see opposite). The main **office** is at 25 rue des Pyramides (daily: May–Oct 9am–7pm; Nov–April 10am–7pm; ⓜ Pyramides). Other useful locations include Carrousel du Louvre, accessed from 99 rue de Rivoli (daily 10am–7pm; ⓜ Palais Royal-Musée du Louvre; ⓦ visitparisregion.com), which also has information on the Ile de France. Montmartre has its own office on place du Tertre (daily 10am–6pm; ⓜ Anvers) and there are booths at the Gare du Nord (daily 8am–6pm) and Gare de l'Est (Mon–Sat 8am–7pm).

Of Paris's inexpensive weekly **listings magazines**, sold at newsagents and kiosks, *Pariscope* has the edge, with a comprehensive section on films. On Wednesdays, *Le Monde* and *Le Figaro* also bring out free listings supplements, while for more detail, the webzines *Paris Voice* (ⓦ parisvoice.com) and the city's municipal website (ⓦ quefaire.paris .fr) cover the latest events.

Travellers with disabilities

While the situation is improving, Paris has never had any special reputation for access facilities. The narrow pavements make wheelchair travel stressful, and the métro system has endless flights of steps. Museums and public transport, however, are getting much better. Up-to-date information is best obtained from organizations at home before you leave.

Festivals and events

Paris hosts an impressive roster of festivals and events. In addition to the festivals listed below, France celebrates thirteen **national holidays**: January 1; Easter Sunday; Easter Monday; Ascension Day; Whitsun; Whit Monday; May 1; May 8; July 14; August 15; November 1; November 11; December 25.

FETE DE LA MUSIQUE

June 21 fetedelamusique.culture communication.gouv.fr

During the annual Fête de la Musique, buskers take to the streets and free concerts are held across the whole city in a fun day of music-making.

PRIDE MARCH

Last Saturday of June

marchedesfiertes.fr

The Marche des Fiertés LGBT, or gay pride march, is a flamboyant parade of floats and costumes making its way from Montparnasse to Bastille, followed by partying and club events.

FETE DU CINEMA

End June feteducinema.com

A superb opportunity to view a wide range of films, from classics to the cutting-edge in French and foreign cinema. Buy one full-price ticket and you can see any number of films during the weekend-long festival for €4.

BASTILLE DAY

July 14

The Big One: on Bastille Day the city celebrates the 1789 storming of the Bastille. The party starts the evening before, with dancing around place de la Bastille; in the morning there's a military march down the Champs-Elysées followed by fireworks.

TOUR DE FRANCE

3rd or 4th Sunday in July letour.fr

Paris stages the final romp home of the Tour de France, and thousands line the route to cheer cyclists to the finish line on the Champs-Elysées.

PARIS PLAGES

Mid-July to mid-August

Three sections of the Seine – from the Louvre to the Pont de Sully, at the foot of the Mitterand National Library near the Josephine Baker swimming pool, and at Bassin de la Villette – are transformed into "beaches", complete with real sand, deckchairs and palm trees. Various extras, from tai chi classes to lending libraries and cafés are available.

JOURNEES DU PATRIMOINE

3rd weekend in September

journeesdupatrimoine.culture communication.gouv.fr

Off-limits and private buildings throw open their doors to a curious public for the "heritage days".

FESTIVAL D'AUTOMNE

Last week of September up to Christmas

festival-automne.com

The Festival d'Automne is an international festival of theatre and music, much of it avant-garde and exciting.

NUIT BLANCHE

Early October paris.fr

Nuit Blanche is a night-long festival of poetry readings, concerts and performance art, held in galleries, bars, restaurants and public buildings across the city.

Chronology

Third-century BC > A tribe known as the Parisii begins to settle on the Ile de la Cité.

52 AD > When Julius Caesar's conquering armies arrive they find a thriving settlement of some 8000 people.

Around 275 > St Denis brings Christianity to Paris. He is martyred for his beliefs at Montmartre.

451 > The marauding bands of Attila the Hun are repulsed supposedly thanks to the prayerful intervention of Geneviève, a peasant girl from Nanterre who becomes the city's patron saint.

486 > The city falls to Clovis the Frank. His dynasty, the feuding Merovingians, governs Paris for the next two hundred years or so.

768 > Charlemagne is proclaimed king at St-Denis. Over the next forty years he conquers half of Europe – but spends little time in Paris.

845–85 > Vikings repeatedly sack Paris.

987 > Hugues Capet, one of the counts of Paris, is elected king of Francia and makes Paris his capital.

1200s > Paris experiences an economic boom, its university becomes the centre of European learning and King Philippe-Auguste constructs a vast city wall.

1330s to 1430s > The French and English nobility struggle for power in the Hundred Years' War.

1348 > The Black Death kills some 800 Parisians a day, and over the next 140 years one year in four is a plague year, and Paris's population falls by half.

1429 > Joan of Arc attempts to drive the English out of Paris, but it is not until 1437 that Charles VII regains control of his capital.

1528 > François I finally brings the royal court back from the Loire to his new palace at the Louvre. He sets about building the Tuileries palace.

1572 > On St Bartholomew's Day, August 25, some 3000 Protestants gathered in Paris are massacred at the instigation of the ultra-Catholic Guise family.

1607 > The triumphant monarch Henri IV builds the Pont-Neuf and sets about creating a worthy capital.

1661–1715 > Louis XIV transfers the court to Versailles, but this doesn't stop the city growing in size, wealth and prestige.

1786 > The wall of the Fermiers Généraux is erected around Paris. The wall has 57 toll gates (one of which survives at place Stalingrad), which levy a tax on all goods entering Paris, a source of irritation in the lead-up to revolution.

1789 > Long-standing tensions explode into revolution. Ordinary Parisians, the "sans-culottes", storm the Bastille prison on July 14.

1793 > The revolutionaries banish the monarchy and execute Louis XVI. A dictatorship is set up, headed by the ruthless Robespierre.

1799 > Army general Napoleon Bonaparte seizes control in a coup and, in 1804, crowns himself emperor in Notre-Dame.

1820s > Paris acquires gas lighting and its first omnibus.

1830 > After three days of fighting, known as *les trois glorieuses*, Louis-Philippe is elected constitutional monarch.

1848 > In June, revolution erupts once again. Louis Napoléon Bonaparte, Napoleon's nephew, is elected president. In 1851 he declares himself Emperor Napoléon III.

1850s and 1860s > Baron Haussmann literally bulldozes the city into the modern age, creating long, straight boulevards and squares.

1863 > At the Salon des Refusés, Manet's proto-Impressionist painting *Déjeuner sur l'Herbe* scandalizes all of Paris.

1870 > Hundreds die of starvation as the city is besieged by the Prussians.

1871 > Paris surrenders in March, but the Prussians withdraw after just three days. In the aftermath, workers rise up and proclaim the Paris Commune. It is speedily and bloodily suppressed by French troops.

1874 > The first Impressionist exhibition is held in photographer Nadar's studio to mixed critical response.

1889 > The all-new Eiffel Tower steals the show at the Exposition Universelle, or "great exhibition".

1894 > Captain Alfred Dreyfus, a Jew, is convicted on the flimsiest of evidence of spying for the Germans. The Dreyfus Affair divides Parisian society into two camps: the Dreyfusards (including republicans and left-wing intellectuals Jean Jaurès, Anatole France and Léon Blum), suspecting a cover-up by the army, and anti-Dreyfusards, including clerics, monarchists and conservatives, who suspect a Jewish conspiracy.

1895 > Parisians are the first people anywhere in the world to see the jerky cinematic documentaries of the Lumière brothers.

1900 > The Métropolitain underground railway, or "métro", is unveiled.

1910 > The Great Flood of Paris: the River Seine bursts its banks, rendering thousands homeless and paralysing the city. Parisians get around by boat and hastily constructed wooden walkways. Damage is estimated at 400 million francs.

1914 > War with Germany calls time on the "belle époque". In September, the Kaiser's armies are just barely held off by French troops shuttled from Paris to the front line, just fifteen miles away.

1920s > In the aftermath of war, the decadent *années folles* (or "mad years") of the 1920s rescue Paris's international reputation for hedonism.

1940 > In May and June, the government flees Paris, and Nazi soldiers are soon marching down the Champs-Elysées. Four years of largely collaborative fascist rule ensue.

1942 > Parisian Jews are rounded up – by other Frenchmen – and shipped off to Auschwitz.

1944 > Liberation arrives on August 25, with General de Gaulle motoring up the Champs-Elysées to the roar of a vast crowd.

1961 > As France's brutal repression of its Algerian colony reaches its peak, at least two hundred Algerians are murdered by police during a civil rights demonstration.

1968 > In May, left-wing students occupying university buildings are supported by millions of striking and marching workers.

1969 > President de Gaulle loses a referendum, and retires to his country house.

1973 > Paris's first skyscraper, the Tour Montparnasse, tops out at 56 hideous storeys. The *périphérique* ring road is completed in April.

1981 > Socialist François Mitterand becomes president but Paris remains firmly right wing, under Mayor Jacques Chirac.

1998 > In July, a multiracial French team wins the World Cup at the new Stade de France, in the suburb of St-Denis.

2002 > Parisians find themselves paying a little extra for their coffees and baguettes with the introduction of the euro, on January 1.

2002 > Far Right candidate Jean-Marie Le Pen makes it through the first round of the presidential elections, sending shock waves through the city. Consequently, some 800,000 people pack the boulevards in the biggest demonstration since 1968. In the second-round run-off Chirac is elected, winning 90 percent of the vote in Paris.

2002 > Mayor Bertrand Delanoë launches Paris's new image by turning three kilometres of riverbank expressway into a summer beach: "Paris Plages" is an immense success.

2005 > In late October, disaffected youths riot in the impoverished Paris suburb of Clichy-sous-Bois. Right-wing interior minister, Nicolas Sarkozy, declares a state of emergency.

2007 > As Nicolas Sarkozy becomes president, Mayor Delanoë continues his greening of Paris: bus and cycle lanes appear everywhere, as do the Velib' rental bikes.

2009 > Paris contemplates its future with an exhibition of architectural visions for the green mega-city of the future. It will incorporate its often-neglected suburbs, and is dubbed "Le Grand Paris".

2012 > Socialist François Hollande is elected president but fails to tackle the country's economic woes, quickly becoming the least popular president in over fifty years.

2014 > Paris elects its first woman mayor, Socialist Anne Hidalgo.

2015 > Paris is shaken by two devastating terrorist attacks. In January, three Paris-born jihadist militants shoot dead seventeen people, including eight journalists at the satirical *Charlie Hebdo* magazine and four people at a Jewish supermarket. In November, 130 people are killed and many more wounded in a series of coordinated terror attacks carried out by members of Islamic State.

French

Paris isn't the easiest place to learn French: many Parisians speak a hurried slang and will often reply to your carefully enunciated question in English. Despite this, it's worth making the effort, and knowing a few essentials can make all the difference. Even just saying "Bonjour monsieur/madame" will usually secure you a smile and helpful service.

What follows is a rundown of essential words and phrases. For more detail, get *French: A Rough Guide Dictionary Phrasebook*, which has an extensive vocabulary, a detailed menu reader and useful dialogues.

Pronunciation

Vowels are the hardest sounds to get right. Roughly:

a as in hat
e as in get
é between get and gate
è between get and gut
eu like the u in hurt
i as in machine
o as in hot
o/au as in over
ou as in food
u as in a pursed-lip, clipped version of toot

More awkward are the combinations in/im, en/em, on/om, un/um at the end of words, or followed by consonants other than n or m. Again, roughly:

in/im like the "an" in anxious
an/am, en/em like "on" said with a nasal accent
on/om like "on" said by someone with a heavy cold
un/um like the "u" in understand

Consonants are much as in English, except that ch is always sh, h is silent, th is the same as t, in some instances ll is like the y in "yes" when preceded by the letter "i", w is v, and r is growled (or rolled).

Words and phrases

BASICS

Yes	Oui
No	Non
Please	S'il vous plaît
Thank you	Merci
Excuse me	Pardon/excusez-moi
Sorry	Pardon/Je m'excuse
Hello	Bonjour
Hello (phone)	Allô
Goodbye	Au revoir
Good morning/afternoon	Bonjour
Good evening	Bonsoir
Good night	Bonne nuit
How are you?	Comment allez-vous?/Ça va?
Fine, thanks	Très bien, merci
I don't know	Je ne sais pas
Do you speak English?	Vous parlez anglais?
How do you say ...in French?	Comment ça se dit...en français?
What's your name?	Comment vous appelez-vous?
My name is...	Je m'appelle...
I'm English/Irish/Scottish/Welsh/American/	Je suis anglais(e)/irlandais(e)/écossais(e)/gallois(e)/américain(e)/
OK/agreed	D'accord
I understand	Je comprends
I don't understand	Je ne comprends pas
Can you speak more slowly?	S'il vous plaît, parlez moins vite
Today	Aujourd'hui
Yesterday	Hier
Tomorrow	Demain
In the morning	Le matin
In the afternoon	L'après-midi
In the evening	Le soir
Now	Maintenant
Later	Plus tard

Here	Ici
There	Là
This one	Ceci
That one	Cela
Open	Ouvert
Closed	Fermé
Big	Grand
Small	Petit
More	Plus
Less	Moins
A little	Un peu
A lot	Beaucoup
Half	La moitié
Inexpensive	Bon marché/ Pas cher
Expensive	Cher
Good	Bon
Bad	Mauvais
Hot	Chaud
Cold	Froid
With	Avec
Without	Sans

QUESTIONS

Where?	Où?
How?	Comment?
How many	Combien?
How much is it?	C'est combien?
When?	Quand?
Why?	Pourquoi?
At what time?	À quelle heure?
What is/Which is?	Quel est?

GETTING AROUND

Which way is it to the Eiffel Tower?	S'il vous plaît, pour aller à la Tour Eiffel?
Where is the nearest métro?	Où est le métro le plus proche?
Bus	Bus
Bus stop	Arrêt
Train	Train
Boat	Bâteau
Plane	Avion
Railway station	Gare
Platform	Quai
What time does it leave?	Il part à quelle heure?
What time does it arrive?	Il arrive à quelle heure?
A ticket to...	Un billet pour...
Single ticket	Aller simple
Return ticket	Aller retour
Where are you going?	Vous allez où?
I'm going to...	Je vais à...
I want to get off at...	Je voudrais descendre à...
Near	Près/pas loin
Far	Loin
Left	À gauche
Right	À droite

ACCOMMODATION

A room for one/ two people	Une chambre pour une/deux personnes
With a double bed	Avec un grand lit
A room with a shower	Une chambre avec douche
A room with a bath	Une chambre avec salle de bains
For one/two/ three nights	Pour une/deux/trois nuit(s)
With a view	Avec vue
Key	Clef
To iron	Repasser
Do laundry	Faire la lessive
Sheets	Draps
Blankets	Couvertures
Quiet	Calme
Noisy	Bruyant
Hot water	Eau chaude
Cold water	Eau froide
Is breakfast included?	Est-ce que le petit déjeuner est compris?
I would like breakfast	Je voudrais prendre le petit déjeuner
I don't want breakfast	Je ne veux pas le petit déjeuner
Youth hostel	Auberge de jeunesse

EATING OUT

I'd like to reserve	Je voudrais réserver
...a table	...une table
...for two people	...pour deux personnes
at eight thirty	à vingt heures et demie

I'm having the €30 menu	Je prendrai le menu à trente euros
Waiter!	Monsieur/madame! (never "garçon")
The bill, please	L'addition, s'il vous plaît

DAYS

Monday	Lundi
Tuesday	Mardi
Wednesday	Mercredi
Thursday	Jeudi
Friday	Vendredi
Saturday	Samedi
Sunday	Dimanche

NUMBERS

1	un
2	deux
3	trois
4	quatre
5	cinq
6	six
7	sept
8	huit
9	neuf
10	dix
11	onze
12	douze
13	treize
14	quatorze
15	quinze
16	seize
17	dix-sept
18	dix-huit
19	dix-neuf
20	vingt
21	vingt-et-un
22	vingt-deux
30	trente
40	quarante
50	cinquante
60	soixante
70	soixante-dix
75	soixante-quinze
80	quatre-vingts
90	quatre-vingt-dix
95	quatre-vingt-quinze
100	cent
101	cent un
200	deux cents
1000	mille
2000	deux mille
1,000,000	un million

Menu reader

ESSENTIALS

déjeuner	lunch
dîner	dinner
menu	set menu
carte	menu
à la carte	individually priced dishes
entrées	starters
les plats	main courses
pain	bread
beurre	butter
fromage	cheese
oeufs	eggs
lait	milk
poivre	pepper
sel	salt
sucre	sugar
fourchette	fork
couteau	knife
cuillère	spoon
bio	organic
à la vapeur	steamed
au four	baked
cru	raw
frit	fried
fumé	smoked
grillé	grilled
rôti	roast
salé	salted/savoury
sucré	sweet
à emporter	takeaway

DRINKS

eau minérale	mineral water
eau gazeuse	fizzy water
eau plate	still water
carte des vins	wine list
une pression	a glass of beer
un café	coffee (espresso)
un crème	white coffee
bouteille	bottle

verre	glass
un quart/demi de rouge/blanc	a quarter/half-litre of red/white house wine
un (verre de) rouge/blanc	a glass of red/ white wine

SNACKS

crêpe	pancake (sweet)
un sandwich/ une baguette	sandwich
croque -monsieur	grilled cheese and ham sandwich
omelette	omelette
nature	plain
aux fines herbes	with herbs
au fromage	with cheese
assiette anglaise	plate of cold meats
crudités	raw vegetables with dressings

FISH (POISSON) AND SEAFOOD (FRUITS DE MER)

anchois	anchovies
brème	bream
brochet	pike
cabillaud	cod
carrelet	plaice
colin	hake
coquilles st-jacques	scallops
crabe	crab
crevettes	shrimps/prawns
daurade	sea bream
flétan	halibut
friture	whitebait
hareng	herring
homard	lobster
huîtres	oysters
langoustines	crayfish (scampi)
limande	lemon sole
lotte de mer	monkfish
loup de mer	sea bass
maquereau	mackerel
merlan	whiting
morue	dried, salted cod
moules (marinière)	mussels (with shallots in white wine sauce)
raie	skate
rouget	red mullet
saumon	salmon
sole	sole
thon	tuna
truite	trout
turbot	turbot

FISH: DISHES AND RELATED TERMS

aïoli	garlic mayonnaise served with salt cod and other fish
béarnaise	sauce made with egg yolks, white wine, shallots and vinegar
beignets	fritters
la douzaine	a dozen
frit	fried
fumé	smoked
fumet	fish stock
gigot de mer	large fish baked whole
grillé	grilled
hollandaise	egg yolk and butter sauce
à la meunière	in a butter, lemon and parsley sauce
mousse/mousseline	mousse
quenelles	light dumplings

MEAT (VIANDE) AND POULTRY (VOLAILLE)

agneau	lamb
andouillette	tripe sausage
bavette	beef flank steak
bifteck	steak
bœuf	beef
boudin noir	black pudding
caille	quail
canard	duck
contrefilet	sirloin roast
dinde	turkey
entrecôte	ribsteak
faux filet	sirloin steak
foie	liver
foie gras	fattened (duck/ goose) liver

gigot (d'agneau)	leg (of lamb)
grillade	grilled meat
hachis	chopped meat or mince hamburger
jambon	ham
lapin, lapereau	rabbit, young rabbit
lard, lardons	bacon, diced bacon
merguez	spicy red sausage
oie	goose
onglet	cut of beef
porc	pork
poulet	chicken
poussin	baby chicken
rognons	kidneys
tête de veau	calf's head (in jelly)
veau	veal
venaison	venison

STEAKS

bleu	almost raw
saignant	rare
à point	medium
bien cuit	well done

GARNISHES AND SAUCES

beurre blanc	sauce of white wine and shallots, with butter
chasseur	white wine, mushrooms and shallots
forestière	with bacon and mushroom
fricassée	rich, creamy sauce
mornay	cheese sauce
pays d'auge	cream and cider
piquante	gherkins or capers, vinegar and shallots
provençale	tomatoes, garlic, olive oil and herbs

MEAT AND POULTRY: DISHES AND RELATED TERMS

aile	wing
blanquette de veau	veal in cream and mushroom sauce
bœuf bourguignon	beef stew with red wine, onions and mushrooms
canard à l'orange	roast duck with an orange-and-wine sauce
carré	best end of neck, chop or cutlet
cassoulet	a casserole of beans and meat
choucroute garnie	sauerkraut served with sausages or cured ham
civet	game stew
confit	meat preserve
coq au vin	chicken with wine, onions and mushrooms, cooked till it falls off the bone
côte	chop, cutlet or rib
cou	neck
cuisse	thigh or leg
en croûte	in pastry
epaule	shoulder
daube estouffade, hochepot, navarin and ragoût	all are types of stew
farci	stuffed
au feu de bois	cooked over wood fire
au four	baked
garni	with vegetables
gésier	gizzard
grillé	grilled
magret de canard	duck breast
marmite	casserole
médaillon	round piece
mijoté	stewed
pavé	thick slice
rôti	roast
sauté	lightly cooked in butter
steak au poivre (vert/rouge)	steak in a black (green/red) peppercorn sauce
steak tartare	raw chopped beef, topped with a raw egg yolk

VEGETABLES (LEGUMES), HERBS (HERBES) AND SPICES (EPICES)

ail	garlic
artichaut	artichoke
asperges	asparagus
basilic	basil
betterave	beetroot
carotte	carrot
céleri	celery
champignons	mushrooms
chou (rouge)	(red) cabbage
chou-fleur	cauliflower
concombre	cucumber
cornichon	gherkin
échalotes	shallots
endive	chicory
épinards	spinach
estragon	tarragon
fenouil	fennel
flageolets	white beans
gingembre	ginger
haricots	beans
verts	string (french)
rouges	kidney
beurres	butter
lentilles	lentils
maïs	corn (maize)
moutarde	mustard
oignon	onion
pâtes	pasta
persil	parsley
petits pois	peas
poireau	leek
pois chiche	chickpeas
poivron (vert, rouge)	sweet pepper (green, red)
pommes de terre	potatoes
primeurs	spring vegetables
riz	rice
safran	saffron
salade verte	green salad
tomate	tomato
truffes	truffles

FRUITS (FRUITS) AND NUTS (NOIX)

abricot	apricot
amandes	almonds
ananas	pineapple
banane	banana
brugnon, nectarine	nectarine
cacahouète	peanut
cassis	blackcurrants
cerises	cherries
citron	lemon
citron vert	lime
figues	figs
fraises	strawberries
framboises	raspberries
groseilles	redcurrants and gooseberries
mangue	mango
marrons	chestnuts
melon	melon
noisette	hazelnut
noix	nuts
orange	orange
pamplemousse	grapefruit
pêche	peach
pistache	pistachio
poire	pear
pomme	apple
prune	plum
pruneau	prune
raisins	grapes

DESSERTS (DESSERTS OR ENTREMETS) AND PASTRIES (PATISSERIE)

bavarois	refers to the mould, could be mousse or custard
brioche	sweet, high-yeast breakfast roll
coupe	a serving of ice cream
crème chantilly	vanilla-flavoured and sweetened whipped cream
crème pâtissière	thick eggy pastry-filling
fromage blanc	cream cheese
glace	ice cream
parfait	frozen mousse, sometimes ice cream
petits fours	bite-sized cakes/pastries
tarte	tart

PUBLISHING INFORMATION

This fourth edition published February 2017 by **Rough Guides Ltd**
80 Strand, London WC2R 0RL
11, Community Centre, Panchsheel Park, New Delhi 110017, India
Distributed by Penguin Random House
Penguin Books Ltd, 80 Strand, London WC2R 0RL
Penguin Group (USA) 345 Hudson Street, NY 10014, USA
Penguin Group (Australia) 250 Camberwell Road, Camberwell, Victoria 3124, Australia
Penguin Group (NZ) 67 Apollo Drive, Mairangi Bay, Auckland 1310, New Zealand
Penguin Group (South Africa) Block D, Rosebank Office Park, 181 Jan Smuts Avenue, Parktown North, Gauteng, South Africa 2193
Rough Guides is represented in Canada by DK Canada 320 Front Street West, Suite 1400, Toronto, Ontario M5V 3B6
Typeset in Minion and Din to an original design by Henry Iles and Dan May.
Printed and bound in South China

208pp includes index
A catalogue record for this book is available from the British Library
ISBN 978-0-24125-616-9

1 3 5 7 9 8 6 4 2

ROUGH GUIDES CREDITS

Editors: Natasha Foges and Neil McQuillian
Layout: Anita Singh
Cartography: Katie Bennett
Picture editor: Aude Vauconsant
Photographers: James McConnachie and Lydia Evans
Proofreader: Diane Margolis
Managing editor: Monica Woods
Production: Jimmy Lao
Cover photo research: Aude Vauconsant
Editorial assistant: Freya Godfrey
Senior DTP coordinator: Dan May
Publishing director: Georgina Dee

THE AUTHORS

Ruth Blackmore is a freelance editor and writer, and longstanding contributor to the Rough Guides to Paris and France.

James McConnachie has travelled all over Europe and beyond for Rough Guides. His non-travel books include *Sex* (Rough Guides) and *The Book of Love: A Biography of the Kamasutra* (Atlantic Books).

HELP US UPDATE

We've gone to a lot of effort to ensure that the fourth edition of **Pocket Rough Guide Paris** is accurate and up-to-date. However, things change – places get "discovered", opening hours are notoriously fickle, restaurants and rooms raise prices or lower standards. If you feel we've got it wrong or left something out, we'd like to know, and if you can remember the address, the price, the hours, the phone number, so much the better.

Please send your comments with the subject line "**Pocket Rough Guide Paris Update**" to mail@roughguides.com. We'll credit all contributions and send a copy of the next edition (or any other Rough Guide if you prefer) for the very best emails.

Find travel information, read inspiring features and book your trip at roughguides.com.

PHOTO CREDITS

All images © Rough Guides except the following:
(Key: a-above; b-below/bottom; c-centre; f-far; l-left; r-right; t-top)

Front cover and spine *View over the city from Notre-Dame* **AWL Images**: Hemis

Back cover *Line of manicured trees in the garden of Palais Royal* **AWL Images**: Danita Delimont Stock

1 Latitude: Andia
2 Corbis: Bertrand Gardel
4 AWL Images: Walter Bibikow
5 Photolibrary: Sylvain Sonnet
6 Photolibrary: Pawel Libera
8 Alamy Stock Photo: Zoonar GmbH (b)
9 iStockphoto.com: Factoria Singular (b)
10 Artist Dran © Getty Images: AFP / Francois Guillot (c). **Musée National Picasso-Paris / Béatrice Hatala (b)**
12–13 AWL Images: Danita Delimont Stock
14 Dorling Kindersley: Valerio Vincenzo
15 iStockphoto.com: Neilerua (b)
17 Alamy Stock Photo: VIEW Pictures Ltd (cb)
19 Alamy Stock Photo: Directphoto Collection (bl). **Getty Images:** Louis-Laurent Grandadam (tr). **L'Arpège:** Aurore Deligny (br). **Semilla** (tl)
24 Alamy Stock Photo: SAGAPHOTO.COM / Stephane GAUTIER
25 Alamy Stock Photo: Ania Freindorf (c); Viennaslide (bl). **Castor Club** (br)
26 Alamy Stock Photo: Marcin Rogozinski
29 Alamy Stock Photo: imageBROKER (c)
31 Corbis: Benjamin Leterrier (bl). **Les Trois Baudets** (cb)
32–33 Dreamstime.com: Dennis Dolkens
34 Photolibrary: Chad Ehlers
37 iStockphoto.com: Lillis photography
39 Corbis: Bertrand Rieger
45 iStockphoto.com: Matthew Dixon
52 Getty Images: J Pratt
56 Alamy Stock Photo: epa european pressphoto agency b.v.
62 L'Arpège: Aurore Deligny
63 Monsieur Bleu: Mathieu Rainaud
71 Alamy Stock Photo: Paris Le Marais
75 Dreamstime.com: Abadesign / Andrey Anisimov
77 Getty Images: Christian Marquardt
79 Photoshot: JB Autissier
81 Dreamstime.com: Infomods
83 Alamy Stock Photo: LOOK Die Bildagentur der Fotografen GmbH
91 Galerie Karsten Greve
94 Alamy Stock Photo: Paris Le Marais
103 Getty Images: David Wolff - Patrick
114 Dreamstime.com: Ukrphoto
123 Alamy Stock Photo: Directphoto Collection
132 Alamy Stock Photo: imageimage
135 Alamy Stock Photo: John Kellerman
141 SuperStock: Carlos S. Pereyra
143 Alamy Stock Photo: Kalpana Kartik
146 Robert Harding Picture Library: Christian Goupi
149 Alamy Stock Photo: Claude Thibault
152 Alamy Stock Photo: Peter Horree
153 SuperStock: Directphoto
155 Getty Images: David Wolff - Patrick
156 iStockphoto.com: Isatis
158 Corbis: Tuul & Bruno Morandi
161 Alamy Stock Photo: Michael Jenner
162 iStockphoto.com: Isatis
164 iStockphoto.com: Anto-Marlot
165 iStockphoto.com: Terraxplorer
166 Robert Harding Picture Library: Gunter Lenz
167 Robert Harding Picture Library: Oliviero Olivieri

Index

Maps are marked in **bold**.

D

E

F

G

H

N

O

P

Q

R

INDEX